The Heart Treasure of the Enlightened Ones

THE HEART TREASURE OF THE ENLIGHTENED ONES

The Practice of View, Meditation, and Action

A Discourse Virtuous in the Beginning, Middle, and End

by Patrul Rinpoche

With commentary by Dilgo Khyentse

Translated from the Tibetan by
The Padmākara Translation Group

SHAMBHALA
Boston & London
1992

Shambhala Publications
Horticultural Hall
300 Massachusetts Avenue
Boston, Massachusetts 02115
www.shambhala.com

16 15 14 13 12 11 10 9 8 7

Printed in the United States of America
∞This edition is printed on acid-free paper that meets
the American National Standards Institute Z39.48 Standard.
Distributed in the United States by Random House, Inc.,
and in Canada by Random House of Canada Ltd

Library of Congress Cataloging-in-Publication Data
O-rgyan-'jigs-med-chos-kyi-dban-po. Dpal-spruel, b. 1808.
[Thog mtha ' ba gsum du dge ba'i gtam. English]
The heart treasure of the enlightened ones / Patrul Rinpoche;
with commentary by Dilgo Khyentse.—1st ed.
p. cm.
Translation of: Thog mtha ' bar gsum du dge ba' i gram.
Includes bibliographical references and index.
ISBN-13 978-0-87773-493-2 (pbk.)
ISBN-10 0-87773-493-3
1. Buddhism—Doctrines—Introductions.
I. Rab-gsal-zla-ba. Dis-mgo Mkhen-brtse. 1910– II. Title.
BQ4138.T55D6513 1992 91-52593
294.3'42—dc20 CIP

Foreword

I am happy to know that this translation of a profound oral explanation by Kyabje Khyentse Dorje Chang of Za Pal-trul Rinpoche's *Thog mtha bar gsum du dge ba'i gtam* is being published under the title: *The Heart Treasure of the Enlightened Ones.* Kyabje Khyentse Dorje Chang is the head of the school of Ancient Transmission.

Za Pal-trul Rinpoche, Jigme Chökyi Wangpo, was a great Bodhisattva who came to the Land of Snows in more recent times. This great, sublime, and learned practitioner gave this teaching, known as the Instruction That Is Good in the Beginning, Middle, and End—the Heart Jewel of the Sacred Practice of the View, Meditation, and Conduct, for the benefit of those desiring liberation. It comprises all the essential instructions and, because of the profound meaning it contains and the beautiful language in which it is expressed, it really is like an elixir for reviving the dead.

I hope and pray that through the publication of this teaching and its explanation, people from both East and West will be able to find mental peace in the unsurpassable happiness of love and compassion.

THE DALAI LAMA

February 8, 1991

Contents

Contents

Translators' Preface

In this book, two great masters of the nineteenth and twentieth centuries describe the entire Buddhist path, starting from the most basic motivation and culminating in the direct experience of absolute reality beyond the reach of the conceptual mind.

The root text is a long poem written in the late nineteenth century by Patrul Rinpoche, one of the most outstanding Buddhist teachers of his time. Patrul Rinpoche was uncompromising in his interpretation of the teachings and lived just as he taught, wandering all over eastern Tibet, finding shelter in mountain caves or under forest trees, free of all the trappings of wealth, position, and self-importance. He was a gruff man who could not bear humbug and hypocrisy, and first encounters with him must sometimes have been unnerving; but no one who got to know him well could fail to be profoundly affected by his wisdom, his learning, his humor, and his deep kindness.

He wrote this poem for one of his close disciples while living in a remote cave near the Chinese-Tibetan border. In it, he first delivers a devastating and unsparing description of the deceit and hypocrisy so prevalent in ordinary everyday life. He concludes that the only solution is to refuse to participate in this quagmire of untruth, and goes on to give a concise explanation of the principal practices of the Buddhist path, starting with the recognition of what is wrong with the ordinary world of delusion and ignorance. He describes the preliminary practices, the stages of development and completion, and the unconceptualized meditation of the Mahāmudrā and the Great Perfection.

Finally, he returns to his original theme, urging us to examine critically our own materialistic preoccupations and think carefully about how we really want to spend what is left of our life.

The language of the text is masterful. Sparkling with wit, alliteration, and sheer poetic genius, it never loses its concise and candid lucidity. We have done our best to convey in English some inkling of the style of the original, but no translation could ever do it full justice. (For those with some background in Tibetan, we include the original root text as an appendix starting on page 169.)

However, there is more than poetic virtuosity behind Patrul Rinpoche's brilliant verses. The point of texts such as this was to provide a concise and, above all, memorable framework which, filled out with personal instruction, might be used to convey the vast body of accumulated experience, knowledge, and wisdom passed down intact from master to disciple over the generations by oral teaching, supervised practice, and personal contact. It was in order to fulfill this need that Patrul Rinpoche wrote these eighty-two succinct and strikingly memorable verses summarizing the teachings, which he then transmitted to his disciples together with a detailed oral explanation.

While many of these verses have become well known individually as quotations in the writings of subsequent authors, it is as a whole and as part of the living oral tradition that they retain their full value. Fortunately, Patrul Rinpoche's disciples practiced, realized, and passed on the tradition as carefully as their predecessors. Today, two generations later, Dilgo Khyentse Rinpoche has been able to transmit to us this same legacy of experience and wisdom.

Khyentse Rinpoche's commentary, therefore, is far from being merely an interpretative amplification of the verses of the root text. It contains the very teaching received by Patrul Rinpoche from his own teachers, going back to Jigme Lingpa, to Longchenpa, to the great gurus Padmasambhava and Vimalamitra.

Although the commentary is presented here in the form of a book, it should not be forgotten that it is not a text that Khyentse Rinpoche wrote down over a period of time and then pondered, corrected, revised, adjusted, added to, and deleted from. He simply spoke it, just as it is, without a single intermission or pause for thought. Anyone who has been present at a teaching of Khyentse Rinpoche will be familiar with this remarkable style. Glancing rarely at the written root text, Rinpoche would speak effortlessly at a steady rate, evenly and without strong emphasis, never pausing or hesitating, as if reading from some unseen book in his memory. Each sentence, however long and complex, would be complete and grammatically perfect. Somehow the subject would always be uniformly covered from beginning to end, in just the allocated time, pitched precisely at the audience's level of understanding. This extraordinary ability was, moreover, by no means confined to the teachings of one particular tradition; Khyentse Rinpoche's eclecticism was such that, wherever he traveled, he could sit down in a monastic center belonging to any tradition and teach exactly according to that particular lineage.

In September 1991, as this translation was in the final stages of preparation, Dilgo Khyentse Rinpoche's extraordinary life came to an end. He was eighty-one years old. From an early age, all his life had been spent studying, practicing, and teaching. Wherever he was, day or night, in the same uninterrupted flow of kindness, humor, wisdom, and dignity, his every effort was directed to the preservation and expression of all forms of the Buddhist teaching, of which he was without doubt one of the greatest exponents of modern times.

In his youth, Khyentse Rinpoche lived and practiced much like Patrul Rinpoche, in the mountains and wilderness. His later life was played out against a wide variety of backdrops, but he never lost his utterly simple style. What these two outstanding masters undoubtedly shared was the uncompromising way in which they both lived and breathed the teachings. Beyond any particular cultural context, they both had the ability to inspire people to question deeply their own choices in life, and then the immense practical experience and wisdom to guide them toward finding their own way of truly practicing the teachings.

The questions with which we are confronted in this book are as fresh and relevant today as ever. Khyentse Rinpoche himself chose this teaching for publication as a text which could inspire anyone to think about his or her life and which at the same time gives a complete overview of the viewpoint and practice of the three great vehicles of the Buddhist teaching. Patrul Rinpoche's fresh and piercing verses, with Khyentse Rinpoche's lucid and down-to-earth comments, make a concise whole that is unusually complete in its scope.

It is in the spirit of these two great teachers' insistence that the teaching be treated as something to be lived to the full, an unceasing breath of fresh air, a way to experience things as they truly are, that we are pleased to present this text for publication in the hope that readers will find in it relevance and inspiration—and truly take it to heart.

Translators' Acknowledgments

At the esteemed command of His Holiness the fourteenth Dalai Lama and Venerable Doboom Rinpoche, His Holiness Dilgo Khyentse Rinpoche gave these teachings at Tibet House, New Delhi, in February 1984. Later, on the occasion of the recitation of one hundred million maṇi mantras in April 1986 at Shechen Tennyi Dargyeling Monastery in Nepal, and again in July 1986 in preparation for the third three-year retreat in Dordogne, France, His Holiness gave further teachings on the same text, which have been included in this volume.

Members of the Padmākara Translation Group who worked on this text include Könchog Tenzin and John Canti, translators; and Michael Friedman, Charles Hastings, Marilyn Silverstone, Daniel Staffler, and Phyllis Taylor, editors.

We are most grateful to Venerable Doboom Rinpoche for permission to use part of the original material of these teachings, which appeared in *Essence of Buddhism* (New Delhi: Tibet House, 1986).

We would like to extend our heartiest thanks, too, to Könchog Lhadrepa, who drew the back cover illustration, and to all those who kindly contributed to the transcription and typing of this text: Christine Fondecave, the late Suzan Foster, John Petit, Anne Munk, and S. Lhamo.

The Heart Treasure of the Enlightened Ones

Introduction

The Right Motivation for Receiving and Studying the Teachings

Of all the countless living creatures throughout the vast reaches of the universe, every single one, right down to the tiniest insect, wants only to be happy and not to suffer. But none of them understand, in their search for happiness, that happiness comes only from positive action; and none of them can see, in their efforts to escape suffering, that what brings suffering upon them is negative actions. So, unwittingly, they turn their backs on happiness and plunge into suffering.

To expect happiness without giving up negative action is like holding your hand in a fire and hoping not to be burned. Of course, no one actually wants to suffer, to be sick, to be cold or hungry—but as long as we continue to indulge in wrongdoing we will never put an end to suffering. Likewise, we will never achieve happiness except through positive deeds, words, and thoughts. Positive action is something we have to cultivate ourselves; it can be neither bought nor stolen, and no one ever stumbles on it just by chance.

Whatever we do involves the use of body, speech, and mind. Of these three, body and speech by themselves cannot initiate any activity; it is mind that determines everything we do and say. Mind, if we give it free rein, will just go on giving rise to more and more negative actions, and this is how we have all come to wander for countless lifetimes in saṃsāra.[1]

In each of these countless lives in beginningless saṃsāra we must have had parents. In fact, we have taken birth so often that, at one time or another, every single sentient being[2] must have been our mother or father. When we think of all these beings who have been our parents wandering helplessly for so long in saṃsāra, like blind people who have lost their way, we cannot but feel tremendous compassion for them. Compassion by itself, however, is not enough; they need actual help. But as long as our minds are still limited by attachment, just giving them food, clothing, money, or simply affection will only bring them a limited and temporary happiness at best. What we must do is to find a way to liberate them completely from suffering. This can only be done by putting the teachings of Dharma[3] into practice.

So, before you receive these precious teachings, first give rise to the appropriate motivation, which is to study and practice not merely for your own sake but primarily to free all beings from the ocean of saṃsāra and bring them to complete enlightenment. This is the vast and perfect attitude of bodhichitta.

Bodhichitta, which means "the thought of enlightenment," has two aspects, one directed toward all beings and one focused on wisdom.

The first aspect is compassion directed impartially toward all sentient beings, without discriminating between those who are friends and those who are enemies. With this compassion constantly in mind, we should perform every positive act, even the offering of a single lamp or the recitation of a single mantra, with the wish that it may benefit all living creatures without exception.

However, to really help all beings it is not enough just to feel compassion for them. A story often told to illustrate this tells of a mother with paralyzed arms helplessly watching her child being swept away by a river; overwhelming though her compassion must be, it does not make it possible for her to save her drowning son. Whatever has to be done to rescue beings from suffering and bring them to enlightenment, we have to actually do it. We should understand that we have had the good fortune to be born into a world where a Buddha has come and taught the Dharma, and we have met a spiritual teacher and received his instructions. Now it is up to us to use this precious human life to make progress on the path of liberation.

It is said, "Human life can lead you to enlightenment; human life can lead you to hell." Depending on our motivation and the direction we take, we could become great sages and attain Buddhahood, or we could become thoroughly evil and when we die go straight to hell. The teachings of the Dharma enable us to distinguish these two directions, showing us clearly what to do and what to avoid.

Right now we lack the ability to help others very much. But if everything we do is motivated by the wish to relieve their suffering, that constant aspiration will eventually be realized. Motivation channels the force of our actions, just as an irrigation canal brings water to wherever it is wanted. Everything depends on our motivation. If all we want is a long and prosperous life, then at the very best that is all we are likely to achieve; but if we yearn to free all beings totally from saṃsāra, we will eventually be able to fulfill that most noble intention. It is therefore very important not to direct our aspiration to lesser goals.

Once, a mother and her young child were crossing a swollen and turbulent river in a small boat. Halfway across, the current became so violent that the boat was about to capsize. Sensing the imminence of disaster, the mother thought, "May my child be saved!" while at that same moment, the child thought, "May my mother be saved!" Though the boat sank and both were drowned, the power and purity of their wishes were such that mother and child were reborn immediately in a celestial Buddhafield.[4]

The second aspect of bodhichitta, the aspect focused on wisdom, is the realization of voidness in order to achieve enlightenment for the sake of others. These two bodhichittas—the skillful means of compassion and the wisdom of voidness—should never be separated. They are like a bird's two wings, both of which are necessary for it to fly; you cannot achieve enlightenment through compassion alone, nor through the realization of voidness by itself.

To do something virtuous with a commonplace motive will certainly bring us some happiness, but only temporarily. Such happiness will soon be gone, and our helpless roaming in saṃsāra will continue. If, on the other hand, everything we do, say, and think is transformed by bodhichitta, our happiness will go on and on increasing and never be exhausted. The fruit of actions motivated by bodhichitta, unlike that of positive actions done with less noble motives, can never be destroyed by anger or other negative emotions.

Whatever we do, therefore, it is the mind that is most important. This is why the Buddhist teachings focus on perfecting the mind. The mind is king, and body and speech are servants which must do its bidding. It is the mind that conceives faith and the mind that conceives doubt; it is the mind that conceives love and the mind that conceives hatred.

So look within and check your motivation, for that is what determines whether what you do is positive or negative. Mind is like a transparent crystal which takes on the color of whatever cloth it rests on—yellow on a yellow cloth, blue on a blue cloth, and so forth. Likewise, your attitude colors the mind, and this determines the true character of your actions, no matter how they may appear. The nature of this mind is not something remote and unknowable; it is always immediately present. Yet, if you look at how it is, you do not find something red, yellow, blue, white, or green; it is not square or round, nor is it shaped like a bird, or a monkey, or anything else. The mind is simply that which conceives and remembers countless thoughts. If the current of thoughts is virtuous, you have tamed the mind; if it is negative, you have not.

Taming the mind and making it positive needs perseverance. Never think, "The Buddha is fully enlightened, and Chenrezi[5] is the very embodiment of compassion; but how could an ordinary person like me ever help others?" Do not be discouraged. As your motivation grows more and more vast, your capacity for positive action will expand too. You may not have the same ability as Chenrezi right now, but the way to develop it is to practice the Dharma. If you maintain the constant wish to benefit others, the power to actually do so will come by itself, as naturally as water runs downhill.

All difficulties come from not thinking of others. Whatever you are doing, look constantly into the mirror of your mind and check whether your motive is for yourself or for others. Gradually you will develop the ability to master your mind in all circumstances; and by following in the footsteps of the accomplished masters of the past, you will gain enlightenment in a single lifetime. A good mind is like a rich ground of gleaming gold, lighting up the whole sky with its golden radiance. But if body, speech, and mind are not tamed, there is very little chance that you will achieve any realization whatsoever. Be aware of your thoughts, words, and actions at all times. If they take the wrong direction, your study and practice of the Dharma will be of no use.

Saṃsāra is the condition of beings who, by acting under the influence of obscuring emotions, perpetuate their own suffering; nirvāṇa is the state beyond all suffering, or, in other words, Buddhahood. If we let the mind follow all its negative fancies, it will naturally take the path of saṃsāra. Now we are at a crossroads. We have had the good fortune to be born a human being in a world where a Buddha has come and has taught the Dharma; we have met a spiritual teacher who can transmit the

Dharma to us, and we have received his instructions; and we are physically and mentally capable of putting his instructions into practice. So now it is up to us to decide: Are we going to climb up the path of liberation with the determination to bring all beings to the supreme level of enlightenment? Or will we descend even deeper into the labyrinth of saṃsāra, from which it is so difficult to escape?

How to Study These Teachings

Through the teachings of Dharma we can bring all beings to perfect Buddhahood. When we receive those teachings, therefore, it is essential that we are free of the habitual shortcomings that might prevent us from understanding them clearly—the three defects, the six stains, and the five wrong ways of retaining the teachings.[6] Otherwise, studying this text will just be a waste of time. Please focus on the teaching which follows with consummate mindfulness and apply the six perfections.[7]

What These Teachings Contain

The teaching we will study here is known as the *Discourse Virtuous in the Beginning, Middle, and End.* It has the additional title *The Practice of View, Meditation, and Action, Which Is the Heart Treasure of the Enlightened Ones.* This text was written by Dza Patrul Rinpoche, Orgyen Jigme Chökyi Wangpo, who was an emanation of the great Bodhisattva Shāntideva.[8] Throughout his life Patrul Rinpoche demonstrated flawless discipline, unlimited compassion, deep knowledge, and a complete renunciation of ordinary worldly concerns.

All the many vast and profound instructions taught by Lord Buddha, with his consummate skill and immense compassion, are collected in the Tripiṭaka.[9] These teachings are explained in the *shāstras,*[10] texts composed not by the Buddha himself but by subsequent generations of Buddhist masters—the glorious paṇḍitas of India and the learned and accomplished sages of Tibet.

This text by Patrul Rinpoche is an example of such a shāstra, or commentary.

All the different Buddhist teachings ultimately lead to liberation. Their great variety and number reflect the varying capabilities and dispositions of practitioners. The *Discourse Virtuous in the Beginning, Middle, and End* is formulated in a way that is particularly easy to understand and practice; nevertheless it contains the quintessence of the teachings of both Hīnayāna and Mahāyāna[11] in their entirety.

As is traditional, this teaching is divided into three sections: the introduction, the main body, and the concluding section. Each section focuses on a specific topic. The first deals with the degenerate ways and intense suffering of beings in this dark age; the second with the view, meditation, and action of the Sūtrayāna and Mantrayāna;[12] and the third with freedom from ordinary worldly concerns.

The first section urges us to reflect on our own defects and on the shortcomings of saṃsāric life. Through this we come to recognize the self-deception and deception of others that characterize our efforts in business and other self-centered activities, caught as we are in our likes and dislikes, attachment to friends, and animosity toward adversaries. Seeing how senseless all this is, we naturally become tired of it and begin to feel a strong desire to be free of it all. This determination to be free is the foundation of all Dharma practice, for it is only when we fully recognize what is wrong with saṃsāra that we feel the irresistible urge to give ourselves completely to the practice.

In the first turning of the wheel of Dharma, the Buddha taught that there is nothing but suffering in saṃsāra. This is the first of the Four Noble Truths.[13] All living creatures are trying to find happiness, but because of their ignorance, what they do is the opposite of what would actually bring them happiness. They fail to understand that true happiness comes only from realizing the Dharma, and they are taken in by the attachments and aversions that their own minds create. Entangled in the web of delusion, they blunder on from suffering to suffering.

The present age is known as the degenerate age[14] or the age of residues, for it retains only residues of the qualities and perfections of the great golden age of the distant past. People these days turn their backs on the teachings of the Buddha, and there are only a very few great beings who really live according to the Dharma. Everyone is desperately thirsting for happiness, but the prevailing views and lifestyles of our times lead only to more suffering.

The intense misery of the lower realms of existence is so great that it is hard for us to even imagine. In the realms of hell, beings are tortured by agonizing heat and cold; in the realms of the hungry ghosts, by inconceivable hunger and thirst. Animals, in blind stupidity, are enslaved and exploited or tormented by fear. Even if we cannot comprehend fully what beings in those realms experience, should we not at least reflect on the suffering our own actions cause in this present life?

As the great Kadampa teachers used to say, "The best teaching of all is one that sheds light on our hidden defects." First we must appreciate that saṃsāra is nothing but suffering. Then, identifying our own errors, we can look for the cause. The root cause of suffering is ignorance, and the root cause of ignorance is the false belief in an "I." As the glorious Chandrakīrti[15] said:

> First conceiving an I, we cling to an ego.
> Then conceiving a mine, we cling to a material world.
> Like water in a water-wheel, helplessly we circle;
> I bow down to the compassion that arises for all beings.

Attached to *my* body, *my* mind, and *my* name, we try to push away whatever is unpleasant and grasp at whatever is desirable. This is the basic process of clinging, the ego, the very root of suffering.

By making us think about how people behave in our decadent age, the first section of the text is intended to clarify our understanding of saṃsāra and inspire in us a deeply felt sadness toward it. This gives us a strong motivation to free ourselves from all the habit-patterns and ignorance that perpetuate suffering. Yet, however strong, motivation by itself is not enough. What we then need is to know how we can actually free ourselves from saṃsāra—in other words, how we can practice the Dharma.

The second section explains how the Dharma, the antidote to all the delusions of saṃsāra, is actually put into practice. It explains the view, meditation, and action of the Mahāyāna, which constitute the core of the Buddha's teachings. Through practicing these instructions, our obscurations and the karma resulting from our deluded actions of the past will be purified, and all the qualities of liberation and enlightenment inherent within us will be revealed. In this text, the instructions are given in the specific context of the meditation on Chenrezi, the Buddha of Compassion.

First of all, it is absolutely necessary to establish the correct *view.* To establish the view means to acquire complete certainty about the absolute truth, which is that the phenomenal world, though obviously appearing and functioning, is utterly devoid of any ultimate reality. This view of all phenomena as appearing yet void is the seed from which the perfect fruit of enlightenment will grow. The first step in establishing the view is to acquire a proper understanding of the teachings about it. Then, to incorporate the view into our inner experience, we put it into practice over and over again; this is the *meditation.* Maintaining our experience of the view at all times and under all circumstances is the *action.* Through the constant combination of these three—view, meditation, and action—the *fruit* of the practice of Dharma will fully ripen. As the saying goes, "When milk is carefully churned, butter is produced."

What are the fruits of practice? Gentleness and self-discipline are indications of understanding; freedom from obscuring emotions is the sign of meditation. These and all the spiritual qualities of liberation will take root in our being and will be expressed effortlessly in our actions. Establishing the view is like recognizing the qualities and usefulness of a particular tool. Meditation is like shopping for this tool, acquiring it, and learning how to use it. Action is like putting it to skillful use all the time. The fruit corresponds to the completed tasks or finished products that come from its use.

The third part of the text shows how the results of the practice find expression in a daily life free from preoccupation with worldly affairs and in harmony with the teachings. As we develop a strong feeling of revulsion for saṃsāra, overcome the delusion that saṃsāra will bring happiness, and immerse ourselves in the practice of Dharma, a growing sense of freedom will naturally arise: we are simply no longer attracted to things that cause suffering. Only by turning our minds away from worldly goals and developing a genuine determination to be free can the goal of liberation be reached.

Opening Verses

The Homage

The text opens with the homage:

NAMO LOKESHVARĀYA

This Sanskrit phrase means "I pay homage to the Paramount Sovereign of the Universe," referring to the great Bodhisattva Avalokiteshvara, or Chenrezi.

Chenrezi's universal compassion embraces all beings, from commoners to kings, from Shrāvakas and Pratyekabuddhas to all the Bodhisattvas of the ten levels.[16] Chenrezi embodies the great compassion inseparable from the vast expanse of the Buddha's mind. Compassion takes such a central position in the Buddha's teaching because it is from compassion that all the vastness and profundity of the Bodhisattva path arises; compassion is the awakened heart itself. In his relative aspect, Chenrezi appears in the universe for the sake of all beings in the form of a Great Bodhisattva of the tenth level, a heart-son of all the Buddhas. In his absolute aspect, he is the very ground from which emanate all the Buddhas and their celestial Buddha-fields, and also all the universal monarchs of this kalpa. He is therefore known as the Paramount Sovereign of the Universe, meaning that he is not just a king in the ordinary sense, but the Lord of Dharma, the sovereign of wisdom and compassion, completely free from the three worlds of saṃsāra,[17] forever beyond the reach of birth, old age, sickness, and death. To meet all the needs of beings he manifests in countless forms, from world rulers to ordinary people and animals. He exemplifies perfect liberation dedicated to the welfare of all.

This is why the opening line is offered in homage to Chenrezi, with great devotion. Then follows a more expanded homage:

> 1. If but a single drop of the nectar of your name
>   were to fall upon my ears,
> They would be filled with the sound of Dharma
>   for countless lives.
> Wondrous Three Jewels, may the brilliance of
>   your renown
> Bring perfect happiness everywhere!

Here, the homage is extended to the Three Precious Jewels: the Buddha, the Dharma, and the Saṅgha. The names of the Three Jewels, which are extremely easy to say, nevertheless possess infinite power to bless living creatures and to deliver them from saṃsāra. These names are like the celestial ambrosia of immortality, amṛita, a single drop of which can soothe the torments of saṃsāra. Simply to hear them plants within us the seed of liberation and ensures rebirth in a place where the Dharma is taught and where progress toward enlightenment is possible.

We should consider the Buddha as the teacher, the Dharma as the path, and the Saṅgha as companions on the path.

At the absolute level, the Dharmakāya, the Buddha's mind is the vast expanse of omniscience which knows all things exactly as they are. At the Sambhogakāya level, beyond birth and death, the Buddha's speech continually teaches the Dharma. At the Nirmāṇakāya level, accessible to the perceptions of ordinary beings like ourselves, the Buddha's body takes form as the

Buddha Shākyamuni, the fourth of the thousand Buddhas to appear in this kalpa.

The Buddha Shākyamuni was born in India as Prince Siddhārtha to King Shuddhodana and Queen Mahāmāyā of the Shākya clan. As a young man, he enjoyed all the pleasures of a princely life, but later he renounced worldly concerns and devoted himself for six years to the practice of austerities. At last, renouncing even these austerities, he achieved complete enlightenment at the foot of the bodhi tree at Vajrāsana.[18] For forty years he taught the Dharma for the benefit of beings. Finally, when their good fortune was exhausted, he passed into the great peace of parinirvāṇa.[19]

Through the power of his omniscience, Lord Buddha saw the vast spectrum of different temperaments and propensities in those he taught. In order to provide each with a means for attaining enlightenment, he expounded eighty-four thousand different sections of Dharma. This teaching, the Dharma, is the second Precious Jewel.

The three cycles of his teachings are known as the three turnings of the wheel of Dharma. In the first turning of the wheel, at Vārāṇasī, he taught the Four Noble Truths common to both Hīnayāna and Mahāyāna. In the second, at Rājagṛiha, or Vulture Peak, he expounded the Mahāyāna teachings on absolute truth—the truth devoid of characteristics and beyond all conceptual categories. These teachings are contained in the *Prajñāpāramitā Sūtra* in One Hundred Thousand Verses. The third turning of the wheel, at several different times and places, was devoted to the ultimate teachings of the Vajrayāna, or adamantine vehicle.

The Dharma consists of the Dharma of Transmission and the Dharma of Realization. The Dharma of Transmission is the word of the Buddha as collected in the Tripiṭaka: the Vinaya, the Sūtras, and the Abhidharma. The Dharma of Realization is the actual realization of the teachings, cultivated through discipline, meditation, and wisdom.

The third Jewel is the Saṅgha, rendered in Tibetan as *Gendun*, which literally means "virtuous community." Traditionally, the Bodhisattvas are the Saṅgha of the Mahāyāna, and the Shrāvakas and Pratyekabuddhas are the Saṅgha of the Hīnayāna. In general, however, all those who listen to the Dharma, contemplate it, and meditate upon it constitute the Saṅgha.

The Three Jewels are the supreme refuge and form the foundation of all Dharma practice. Homage to the Three Jewels is at once homage to all teachers, Buddhas, and Bodhisattvas.

The Author's Motive in Writing This Text

Because Patrul Rinpoche himself regarded the Three Jewels as his supreme teacher, his mind was completely imbued with the Dharma, and he led a life of perfect purity. His teachings are therefore completely pure and authentic, and this text he composed out of sheer compassion, without any arrogance or pride. Nevertheless, he says with great humility:

> 2. Like some persimmons in the autumn
> Which, though inside still unripe, look ripe outside,
> I myself am just the semblance of a Dharma practitioner,
> And since my mind and the Dharma haven't mixed, my Dharma teaching won't be up to much.

As summer turns to autumn, persimmons can be found at different stages of ripeness. Some persimmons look ripe, but inside they are still green. They are like people who pose as exemplary Dharma practitioners but, full of poisonous thoughts, are in fact preoccupied with accumulating wealth, performing village ceremonies, and making a name for themselves.

Others, on the contrary, still look green outside, but inside they are already ripe. These are like people who, though appearing to be ignorant, humble beggars, are totally free from saṃsāric concerns, are full of faith, and have achieved genuine meditative experience and realization.

Other persimmons, both outside and inside, are green and unripe all the way through. They are like people who have never entered the Dharma, know nothing about it, and have no faith in it.

Finally, some persimmons both look ripe and actually are ripe. These are like the great Bodhisattvas, inwardly full of wisdom and compassion and outwardly displaying infinite ways of helping beings. In truth, Patrul Rinpoche was without doubt one of these perfect Bodhisattvas. Jamyang Khyentse Wangpo[20] had this to say about him:

> I pray to Jigme Chökyi Wangpo, Fearless Lord
> of Dharma;
> Outwardly he is the Bodhisattva Shāntideva,
> Inwardly he is the mahāsiddha Shavaripa,
> And in his absolute nature he is the Spontaneous
> Liberation of Suffering.[21]

This is by no means just token praise. As his life story demonstrates, everything that Patrul Rinpoche thought, said, or did was completely consistent with the Dharma. Indeed, it is precisely from this standpoint that he makes such a humble disclaimer.

Anyone who wants to teach the Dharma must first make it an integral part of his being; it would be no good just repeating the words, like a deaf musician playing tunes that, however beautiful, he cannot hear himself. To receive the teachings, our motive should be a sincere aspiration to apply them to ourselves; if we are just trying to acquire something that we can teach to other people, like the music a beggar plays to get money, receiving teachings will be useful neither to ourselves nor to others. It is equally wrong to collect knowledge of the Dharma for the sake of our own fame and importance. As the saying goes, "Greater knowledge, greater pride; further from home, further from honesty." How can we help others before we have tamed the negative forces hidden within ourselves? That would just be a joke, like a penniless beggar talking of feeding the whole village. To secure the genuine welfare of others we must first perfect ourselves until we can emulate Patrul Rinpoche, who modestly claims he has no realization, yet whose whole being is saturated with the meaning of the Dharma.

3. But since you, worthy friend, entreat me insistently,
I cannot refuse—I will speak out frankly.
Unusual though it is in this decadent age,
I offer you these words without treachery, so
listen well.

If you point out someone's faults, he will become quite upset—even if he is your own child or student. If you flatter him, however, attributing to him qualities he does not possess, he will be delighted. But as a saying goes, "Though it sounds impressive, the rumble of thunder is just noise." If people always agree with us and flatter us, it may make us feel good but it will not help us to develop the qualities of a Dharma practitioner. What will truly help us most is to have our faults pointed out and the right way to deal with them shown to us. Gold, through repeated beating and melting, becomes more and more refined. In the same way, by continually recognizing our own faults and applying the teacher's instructions, we will be able to transform our negative qualities into the path of liberation.

When a troublemaker is identified and apprehended, peace returns to the village; similarly, when our faults are unearthed by a truly kind teacher, enabling us to recognize and eradicate them, peace returns to our being. Here, as in his famous *Kunzang La-me Shelung*,[22] Patrul Rinpoche speaks frankly, striking at the core of our defects in order to lead us to the right path. He expresses only the very essence of the Dharma, for we do not need to know many details; all we really need is the heart of the teachings leading to enlightenment.

In these verses, Patrul Rinpoche says that although he does not have any great realization, at least if he can inspire in us the determination to be free of saṃsāra and stimulate an attitude of compassion, writing this text will not have been in vain.

Part One

The Shortcomings of Our Decadent Age

Having paid homage to the Three Jewels, Patrul Rinpoche begins the first section of the text:

4. The True Ṛiṣhi, the Munīndra, god of gods,
Attained the true level through the true path,
And truly showed this true and excellent path
to others.
Isn't that why he's known as the True Ṛiṣhi?

In ancient India, ṛiṣhis were long-haired ascetics living in forest retreats, sustaining themselves with whatever alms might come their way, and remaining aloof from family life, trade, farming, and other ordinary worldly activities. They were called ṛiṣhi, in Tibetan *trangsong*, which literally means "straight" or "true," because their conduct was upright and true and made them worthy of respect and veneration.

These ṛiṣhis, of whom some were Buddhist and some were not, varied greatly in their degree of accomplishment and realization. There were some who had achieved miraculous powers through concentration and meditation and were known to live for a kalpa,[23] to be clairvoyant, and to be able to fly or levitate with ease. But even such accomplished ṛiṣhis had not yet cut the root of the obscuring emotions, and so they remained vulnerable to pride and attached to praise and recognition. Lord Buddha, on the other hand, the unequaled prince of the Shākyas, totally eliminated ego-clinging at its very root from the very moment he conceived the thought of enlightenment.[24] How was it that he was able to do this? It was because he sought enlightenment exclusively for the sake of others. That is why he is called the True Ṛiṣhi.

When the thousand and two Buddhas each made their prayers of aspiration to benefit beings, Buddha Shākyamuni vowed to help those of our present dark age. He was undaunted by the fact that this would be the age of the five degenerations[25] and that the minds of beings, obscured by gross emotions and tossed by the strong winds of passion, would be wild and difficult to tame. Such is the nobility of this aspiration that, of all the Buddhas of the kalpa, Buddha Shākyamuni stands out like a brilliant white lotus.

From the moment the bodhichitta arose in his mind, he gave up all traces of selfishness and considered only the welfare of others. For three great kalpas and over hundreds of lifetimes he accumulated merit and helped living creatures in every possible way with a determination and resourcefulness that knew no limits. For example, once as a young prince, while walking in the forest, he came upon a tigress so weakened by hunger that she could not feed her cubs. Overwhelmed by great compassion he offered her his own flesh, but she did not even have enough strength left to eat it. So he cut his wrists and nourished her with his own blood; and when she had revived, he gave her his entire body on which to feed.

Through his extraordinary compassion and unfaltering diligence, he finally attained the fruit, perfect enlightenment. Following the true path to its end, his ego-clinging utterly extinguished, Lord Buddha was like a great sun illuminating the whole universe for the benefit of beings.

All this he accomplished solely for the good of others, and it is through his perfect example and flawless teaching that we now have a chance to blend our own minds with the true Dharma and attain Buddhahood. By adopting the right attitude and following the true path we can achieve the true result; like the Buddha, we will no longer be deceiving either ourselves or others. Since Lord Buddha himself was true, he spoke the truth as it is. To those with faults he pointed out what was wrong with them. To those who wished to devote their lives to the Dharma he said, "Go from home to homelessness, take up the three monastic robes, and immerse yourselves in study, reflection, and meditation." To householders he explained how to give up the ten negative actions[26] and cultivate the ten positive ones. In these ways he enabled people of different capacities to lead their lives in the right way and practice the Dharma correctly.

Followers of the Buddha—whether learned sages, accomplished meditators, or just ordinary people like ourselves—should follow the path properly. Even in ordinary life people respect someone whose mind and behavior are straightforward and true; but a dishonest person is trusted by no one.

We should pray that our teacher will clearly show us our mistakes and defects. When he does so, we must gratefully accept his criticism and use it to rid ourselves of our faults. Here the words of Patrul Rinpoche come down in a direct lineage from the teachings of Shākyamuni—they are the words of the Buddha himself.

5. Alas for people in this age of residues!
The mind's wholesome core of truth has withered,
and people live deceitfully,
So their thoughts are warped, their speech is twisted,
They cunningly mislead others—who can trust them?

In the golden age, the age of perfection, there was no need for sunlight or moonlight, for beings radiated light from their own bodies. They could move miraculously through space, and they lived without needing any solid food. All creatures naturally abided by the ten virtues. But, as time passed, they began to harm each other, to be ruled by their desires, to steal, and to lie. They lost their natural radiance and had to depend on sun and moon for light; they lost their ability to fly; they began to need solid nourishment, and when eventually the spontaneous harvest and the bountiful cow[27] disappeared, they had to toil to produce their food. Now in our present epoch, all that remains of the qualities of the golden age are residues, like the unappealing left-over scraps of a sumptuous feast. Anyone with eyes of wisdom seeing the miserable condition of people in this decadent age cannot help but feel great compassion.

In this age of conflict people are ill intentioned and full of deceit. They put themselves first and disregard the needs of others. Whoever flatters them they regard as a friend; whoever contradicts or opposes them they see as an enemy. As these attitudes gradually distort all their actions, words, and thoughts, people become more and more warped and twisted, like crooked old trees, until finally their mentality degenerates so far that any notion of right and wrong is completely lost.

We are in an age when anger, craving, ambition, stupidity, pride, and jealousy are the rule of the day. It is an age when the sun of Dharma is already sinking behind the shoulders of the western mountains, when most of the great teachers have left for other realms, when practitioners go astray in their meditation, and when neither lay people nor the ordained act according to the Dharma. People may obtain some transient advantage from the misguided values of these times, but ultimately they are cheating no one but themselves.

The poisonous emotions that saturate people's minds in this dark era are the principal cause of their wandering in the endless cycle of saṃsāra. To deal with those emotions we need to keep a constant vigilance, following the example of the Kadampa masters, who used to say:

> I will hold the spear of mindfulness at the gate of
>   the mind,
> And when the emotions threaten,
> I, too, will threaten them;
> When they relax their grip, only then will I relax mine.

6. Alas! How depressing to see the beings of this
   degenerate age!
   Alas! Can anyone trust what anyone says?
   It's like living in a land of vicious man-eating
   demons—
   Think about it, and do yourself a big favor.

If you were to find yourself in a land of man-eating demons, you would find it hard to feel relaxed, knowing that however friendly and polite they pretended to be, they might attack and eat you up at any time. In the same way, however agreeable ordinary people may seem, you are sure to end up in trouble if you listen to the advice they give you. And if you should try to give them advice, that will only lead to trouble, too. It would be much wiser to concentrate on your own shortcomings. Numerous as they may seem to be, they cannot be permanent, and it is always possible for you to transform them. Replace negative thoughts with faith and love, ordinary gossip with prayers, pointless activities with prostrations and circumambulations, and you will be doing yourself a favor. To take monastic vows, respect your teacher, and make serious efforts in study, reflection, and meditation, working on all your defects, is to do yourself an inestimable service. Just as the application of a drop of gold can transform an entire painting, so too the application of the teachings will completely transform your mind.

To do yourself a favor in this sense does not mean to be selfish. It means that rather than perpetuating your own and others' suffering by allowing yourself to be taken in by the ways of saṃsāra, based as they are upon deluded attachments and aversions, instead consider carefully what the best way to use your life might be. The true goal of the Bodhisattva is to free all beings from saṃsāra, but to be able do that he must first free himself; and to free himself from saṃsāra he first has to understand clearly what is wrong with it. As it is said:

Whatever is born will die,
Whatever is gathered will be dispersed,
Whatever is joined together will come apart,
Whatever goes up will fall down.

Like a pit of burning coals, a nest of vipers, or a city of demons, ordinary worldly life inevitably brings tremendous suffering. Imagine 360 holes pierced in your body, each with a burning wick set in it; the terrible pain you would feel is nothing compared to the inconceivably intense suffering caused by even a single spark of the fires of a hell realm. Whatever suffering we may experience now, we should use it to remind us of compassion and love, to sweep away our evil deeds and obscurations, and to spur ourselves on as we travel the path of deliverance. We must understand the nature of saṃsāra and see clearly that its only antidote is the practice of Dharma.

7. Not long ago, your consciousness was wandering
 alone.
 Swept along by karma, it took this present birth.
 Soon, like a hair pulled out of butter,
 Leaving everything behind, you'll go on again
 alone.

Be careful—a powerful enemy is approaching. Not an ordinary enemy, but an invincible one: death. No plea, however eloquent, can persuade death to hold off for a few years—or even for a second. Not even the most powerful warrior, at the head of all the armies on earth, can make death turn a hair. Death cannot be bribed by wealth, however vast, nor stirred by even the most enchanting beauty.

The best approach, you might think, would be to spend about ten years trying to get somewhere in the world, so that you would then be set up to spend another ten practicing the

Dharma. But who can say with certainty that he will live twenty more years? Who can say that he will definitely see tomorrow's sunrise? Who can even be sure that he will draw his next breath? As you light the fire in your mountain retreat, think to yourself, "I wonder if I'll be lighting a fire like this tomorrow?" Some people die while sleeping, some while walking, some while eating, and some at war; some die young and some die old. Any circumstance of life may turn out to be the cause of death. In a hundred years' time, how many of all the people now living on earth will still be alive?

We were born alone and we will die alone. Yet even while alone we still have our shadow with us; and alone after death, our consciousness will still have with it the shadow of our actions, good and bad. By the time we are just about to enter the bardo, the intermediate state between death and birth, it will be far too late to begin our Dharma practice. But if we have already prepared ourselves, if we feel confident in our practice and know how to go to a Buddha-field, there will be no suffering in death.

Today you are alive and well in a place where you are free to cultivate the Dharma. No one is telling you that your religion is forbidden, or that you are not allowed to recite the *maṇi*, the six-syllable mantra of Chenrezi. So now is the time to prepare for death. In general, we are always very worried about the future. We make strenuous efforts to ensure that in the future we will not run out of money, run out of food, or be without clothes. But of all future events, isn't death the most crucial? Out of fear of assassins, kings and presidents surround themselves with guards; but what about the most lethal assassin of all, who can move in at any moment with no one to stop him?

We came into the world without husband, wife, friend, or companion. We may have many friends and acquaintances at the moment, and perhaps many enemies too, but as soon as death falls upon us we shall leave all of them behind, like a hair pulled out of a slab of butter. Not one of our friends and relatives will be able to help us; we have no choice but to face death all alone. This body of ours, which finds even the pain of a pinprick or a tiny spark of fire really hard to bear, is going to experience death. This body of ours, which we cherish so dearly, will turn into a corpse that our friends and relatives will only want to dispose of as quickly as possible.

In the bardo we will wander, naked and frightened, with no idea of where we are going, all alone, carrying the burden of our past deeds. In front of us, we will face unfathomable darkness; from behind, the red wind of our karma will sweep us on; and, on all sides, we will be surrounded by messengers of Yama, the Lord of Death, shouting, "Catch him, kill him!" If at that time we can remember our teacher for even an instant, the frightful experiences of the bardo will fade away and we will be reborn in a Buddhafield. At the very least, we will again obtain a human life. But if our mind is so heavily burdened by our negative actions that we can apply nothing of the teachings, any hopes of being reborn in the higher realms will be utterly dashed. Like a stone falling from the top of Mount Meru, we will plummet helplessly to the lower realms. We, who in this life find it so hard to bear even the slightest pain, will be plunged into ceaseless torment.

The powerful may have acquired their wealth by force, and the corrupt may have made themselves rich by imposing unnecessary taxes or making a profit at others' expense. But at the moment of death, when all this wealth, power, and influence, together with whatever short-lived satisfaction it may have brought during life, is left behind, the effect of the negative actions through which it was acquired will persist and cause future misery. At death only the effect of our actions, good and bad, stays with us, and only the Dharma can protect us. If we ignore the Dharma now and fall under the influence of the limited concerns of everyday life, we are sure to be carried away by poisonous emotions and accumulate karmic debts. Without the Dharma we will be completely helpless. Instead of concentrating on worldly concerns, shouldn't we do everything we can to practice it right now?

This is the most important task in your life, and you shouldn't be indecisive about it. If you think you will practice later when you have more free time, when you are older, or when you find a more suitable place, you may never get down to practicing at all. As Padampa Sangye said:

> If you wait till you're no longer busy, you'll never get
> around to the Dharma;
> The moment you think of it, quick, do it, Tingri folk!

So, to do something really useful with whatever time may be left before we die, we must turn to the Dharma, as the next root verse explains.

> 8. Of course what we want is our own good,
> So we have to be honest with our own selves:
> If we don't accomplish the essence of the Dharma
> for our own sake,
> Won't we be ruining our own life?

No one is ill intentioned toward himself. People never think to themselves how nice it would be to get sick, nor do they long to be crippled and poor or look forward to being robbed; what they think is how much they want to be happy, and what a pleasure it would be to be rich and comfortable. But where do these ideas come from? They come from the belief in an "I." It is because of this deeply rooted belief that we are preoccupied primarily with our own happiness. In this frame of mind we will never be satisfied. Even if we were crowned emperor of the whole universe, we would still yearn for more power, wealth, and pleasure.

The same process is at work in our feelings about those close to us: husband, wife, children, and friends. Because we love them, we favor them over all others, and should anyone praise or help them we feel quite inordinately pleased. But this is not true love; it is based on thinking they are ours.

Although we love ourselves so dearly, we have no idea at all where to find real happiness. We are about as capable of looking after ourselves as a lunatic. We search for happiness in pleasure, fame, and wealth, oblivious to the fact that death will soon take all those things away. When we cross the threshold of death, we will not be able to take with us even one of the possessions we have worked so hard to obtain. At the most, all our strenuous exertions may have produced a few brief moments of enjoyment—a small result from such a huge amount of effort.

The only sure way to obtain the real and lasting happiness we seek is simply to pray from the bottom of our hearts to our teacher and practice the Dharma in the proper way. Through the natural law of cause and effect and through the blessings of the Three Jewels, in all our future lives we will be born where the Dharma flourishes, we will always meet spiritual teachers, and we will continually make progress toward enlightenment—a huge result from such a small amount of effort.

If, on the other hand, we think that practice and positive actions are meaningless, and that there is no harm in doing wrong, if we think that the main thing is to enjoy this life as much as we can, we are sure to be reborn in the lower realms or in a place where even the word "Dharma" is never heard.

Ordinary convention leads us to believe that the most admirable thing we can do is to look after those dear to us and try to overcome those we don't like. This is mistaken. If you really wish to do something worthwhile with your life, devote yourself to the Dharma.

In the first stages of the path of Dharma, it is essential to put our energy and determination into working on ourselves rather than trying prematurely to help others. At the moment, we are a long way from having rooted out ego-clinging; until we have tamed our own mind, to try to help others would be ludicrous. That is why the teachings talk about "realization for oneself, compassion for others." Through cultivating the view, meditation, and action, we can eliminate our ego-clinging and negative emotions and thus become truly able to help others. As we tame the wildness of our minds with the appropriate discipline, all our defects will gradually disappear and all the qualities of a Bodhisattva will bloom. As Nāgārjuna said:

> Someone who has acted carelessly,
> But later becomes careful and attentive
> Is as beautiful as the bright moon emerging from
> the clouds.

However intractable our ego-clinging might seem, it is possible to free ourselves from it and develop compassion.

To receive any of the prātimokṣha vows[28] provides a firm foundation for taming the mind. Through the pure discipline of the vinaya, we develop the ability to discriminate between what should be included on the path and what should be rejected. It would be difficult at this point to master the whole vast spectrum of Buddhist teachings, but if we can find an authentic teacher; attend and serve him in the right way; receive his teachings on the view, meditation, and action; and put them into practice, we will certainly be able to accomplish the essence of the Dharma.

If you have complete confidence in your teacher, all of his spiritual qualities will steadily develop in you, in the same way that even the ordinary trees in the sandalwood forests of the Malaya Mountains, after years of being impregnated with the fragrant drops that fall from the sandal leaves, eventually carry the beautiful scent of sandalwood. If, however, instead of finding a true spiritual guide, you rely on confused friends who only show you how to accumulate more negative actions, you will be as difficult to cleanse as a piece of kusha grass[29] that has fallen into a sewer. That is why it is said:

> First, be judicious in finding a teacher;
> Then, be judicious in attending him;
> Finally, be judicious in practicing his teachings.
> Whoever is judicious in these three ways will make unerring progress on the path of liberation.

In this decadent age, because of their limited intelligence and lack of determination, people need to practice the Dharma in an essentialized form. The practice of combining devotion to the teacher as inseparable from Chenrezi with the recitation of the six-syllable mantra fulfills this need. This six-syllable mantra, the maṇi, is so easy to recite, yet it concentrates within it the substance of all the Buddhist scriptures. It is the essence of Chenrezi's heart, and the blessings it brings are infinite. If you make it your main practice, humans, celestial beings, and even harmful spirits will be well disposed to you, and you will have a long life free from illness and obstacles. In your next life you will be born in the Blissful Buddha-field of the Potala Mountain, or at the very least in a place where the Dharma prevails. This is because Chenrezi's mantra contains the infinite blessing and compassion of the Buddhas.

The key to success in any endeavor is inner determination. If you are determined to be rich, starting out with even a small sum you can end up a millionaire. If you are determined to study, in time you can become very learned. If you are determined to meditate, you will eventually find a way to free yourself entirely for the practice of Dharma. It is up to you to choose the right goal. Through the practice of Dharma, like an invincible king conquering his ancestral adversary, you will overcome once and for all the ego-clinging that has so tormented you for innumerable lifetimes.

> 9. In this dark age, what people think and do is vile.
> None of them will help you, they'll deceive and
> trick you;
> And for you to be of any help to them will be hard;
> Wouldn't it be best to quit the whole rat race?

In this age, not even our parents can be relied on to show us how to live according to the Dharma. For the most part, what our family and friends see as worthwhile—though with the best of intentions—is only to accumulate wealth, to overpower enemies, and to protect their own interests; they pursue these values perpetually, their thoughts a continual stream of attachment and hostility. They think all the time about how their parents are ill, how ungrateful the children are, how the house needs repairing, and so on. But if our minds continually revolve around such thoughts, we have lost hold of the Dharma. Of course, it is natural that we should care about our parents and relatives and help them however we can, but it is important that we keep our body, speech, and mind attuned to virtue and try to practice the Dharma as much as possible.

Confronted with the chance of some pleasurable experience, even something as small as tasting a spoonful of food, we would hardly ever prefer that someone else might enjoy it instead. We want to keep it for ourselves. In fact, such selfish desires make no sense at all; not only do they make others suffer, but in the long run they bring us suffering too. To think only of ourselves is to abandon the transcendent activities of the Bodhisattva. Would it not be better to put our trust in a spiritual guide and give up all that selfish obsession with wealth, food, clothing, and companions?

If you follow the example of most people of this decadent

age, you will end up being just like them—an expert fraud. You will waste your life chasing after the unattainable. You will be like children who are so busy playing that they are indifferent to hunger and cold and don't notice the day passing—until it gets dark and they suddenly remember their mother and start to cry. If you genuinely want to help beings, you must first perfect yourself. If you make a lot of ambitious plans, doing business, collecting disciples, and setting yourself up as a teacher, you will end up like a spider caught in its own web. Spending your life spinning such webs, you won't notice how fast time is passing until you suddenly realize that death is at hand. You will have used all your energy and gone through all sorts of hardships, but these hardships, unlike the trials of spiritual practice, will not have helped you in the least to improve yourself.

The holy Kadampa teachers used to practice in a very humble way, completely disregarding comfort and entertainment. And our teacher, Buddha Shākyamuni, left the pleasures of his palace behind and practiced austerities for six years. Since we are his followers, should not we, too, relinquish all worldly concerns, forget the endless distractions of our friends and relatives, and wholeheartedly follow the instructions of a genuine teacher?

What is the good of getting involved in saṃsāric issues? Everything in saṃsāra undergoes constant upheaval. Millionaires become beggars, and beggars become millionaires. Whatever happens, people are never content—if they make a million they want to make two, and if they make two million they want to make three. How will you ever be satisfied like that? There is only one thing of which you should never feel you have had enough—your Dharma practice. Be like a hungry yak, who as he grazes is always looking ahead to see where more grass can be found. If you practice in this way, you won't be disappointed.

If you actually tried to achieve everything you want for this life, there would never be enough time. It is said: "All those plans are like children's games. If we put them into action they will never be finished, but if we just drop them, they are all finished at once!"

> 10. Though you serve your superiors, they will never
> be pleased;
> Though you look after your inferiors, they will
> never be satisfied;
> Though you care about others, they won't care
> about you.
> Think about it, and make a firm decision.

No matter what you do, you will never be able to satisfy everyone. The powerful of this world are no different from ordinary people—however hard you might try to please and serve them, they won't really appreciate it. What is more, they can easily become irritated by some small mistake and have you punished, beaten, or thrown in jail. And as for those who depend on you, however much you may take care of them you will never be able to satisfy them fully. However well intentioned your friends may be, in most cases if you follow their advice you will just become more and more tangled in the web of saṃsāra. There is no end to overcoming adversaries and looking after kin. It is all a waste of time. To help others you must first perfect yourself, and to perfect yourself you first have to cut these three ties: obeying important people, getting entangled in futile attempts to help others, and listening to what people say.

Trying to gratify important people only leads to emotional upheavals. Trying to help people with the things of this life only fuels the fires of saṃsāra. At best, whatever satisfaction you may bring about in these ways will only be temporary; it won't help anyone at the moment of death. These, in fact, are mistaken notions of compassion. True compassion is to establish beings in the deathless bliss of perfect Buddhahood.

Trapped in saṃsāra, you should feel like a prisoner in a dungeon who thinks of nothing but how to escape. Recognizing the futility of ordinary occupations, the Kadampa masters used to say:

> Base your mind on the Dharma,
> Base your Dharma on a humble life,
> Base your humble life on the thought of death,
> Base your death on a lonely cave.

To dwell in remote retreats, free from distractions, is the best way to ensure that you will actually practice the Dharma.

Shouldn't we keep all this in mind and work on perfecting ourselves? That is the first step toward truly helping others.

> 11. Being learned these days doesn't help the
> teachings—it just leads to more debate;
> Being realized these days doesn't help others—
> it just leads to more criticism;
> Being in a responsible position these days doesn't
> help govern the country well—it only spreads
> revolt.
> Think about these times with sorrow and disgust.

Although great and highly realized teachers do appear among the confused people of this degenerate age, they are like drops of mercury that have fallen in the dust. They have complete mastery of the five branches of knowledge[30] and teach the Dharma generously, but most people either have distorted views and are inclined to criticize or else show no interest in the Dharma at all. Even the few who do listen become bored after a day or two, not realizing how rare and precious it is to receive such teachings.

If those who receive the teachings do not practice them, they may acquire a superficial knowledge, but it only increases their arrogance. They may develop a certain degree of discipline, but it only increases their infatuation with their own virtue. They may reach a high position, but it only propagates greed, abuse, and revolt. Such disciples are no better than ordinary people; they neither serve the Dharma nor help others.

In the past, qualified teachers would flawlessly expound the teachings, conduct debates to correct any deviations in meaning, and compose commentaries to explain that meaning. These three activities, like the different steps in refining gold, would preserve and spread the teachings, leading people to genuine spiritual practice, culminating in enlightenment. But nowadays these activities just lead the various traditions to the peak of pride and jealousy, where they burn with rivalry, criticism, and spite, poisoning the peaceful atmosphere of authentic spiritual practice with breaches of samaya.[31]

Even in the case of fully realized beings like Guru Rinpoche and Vimalamitra,[32] who had the power to display miracles, who attained the five kinds of supernatural knowledge,[33] and who had the ability to bring to the path of liberation anyone who so much as saw, heard, or thought of them, there were people who nevertheless managed to find fault, doubting the reality of their accomplishments and thinking, "This is all lies and sorcerers' tricks."

In this decadent age disciples have such distorted ways that they only cause breaches of samaya. Because of this, great beings may not be able to benefit others fully, and so the Dharma will be prevented from spreading and flourishing.

Even those who govern cities and countries wisely and with a good heart find that people rise against them and sometimes even try to kill them. As the saying goes, "The higher your rank, the greater your suffering."

Why is it so difficult, even for highly realized beings, to help people? The next verse of the root text explains.

12. Though you explain, people miss the point or
    don't believe you;
    Though your motivation is truly altruistic, people
    think it's not.
    These days, when the crooked see the straight as
    crooked,
    You can't help anyone—give up any hope of that.

When you explain the Dharma these days, people say, "What a fool! He knows a bit about Dharma but nothing about ordinary life." If you explain how to achieve real happiness and how to escape rebirth in the lower realms, people simply do not believe you. Because of their jaundiced views they misinterpret everything you say. When, in broad daylight, a group of blindfolded people agree that it's dark, the problem is surely their mistaken perception. The attitudes that are current these days cut people off from their inherent sanity.

If, with the purest of motivations, you give people sound advice, they think you are trying to take advantage of them in some clever way. If you tell people to practice the Dharma, they think, "This will be the end of my job and family life, and eventually I'll have nothing left at all!" They cannot even recognize that you are trying to help them. If you teach a lot, people just say, "Oh, he's so silver-tongued, isn't he!" but they won't consider the actual meaning of your words. Unable to see what would be best for themselves in the long run, they think you are trying to harm them. They are as twisted as crooked old trees, so whatever their minds perceive becomes distorted too.

In the past golden age, when parents gave advice their children followed it. These days it is not like that, so it is better to keep quiet. Hardly anyone tries to put his guru's teachings into practice. Most people's efforts go into earning money, doing well in business, and trying to reach a position of success. Motivated by these goals, people become warped by attachment and malevolent ambition. In order to get ahead they cheat and consider only their own selfish motives. How could such crooked people ever help each other?

If you carefully examine this sad state of affairs, it will become clear to you just how empty and meaningless all the frenetic activity of saṃsāra really is. You will feel more and more certain that the only worthwhile pursuit is to engage in spiritual practice. Wouldn't it be best to follow the example of Jetsun Milarepa, who cut himself off from all worldly distractions and devoted himself single-mindedly to practicing Dharma in solitary retreats? If you do the same, what you will achieve is something no one can take away from you.

How should we practice the Dharma? The great Kadampa teachers considered the most precious teaching to be the inseparability of voidness and compassion. Over and over again, they cultivated love, compassion, joy, and equanimity—the four limitless thoughts out of which the ability to help others arises effortlessly. Famous for practicing in uncompromising adherence to the teachings, these masters trained themselves first through careful study of the Dharma and then through direct experience in meditation. That is the right way to make progress on the path that leads to the great bliss of ultimate Buddhahood.

The glorious paṇḍita Atīsha, founder of the Kadampa lineage and renowned as the "Second Buddha," brought the teachings on bodhichitta and mind-training to the Land of Snows. In his own practice he constantly cultivated heartfelt love and compassion. If, like him, motivated by compassion for all beings, we establish firmly in our hearts the intention to attain enlightenment for the sake of others, there is nothing that we cannot accomplish. But without this intention, our compassion will be a pale imitation of the real thing. It is said, "To wish happiness for others, even for those who want to do us harm, is the source of consummate happiness." When finally we reach this level, compassion for all beings arises by itself in a way that is utterly uncontrived.

When Lord Buddha was in the Tuṣhita heaven, soon to

become the fourth Buddha of this kalpa, he announced that the time was coming for him to incarnate in the land of Jambudvīpa and display the deeds of a Buddha. The Bodhisattvas and celestial beings tried to dissuade him; now was the dark age, they said, with heretical views predominating everywhere. But the Buddha replied that he was certain he would be able to realize his aspiration to benefit beings. How was it that he could have such confidence? It was because his compassion was boundless, and he knew that with the power of compassion there is nothing that cannot be accomplished. Then, as confirmation of his words, he blew a conch, the sound of which surpassed in beauty and splendor all the music of all the celestial beings put together.

In order to develop this magnitude of compassion, we must abandon ordinary worldly ways and work on taming our stubborn, wild minds. If we try to mix Dharma practice with ordinary pursuits, our realization will be imperfect, like a piece of gold still tarnished and stained. Rather than rushing into undertakings which would, in fact, only be feeble reflections of true Bodhisattva activity, we should first work on our own minds. Then, when we have realized the inseparability of voidness and compassion, we will be able to follow effortlessly in the footsteps of the Buddhas and Bodhisattvas.

If you examine closely the ordinary values that underlie your urge to pursue worldly goals and try to discover where they come from, you find that their source is a failure to investigate things properly. Normally we operate under the deluded assumption that everything has some sort of true, substantial reality. But when you look more carefully, you find that the phenomenal world is like a rainbow—vivid and colorful, but without any tangible existence.

The ways we delude ourselves about the nature of the phenomenal world can be divided according to the different sorts of phenomena: physical, verbal, and mental. About the delusion of physical phenomena, the root text has this to say:

13. "All phenomena are like magical illusions," said the
Buddhas;
But these days the illusions are more illusory than
ever,
Trickeries conjured up by devious illusionists—
Beware of the illusions of this degenerate age's ways.

All the infinite phenomena of saṃsāra and nirvāṇa are like magical illusions. Nowhere in the whole universe is there a single permanent, intrinsically existent entity to be found. There has never been a king who kept his kingdom forever; never someone born who did not die; never a crowd that did not disperse. Everything is like a drama in which actors play out wars, passions, and death. Everything is like a dream, sometimes good and sometimes a nightmare.

But it is in this degenerate age that we have reached the peak of illusion. People have long forgotten the purity of the golden age. They disregard their future lives and are preoccupied only by immediate gratification; unreliable and capricious, they bury the Dharma under a great heap of harmful and negative actions. The world and beings change direction every moment like stalks of wheat swaying to and fro in the wind, and what was true this morning is untrue by this evening. Untimely rain, snow, hail, heat, and cold upset the natural course of the seasons. Seeing all this, we must understand that there is no point in being excessively glad when something good happens to us, as it may well turn into its opposite at any time; and we must understand that there is no point in being too depressed by bad circumstances, as our difficulties are minute compared to those endured by countless beings in the lower realms.

A magician is never deceived by his own tricks. When he conjures up the illusion of horses, oxen, chariots, or whatever, realistic though they may be, he knows that they do not actually exist. Just as a magician cannot be fooled by illusions that he knows he created himself, a Bodhisattva who has realized the emptiness of all phenomena and who recognizes all worldly pursuits to be illusory, even if he lives as a householder, is not affected by negative emotions or ego-clinging. Understanding the void nature of ordinary worldly activities, he is neither attracted to them nor afraid of them. He neither hopes for success nor fears failure; and he has such confidence in his study, contemplation, and practice that whatever he does brings him closer and closer to complete liberation.

However, these days such understanding is rare. Delusion is piled upon delusion and proliferates like the antics of monkeys imitating one another; it has gone so far that it is hard for us to find a way out of it all. We have lost sight of the true nature of things, so it is difficult for us not to waste our lives. But, as the Buddhas of the past have said, "All phenomena are compounded; everything compounded is impermanent; impermanence is suffering." So we should recognize worldly values for what they are; let go of all consideration for wealth, food, and clothes; stop taking advantage of others; and strive to mix our minds with the Dharma. If we can abandon all the busy activities of ordinary life our Dharma practice will progress straight to its goal. Dharma practice and positive actions are also no more real than illusions and dreams, but through these dreamlike merits we will reach the dreamlike fruit of enlightenment.

We must apprehend the nature of everything in the light of the two kinds of truth, relative and absolute. In brief, relative truth is the domain of manifest phenomena, which arise through a combination of causes and conditions in a sequence of interdependent events. Now, since all phenomena are interconnected in this way, it follows that within the realm of relative truth the law of cause and effect is inescapable: positive and negative actions will inevitably result in happiness and suffering. Once the causes and conditions are present, nothing can prevent the result from being produced, just as in the spring if there are seeds in the ground and if the sun gives warmth and the rain moisture, flowers and fruits will appear. That is why we should always be aware of the potential of even the most minute of our actions. We should also realize how rare and precious is the opportunity to be able to practice the Dharma. We may have this opportunity in our hands now, but at any moment it could be taken away from us by death; we must not waste time. The constant thought of impermanence should spur us on to practice. As Lord Buddha said, "Of all footprints, the largest is the elephant's; of all considerations, the foremost is to remember impermanence."

To understand the impermanence of everything is also the key to understanding the void nature of all phenomena. This is absolute truth, and it can only be apprehended by those who have achieved full realization. Ultimately, the two truths are understood to be one within the unity of appearance and voidness.

On the delusion of verbal phenomena, the root verse says:

14. "All talk is like an echo," said the Buddhas,
But these days it's more like the re-echo of an echo.
What the echoes say and what they mean are not the same,
So don't take any notice of those insidious echo-words.

All the words and attitudes of saṃsāric life, whether pleasant or unpleasant, kind or critical, are just the echoes of emptiness. If you shout either insults or flattery at a cliff and the words are echoed back to you, is there any reason to feel depressed or elated? The sounds of the universe—fire, wind, water, the cries of animals, human speech—are all without any real essence. They are just ungraspable empty echoes.

Stories of past events, talk about the present, and discussion of future plans are for the most part expressions of meaningless attachment or hatred. The words come and go, without any real basis, leaving no trace. You may hear somebody being praised in the morning and castigated in the afternoon. People say sweet things when their thoughts are actually unkind; and conversely, when their intentions are good, their words may be cruel. If you take any notice of all this, you are bound to be misled. So ignore ordinary worldly talk, and instead recite prayers and mantras, and read the scriptures aloud.

The happiness and suffering created by praise and criticism are ephemeral. When you are complimented, instead of feeling proud just regard the praise as if it were something you were hearing in a dream or a fantasy. Tell yourself that it is not you that is being praised but the good qualities you may have developed through spiritual practice. In fact, the truth is that the only people really worthy of praise are those who have attained liberation.

When you are criticized, accept it as an opportunity to acknowledge your hidden faults and increase your humility. As it is said, "Blame and ill treatment are the roots of the meditation flower." They are your teacher, destroying attachment and craving. If brought to the path, harsh words and blame will inspire your practice and strengthen your discipline. How can you ever repay such kindness?

For a Bodhisattva who has realized the dreamlike nature of speech, criticism and abuse can only enhance his meditation practice. It does not matter whether he encounters good or bad circumstances, as both help to increase his merit and wisdom. He is never swept away by worries and desires because his mind remains undisturbed in the perfect view. Having let go of all worldly values, he obtains the esteem of others without seeking it.

As for us, even if we were to single-mindedly put everything we have into achieving fame throughout the world, there would always be someone to denigrate us. And even were we to succeed, whatever fame we might achieve, whether for our courage, physical beauty, or power, would only be temporary.

So when you are complimented, think that it is solely because you have done what the Dharma teaches. When you are criticized, let it remind you to increase your compassion for others and to renounce your saṃsāric ways.

> 15. Whoever you see isn't human, but a fraud;
> Whatever people say isn't right, but just lies.
> So since these days there's no one you can trust,
> You'd better live alone and stay free.

To live in this age is like being stranded on an island populated by man-eating demons—we can never relax our guard. Any circumstance we come across can easily turn into a source of misery, and anyone we meet is likely to lead us astray. One thing is certain: only a spiritual teacher can give us valid advice. This should be clear in our minds.

Since the mind is so easily fooled by its deluded perception of physical phenomena, and so easily entangled by deluded worldly talk, wouldn't it be better to go away to a solitary place and meditate? That is the best way to develop love and compassion toward sentient beings. If you continue to practice in that way, day in and day out, you will eventually be able to act with the inexhaustible compassion of a Bodhisattva.

It is very important to meditate with your whole being on bodhichitta until it becomes clear just how meaningless and frustrating the activities of this life really are. You will be touched and saddened by the debilitated condition of beings in this dark age, and a strong feeling of determination to be free from saṃsāra will arise. If these attitudes truly take root, the qualities and achievements of the Mahayāna, the great vehicle, are sure to grow from them. But if that genuine determination to be free from saṃsāra is not firmly implanted in your mind, your Dharma practice will never be able to fully develop.

16. If your actions conform with Dharma, you'll
    antagonize everyone;
    If your words are truthful, most people will get
    angry;
    If your mind is truly good and pure, they will
    judge it a defect.
    Now is the time to keep your own way hidden.

The time is not yet ripe to let others see our worth. Nor is it the moment to give them advice in the hope that they might change for the better—that will only irritate them. Now is the time, rather, to check our own defects and work on ourselves.

We live in a time when most people's minds are quite deranged; what they do or say rarely corresponds to what they actually think. People and events change so fast that it is impossible to rely on anyone or anything. In fact, no one can give us reliable advice except an authentic spiritual master.

In the past, anyone who took monastic vows, wore robes—the glorious emblem of the Buddha's teachings—and practiced the Dharma properly would earn everyone's approval, respect, and support. But if anyone does that nowadays, people assume either that he is showing off or that he is some inadequate personality who cannot adjust to the world.

If with a pure heart you do something helpful for other people, they suspect you must be trying to fool them. If you speak out truthfully, you are bound to highlight people's shortcomings—and no one likes that. Instead, you had better keep your true worth concealed, like live embers buried under the ashes. How to do that is explained in the next verse.

17. Hide your body by staying alone in a mountain
    wilderness;

Hide your speech by cutting off contact and saying
very little;
Hide your mind by being continuously aware of
your own faults alone.
This is what it means to be a hidden yogī.

You will never be free from delusion as long as you are caught up in all sorts of distracting activities; so it is important to live alone in places far from worldly diversions. There is no better place to live and die than a secluded cave in an uncharted valley, where you will meet only wild animals and birds. In such surroundings your loving-kindness and compassion will increase, attachment and hatred will disappear from your mind, and your meditation will not be dissipated by distractions.

The mouth is the doorway of sin. Words tumble out of our mouths with the greatest of ease, yet the consequences they bring can be far-reaching and heavy. Most ordinary conversations are mainly expressions of attachment and animosity. If you speak too much, you will run into trouble, just as a parrot ends up in a cage. So give up unnecessary chatter.

It is the mind that makes us wander in saṃsāra. It is the mind that, by continuously generating the five poisons—attachment, hatred, stupidity, pride, and jealousy—is responsible for the delusion that pervades the three worlds. Instead of letting this troublesome monkey of a mind abuse us as it wishes, we should constantly scrutinize our own faults and, as soon as poisonous thoughts arise, apply the proper antidote. For example, to counteract attachment cultivate disinterest; to counteract hatred cultivate loving-kindness; to counteract ignorance reflect on how the chain of interdependent events[34] creates saṃsāra. The crux of positive action is taming the mind; that is why it is said:

The point of asceticism is to safeguard the mind;
Apart from that, what need would there be for
asceticism?

Check constantly whether your mind is in a state consistent with the teachings or whether it has been invaded by poisonous emotions. If the mind is disciplined and aware, body and speech will naturally follow suit. This inner control of the mind is the true spiritual master. The Dharma is something to be applied all the time—if not, what use can it be?

A hidden yogī is a practitioner who does not mix with other people and become involved in worldly activities, and who seeks neither fame nor followers. He burns with an irresistible longing for spiritual practice and has seized the root of Dharma—the determination to be free from saṃsāra. Now, you might think: "If I renounce all worldly activity now, what will happen to me later? How am I going to find food, lodging, and all the rest of it?" But such deluded hesitations and anxieties could, if you allow them, dominate the rest of your life, pulling the net of saṃsāra tighter and tighter. As long as these inveterate tendencies continue, so will suffering. You will never be a good Dharma practitioner until you are truly sick of ordinary life and know how to be satisfied with whatever you have.

18. Disgust, because there's no one to be trusted,
Sadness, because there's no meaning in anything,
Determination, because there'll never be time to get
everything you want;
If you always keep these three things in mind,
some good will come of it.

We usually see those who are nice to us as friends and those who get in our way as enemies, but these judgments are highly unreliable. Those we now consider friends could easily become enemies in the future, and vice versa. Nothing is ever completely fixed and dependable.

The ordinary concerns of saṃsāra will finally leave no more permanent traces than finger-paintings on a pool of water.

However hard we strive for success and happiness in this life, even if we work till we drop from sheer exhaustion, it will all be for nothing—for what can we take with us across the threshold of death?

When we are involved in some project, the mind, full of thoughts about past events and preoccupied with thoughts of the future, loses any clear mindfulness of the present; this is hardly the way to gain freedom from the bondage of the emotions. In any case, in this life there will never be time to realize even half of all our plans and ideas. Recognizing how futile it all is, and feeling sick and tired of all the ordinary activities of this life, shouldn't we just stick to Dharma practice?

There has never been anyone who did not die. Even Lord Shākyamuni, the Enlightened One, endowed with the thirty-two major and eighty minor marks of Buddhahood, left his body behind to remind beings of impermanence. If Brahmā, Indra, and the other celestial beings who can live for a kalpa in the highest state possible in saṃsāra must nevertheless eventually die and be reborn in the lower realms because they have not eradicated their obscuring emotions, what can we say about ourselves, with our frail human body, loaded down as we are with so many imperfections?

If you are full of your own greatness and irritated by the slightest discomfort, you will never be a true practitioner. Until now we have been preoccupied exclusively with our own comfort, success, family, and friends. For countless lifetimes we have wanted happiness for ourselves alone; now it is time to start wanting what is best for others. Our own present joys and sorrows are just the fruit of seeds we ourselves planted in the past, and it is pointless to be obsessed by hopes and fears about them. Compared to the welfare of the infinity of beings, they are completely insignificant. So welcome suffering as a reminder of saṃsāra's imperfections, as an inspiration to practice, and as an occasion to take the suffering of others upon yourself. Use happiness, too, to nurture your strength to strive toward enlightenment, and to increase your loving-kindness.

Contemplating all this, sadness, revulsion, and determination will rise simultaneously: sadness at seeing the condition of beings and your inability to help them, revulsion at the thought of continuing to go round in this vicious circle, and determination to do something about it by practicing the Dharma.

> 19. There's no time to be happy; happiness is over just like that;
> You don't want to suffer, so eradicate suffering with Dharma.
> Whatever happiness or suffering comes, recognize it as the power of your past actions,
> And from now on have no hopes or doubts regarding anyone at all.

Right now, you may be experiencing all sorts of happiness and pleasure; but this won't last, so do not become attached to it. In this life you are bound to experience all sorts of difficulties, sickness, and other troubles; it is important to see in them the truth of the teachings.

Whenever we experience pain or pleasure, misery or contentment, it is due to our actions in past lives. If you are now healthy, famous, or rich, it is because of meritorious actions you performed in the past. If you suffer from illness, obstacles, or troublesome circumstances, that is the result of your past negative actions. But whatever circumstances you find yourself in, you can purify your mind; when in pain, you can pray from the core of your heart that your suffering may be a substitute for the suffering of others, so that all their pain and suffering will be exhausted forever. The more you suffer, the more you can practice taking on the suffering of all beings.

When difficulties act in this way as an incentive to practice the Dharma, they become a help rather than a hindrance. The way the great Jetsun Milarepa turned all the pain and hardship he endured into the path of enlightenment is a perfect example. Like him, shouldn't we give up all concern for the happiness and comfort of this life and welcome whatever circumstances we encounter as sustenance for our practice?

> 20. Expecting a lot from people, you do a lot of smiling;
> Needing many things for yourself, you have many needs to meet;
> Making plans to do first this, then that, your mind's full of hopes and fears—
> From now on, come what may, don't be like that.

To be rich and powerful, you have to flatter important people. You smile obsequiously and hypocritically, hoping you'll get what you want. As soon as you step into the world of power and affluence, your mind is full of worries, constantly preoccupied with the past, the present, and the future.

In the end, however important and wealthy we may become, it never seems enough. We are never satisfied with what we already have. As the saying goes, "Craving is like a hungry dog." If we could taste the ambrosia of the gods, we would long for something even more delicious; if we could wear their exquisite apparel, we would crave something still finer. So don't exhaust yourself uselessly, like a child running to find the end of the rainbow! Ordinary goals are completely futile; develop the conviction that the only worthy aim in life is to practice the Dharma in order to help all beings.

The essential point of the Dharma is to stay clear of hope and fear about life's joys and sorrows. Living alone in the wilderness, content with whatever you have, you are safe from the torment of wants and needs. Practice comes easily, without many obstacles, distractions, or conflicts. Spending all your life trying to achieve ordinary worldly goals, on the other hand, would be like trying to net fish in a dry riverbed. Clearly understanding this, make a firm decision not to allow your life to pursue such a useless course.

21. Even if you die today, why be sad? It's the way
 of saṃsāra.
 Even if you live to be a hundred, why be glad?
 Youth will have long since gone.
 Whether you live or die right now, what does
 this life matter?
 Just practice Dharma for the next life—that's
 the point.

If you have practiced the Dharma, your life has been meaningful, and even if you are suddenly struck and killed by a thunderbolt this very day, you need have no regrets.

And if you have not practiced the Dharma, there is at least one thing you do not need to worry about—leaving saṃsāra behind. There is no chance of that; you are in it now, and you will be in it for many more lifetimes, like a bee trapped in a jar, flying sometimes up and sometimes down but never escaping. It makes little difference in the end whether you live a few more years or a hundred, if all you are going to do is to fritter your time away.

Now, you may have wasted your life so far; but once you start to practice the Dharma, then, however long you live, every instant of every day will be an immeasurably precious chance to be with your teacher, to receive his instructions, and to practice them wholeheartedly until the day of your death. Then you will know clearly that there is nothing more worthwhile than the Dharma and that practicing it to perfect yourself is a precious investment for this life and all your lives to come.

When death finally comes you will welcome it like an old

friend, being aware of how dreamlike and impermanent the whole phenomenal world really is. As the peerless Gampopa said, at death the best practitioner, having exhausted all saṃsāric tendencies, will merge with the great luminosity; the middling practitioner will have no fear, being confident that he will go straight to a Buddhafield; the inferior practitioner, having practiced some Dharma, will at least have no regret, knowing that he is safe from rebirth in the lower realms.

Even if you are strongly attached to the things of this life, there is simply no way for you to keep them. Youth, with all its pleasures, passes quickly, and without the Dharma, living till you are a hundred will only draw out the suffering of old age. As long as your mind is contaminated by the eight ordinary concerns,[35] no amount of study, contemplation, or meditation will ever lead to liberation. Worldly goals are endless and have no true value. But to practice with the idea of gaining enlightenment solely in order to benefit others is to aspire to the most noble and worthwhile goal of all. This is bodhichitta, the essence of all paths, the one Dharma that accomplishes them all.

There is a right time for everything. Farmers know when the time has come to plough, to sow, or to harvest, and they never fail to do each job when it is necessary. Now that you are in full possession of your faculties, have met a teacher, and have received his instructions, will you let the field of liberation lie uncultivated?

Most people, thinking of the future, make a lot of plans—but the future they plan for is only the very few years of this life. This is very shortsighted; we have such a long way to go in lives to come. Death is just the threshold, which we have to cross alone, aided only by our faith in the teacher and the Three Jewels and by our confidence in the practice. Relatives, friends, power, wealth, and whatever else we have become so used to leaning on will simply no longer be there. So if you waste your life now on endless minor tasks, you can be sure that at the time of death you will weep with regret and be stricken with intense anxiety, like a thief who has just been thrown into jail and anxiously anticipates his punishment. As Jetsun Milarepa said to the hunter Chirawa Gönpo Dorje:

> To have the freedoms and fortunes of human birth
> is usually said to be precious,
> But when I see someone like you it doesn't seem
> precious at all.

A person might find himself with nothing to eat, no clothes to wear, and no house to live in; but if his mind is filled with faith in his guru and the Three Jewels, that person will both live and die with his heart always joyful and confident.

This first section is set out in terms of the Four Noble Truths, the teaching given by Lord Buddha in his first turning of the wheel of Dharma. It corresponds to the first of the three paths, the Hīnayāna. Pointing out the faults of saṃsāra in general, it urges us in particular to revolt against the negativity of this dark age. This determination to be free from saṃsāra is the foundation of all Dharma practice. The second section now goes on to explain the antidote to saṃsāra: the view, meditation, and action of the Mahāyāna.

Part Two

The View, Meditation, and Action of the Mahāyāna

The Three Paths

The first section, outlining the preliminary path, the Hīnayāna, was intended to engender in us a feeling of weariness and revulsion toward the conditions in which we find ourselves, in saṃsāra generally and more particularly in this decadent age. The second section goes on to define the remedy for this situation: the view, meditation, and action according to the great vehicle of the Buddha's teachings, the Mahāyāna. These are explained in two sections: first the intermediate path, the Sūtrayāna, and second the extraordinary path of skillful means, the Mantrayāna.

The Path of the Sūtras

Taking Refuge

Saṃsāra, as we have seen, is nothing but suffering, and so we feel determined to free ourselves from it. To actually do so, however, we need help. Clearly, our only hope for the help we need lies in a fully enlightened being, himself totally free from saṃsāra. This is why Patrul Rinpoche now appeals to the Buddha of Compassion, Chenrezi:

> 22. Ah! Fount of compassion, my root teacher,
>   Lord Chenrezi,
> You are my only protector!
> The six-syllable mantra, essence of your speech,
>   is the sublime Dharma;
> From now on I have no hope but you!

Chenrezi is a fully enlightened Buddha who, in order to benefit beings, takes on the form of a Bodhisattva. All the Buddhas have but one nature, and their compassion is embodied in Chenrezi. As the embodiment of the compassion of all the Buddhas, Chenrezi is at the same time the source of all Buddhas and Bodhisattvas, since compassion is the very root of enlightenment. Chenrezi is compassion itself in the form of a deity. Chenrezi is the Buddha, Chenrezi is the Dharma, Chenrezi is the Saṅgha; Chenrezi is the Guru, Chenrezi is the Yidam, Chenrezi is the Ḍākinī; Chenrezi is the Dharmakāya, Chenrezi is the Sambhogakāya, Chenrezi is the Nirmāṇakāya; Chenrezi is

Amitābha, Chenrezi is Guru Rinpoche, Chenrezi is Ārya Tārā; and above all Chenrezi is our own Root Teacher. Like a hundred streams passing under a single bridge, Chenrezi is the union of all the Buddhas. To receive his blessings is to receive the blessings of all the Buddhas, and to realize his nature is to realize the nature of all the Buddhas.

Chenrezi has appeared in this dark age in the person of Guru Rinpoche, whose wisdom, compassion, and power are swifter than those of any other Buddha, for it was specifically to benefit the beings of this age that he made his prayers of aspiration. Chenrezi manifests infinite forms: kings, spiritual teachers, ordinary men and women, wild animals, even mountains, trees, bridges—whatever is necessary to fulfill sentient beings' needs. Even a cool breeze in scorching weather or a soothing moment of relief during a painful illness are manifestations of Chenrezi's compassion.

Similarly, Chenrezi's six-syllable mantra, OṂ MAṆI PADME HŪṂ, is the compassionate wisdom of all the Buddhas manifested as sound. Within it is contained the essential meaning of all eighty-four thousand sections of the Buddha's teachings. Of all the many mantras of various kinds, such as awareness mantras, dhāraṇīs, and secret mantras,[36] not one is superior to the six syllables of Chenrezi. The great benefits of reciting this mantra, commonly known as the *maṇi,* are described again and again in both sūtras and tantras. It is said that to recite the maṇi even once is the same as reciting the whole of the twelve branches of the Buddha's teachings.[37] Reciting the six syllables of the *maṇi* perfects the six pāramitās and firmly blocks any possibility of rebirth in the six realms of saṃsāra. It is a simple practice, easy to understand and accessible to all, and at the same time it contains the essence of the Dharma. If you take the maṇi as your refuge both in happiness and in sorrow, Chenrezi will always be with you, you will feel more and more devotion without any effort, and all by itself the realization of the Mahāyāna path will arise in your being.

According to the *Kāraṇḍavyūha-sūtra,*[38] if you recite one hundred million maṇis, all the myriad living organisms in your body will be blessed by Chenrezi, and when you die even the smoke from the cremation of your corpse will have the power to protect whoever inhales it from rebirth in the lower realms.

Even a single syllable of the mantra by itself—OṂ, MA, or ṆI—carries unimaginable power to bless and liberate beings. It is said that a Buddha is capable of extraordinary feats beyond the capacity of any other being, such as stating exactly how many drops of rain would fall during a rainstorm lasting twelve years, but that even he would not be able to fully describe the merit generated by a single recitation of the maṇi. Were he to so much as begin such a description, even if all the forests on earth were made into paper, there would never be enough to write down more than the minutest part.

There is nothing in the whole world that can actually frighten away the Lord of Death, but the warm radiance of Chenrezi's compassion can completely dispel the dread felt by anyone as Death approaches. This is what is meant by "undeceiving refuge." Totally free from saṃsāra, Chenrezi is always ready to help sentient beings, and even his slightest movement—a gesture of his hand, a blink of his eyes—has the power to free us from saṃsāra. When we invoke him by reciting the maṇi, we should never think that he is too far away to hear us, in some distant Buddhafield; Chenrezi is always there with whoever has faith in him. Our own obscurations prevent us from actually going to the Potala Mountain in the Blissful Pure Land of Sukhāvatī to meet him face to face, but in truth his compassion never forsakes a single being. He manifests himself constantly in whatever form may benefit beings most, particularly in the form of great spiritual teachers; so we should understand with complete conviction that Chenrezi, the supreme protector who shows all sentient beings the path to liberation, is in fact none other than our root teacher.

The rain of Chenrezi's compassion falls everywhere on the

fields of sentient beings impartially; but the crop of happiness cannot grow where the seeds of faith have been shriveled. To lack faith is to close yourself to the radiant sun of his blessings, as if you were shutting yourself away in a dark room. But if you have faith, there is no distance, no delay, between you and Chenrezi's blessings.

Lord Buddha's teachings are inconceivably extensive and profound. To attain an exhaustive intellectual understanding of them would indeed be a rare and remarkable achievement. But even that would not be enough by itself. Unless we also achieve inner realization by actually applying the teachings and mingling them with our minds, whatever knowledge we may gain remains theoretical and will only serve to increase our self-infatuation.

We have read a lot of books and heard a lot of teachings, but it hasn't been of much benefit in really transforming our being. Leaving the doctor's prescription by the bedside will not cure the illness. So turn your mind inward and ponder deeply the meaning of the Dharma until it permeates your whole being.

This is why Patrul Rinpoche says:

23. Whatever I know I've left it as theory;
 it's no use to me now.
Whatever I've done I've spent on this life;
 it's no use to me now.
Whatever I've thought was all just delusion;
 it's no use to me now.
Now the time has come to do what's truly
 useful—recite the six-syllable mantra.

Like waves, all the activities of this life have rolled endlessly on, one after the other, yet have left us empty-handed. Myriads of thoughts have run through our minds, each one giving birth to many more, but all they have done is to increase our confusion and dissatisfaction. Wouldn't it be better to meditate on the essence of the teachings and recite the maṇi?

As we are now, bogged down in a swamp of habitual tendencies and trapped in the bonds of our passions, we are neither free enough nor strong enough to be able to liberate sentient beings from saṃsāra. We have to look for help—not just any kind of help, but the unfailing help of Chenrezi:

> 24. The only never-failing, constant refuge is the
> Three Jewels;
> The Three Jewels' single essence is Chenrezi.
> With total, unshakable trust in his wisdom,
> Convinced and decisive, recite the six-syllable
> mantra.

Seeking refuge in gods such as Brahmā or Indra, since they are themselves still trapped in the net of saṃsāra, can be of no real help. Seeking refuge in the powerful and influential people of this world, or in friends and relatives, will bring only the most limited protection. Nor can mountains, stars, or any other natural phenomena provide true security. None of these are ultimate sources of refuge. If you were in jail and wanted to be released, you would have to seek help from someone who had the power to free you, not from another prisoner.

To be able to free us from the whirlpool of saṃsāra, the basis of the refuge we seek must be something itself already totally free. There is only one source of refuge free from all the limitations of saṃsāra, complete with all the qualities of ultimate realization, and possessing the limitless compassion that can respond universally to the needs of sentient beings and lead them all the way to enlightenment: the Three Jewels.

The Three Jewels are the Buddha, the Dharma, and the Saṅgha. The Buddha is the teacher, who displays the four kāyas and five wisdoms.[39] The Dharma is the path, the teachings that are transmitted and realized. The Saṅgha are the companions on the path, those who understand the meaning of the teachings and who as a result are liberated.

Through faith and devotion in the Three Jewels, we will come to realize that they are not three separate entities, but the body, speech, and mind of Chenrezi, the Buddha of Compassion. His mind is the Buddha, his speech the Dharma, and his body is the Saṅgha. Even though at present we cannot meet Chenrezi in person, we should be aware of his limitless qualities as they are described in the sūtras and tantras. We should also remember that Chenrezi is inseparable from our teacher, who instructs us in the precious Dharma. Deeply appreciating this great kindness, praying to him and reciting the six-syllable mantra, there is no doubt that all our karmic obscurations and negative emotions can be cleared away. The time will come when we will actually be in the presence of Chenrezi in his Buddhafield, where he turns the wheel of the Mahāyāna Dharma for his retinue of Bodhisattvas.

Taking refuge is the gateway to the Dharma. It is common to all three vehicles and is the foundation on which all practice depends. The attitude to saṃsāra that motivates people to take refuge, however, is not always the same. To be afraid of suffering in saṃsāra and therefore to take refuge for one's own sake would be an inferior motivation. The best motivation would be the wish to liberate all sentient beings completely from the suffering of saṃsāra and to establish them in the state of enlightenment. To take refuge with that thought is the attitude of the Mahāyāna.

If the taking of refuge is to be genuine and true, unshakable faith needs to be developed. Faith is a vital element in the path, opening us to the Buddha's blessings. Expecting to attain realization without having faith would be like sitting in a north-facing cave waiting for the sunshine to pour in.

There are four stages in the development of faith: clear faith, longing faith, confident faith, and irreversible faith. When you first realize what wonderful and extraordinary qualities the Buddha, Chenrezi, and your teacher possess, your mind becomes very clear and joyful. This is clear *faith.* When this clear faith inspires you to obtain Chenrezi's perfect qualities for yourself, and you think what an infinite number of beings you would be able to help if you had those qualities, it has become longing *faith.* When you know with complete certainty that Chenrezi's qualities are truly as they were described by the Buddha himself, it has become confident *faith.* Finally, when faith has become so much a part of yourself that, even at the cost of your life, there is no way you would ever renounce it, it is then irreversible *faith.* When your faith reaches this point, whatever circumstances you may meet you will always be completely confident, thinking, "Chenrezi, you know everything; no matter what happens, I rely entirely upon your wisdom and compassion." From then on the blessings and guidance of Chenrezi will always be with you, and there is no doubt that even the sound of his name will have the power to free you from the lower realms. It is this irreversible faith that is needed for the taking of refuge to be truly authentic.

There is a saying: "Faith is the precious wheel that rolls day and night along the path of liberation." Faith is the foremost of the seven noble qualities. The sun's rays fall everywhere uniformly, but only where they are focused through a magnifying glass can they set dry grass on fire. In the same way, Chenrezi's compassion radiates to all beings equally, but only in those who have the magnifying glass of faith will the flame of his blessings be kindled.

It would be shortsighted to take refuge for this lifetime only, or just until you are cured of all your present ills. Your commitment should be to take refuge until all sentient beings have attained enlightenment. When you are able to offer body, speech, and mind to Chenrezi with genuine faith, relying upon him totally, whether in good or bad circumstances, then you are taking refuge in the fullest sense—the genuine refuge of the Mahāyāna.

Taking refuge in Chenrezi may be according to outer, inner,

and secret perspectives. In his outer aspect, Chenrezi is the Three Jewels—the Buddha, the Dharma, and the Saṅgha. From an inner perspective, he is the Three Roots—the Guru, the Yidam, and the Ḍākinī. And from the secret point of view he is the three kāyas—the Dharmakāya, the Sambhogakāya, and the Nirmāṇakāya. Taking refuge is therefore by no means only a preliminary or beginners' practice; in fact it includes the whole path in all its profundity, right up to enlightenment. However, although many levels of taking refuge can be distinguished, we can fulfil them all by simply reciting the six-syllable mantra with the faith and conviction that our teacher, inseparable from Chenrezi, is the single essence of the Three Jewels in all their aspects.

Lord Atīsha, whose peerless knowledge and realization had brought him acclaim throughout northern and eastern India as the "Second Buddha," traveled to Tibet, where he taught the benefits of taking refuge so many times that everyone started to call him the "Refuge Paṇḍita." On hearing that this was the name his students had given him, he exclaimed, "To be given this name is an honor, indeed—for what could be more excellent than taking refuge in the Buddha?"

The Thought of Enlightenment

Having realized the importance of faith and of taking refuge, we now come to the essence of Mahāyāna, the thought of enlightenment.

25. The basis of the Mahāyāna path is the thought of
    enlightenment;
    This sublime thought is the one path trodden by
    all the Buddhas.
    Never leaving this noble path of the thought of
    enlightenment,

With compassion for all beings, recite the six-syllable mantra.

The "thought of enlightenment," *bodhichitta* in Sanskrit, is the wish to attain enlightenment for the sake of all sentient beings. Bodhichitta has two aspects, the relative and the absolute. Absolute bodhichitta is the recognition of the Buddha-nature inherently present in each being and can be grasped only by those who realize the void nature of all phenomena; since it is not easy to understand fully, we usually begin with the practice of relative bodhichitta, which is less difficult.

Relative bodhichitta is also divided into two: aspiration and application. The first is the wish to attain enlightenment for the sake of all beings, and the second is putting this wish into action through the practice of the six pāramitās. In other words, aspiration bodhichitta is what identifies the goal, and application bodhichitta is the means by which the goal is attained. The key point of the Mahāyāna is that both aspiration and application are directed not toward oneself but toward all sentient beings, for however long saṃsāra may last.

How does one start to generate aspiration bodhichitta, the feeling of compassion for all beings that inspires in us the wish to attain enlightenment for their sake? First, take Chenrezi as a witness of your determination to attain realization in order to benefit others. Next, try to overcome the attitude of only wanting to help those close to you while rejecting the needs of people you dislike. This becomes possible when you realize that, in all your infinite previous existences, every being, without exception, must have been your mother or father at least once. Each one of those beings, down to the smallest insect, wants only to be happy and not to suffer; but what none of them know is that suffering is caused by negative actions and happiness is generated by a virtuous mind. When you think about all those beings who are sinking hopelessly in suffering like blind people lost in a vast desert, you cannot help but feel great compassion for them all.

To develop this compassion further, imagine yourself in the realms of hell; suddenly, before your eyes, your own parents are dragged in by the henchmen of Yama, the Lord of Death,[40] who savagely beat them, slash them with sharp weapons, scald them with molten bronze, and crush them beneath slabs of red-hot iron. Watching their terrible agony, would you not feel overwhelming compassion and the irresistible urge to rush immediately to their rescue? When this strong feeling of compassion arises clearly, reflect a little. Your living parents are only two out of the vast infinity of living beings. Why should the infinite number of other beings not deserve your compassion too? Realizing that in fact there is no real reason, gradually try to extend your compassion, first to your closest friends and relatives, then to everyone you know, to the whole country, the whole earth, and finally to the infinite number of sentient beings in the three realms of saṃsāra. Only when your compassion really reaches this vast extent can it be called true compassion.

All sentient beings are the same in wishing to be happy and not to suffer. The great difference between oneself and others is in numbers—there is only one of me, but countless others. So, my happiness and my suffering are completely insignificant compared to the happiness and suffering of infinite other beings. What truly matters is whether other beings are happy or suffering. This is the basis of bodhichitta. We should wish others to be happy rather than ourselves, and we should especially wish happiness for those whom we perceive as enemies and those who treat us badly. Otherwise, what is the use of compassion?

To feel compassion for all beings is the starting point. You then have to be able to translate your wishes and aspirations into action. But, as Lord Atīsha said, "It is the intention that counts." If your mind is always filled with the intention to benefit others, then, no matter what your actions may look like on the surface, the application bodhichitta will take care of itself. If you can maintain this attitude of bodhichitta, not only will you never stray from the path, you will also definitely make progress along it. When your body, speech, and mind are completely saturated with the wish to help all sentient beings, when your aim both for others and for yourself is perfect Buddhahood, then even the smallest action, a single recitation of the maṇi or a single prostration, will swiftly and surely bring the fulfillment of your goal.

The six syllables of the maṇi, the essence of Chenrezi's being, are the six pāramitās in the form of mantra. When you recite the mantra, the six pāramitās spontaneously arise and the application bodhichitta is accomplished.

It is said that when those who are afflicted in the prison of saṃsāra generate the thought of enlightenment, they are instantly adopted by the Buddhas as their sons and daughters, and they are praised by both men and gods. The whole of their existence takes on a new meaning. This is all due to the measureless power of the jewel-like bodhichitta. Bodhichitta is the essence of the eighty-four thousand sections of the Buddha's teachings, but at the same time it is so simple, so easy to understand and practice, even for a beginner.

Absolute Bodhichitta is the inseparability of voidness and uncontrived compassion. It is the simplicity of the natural state, beyond all concepts and intellectual limitations, out of which spontaneous, objectless compassion arises, benefiting all sentient beings.

As you make progress in your practice, the two aspects of bodhichitta reinforce one another. To catch even a glimpse of the absolute nature of mind gives you the proper perspective to practice relative bodhichitta, and, in turn, the practice of relative bodhichitta broadens your realization of absolute bodhichitta.

Purification

Having developed the right attitude of bodhichitta, we now need to clear away whatever might hinder our progress on the path to enlightenment:

> 26. Wandering in saṃsāra from beginningless time until now,
> Whatever you've done was wrong and will lead to further wandering.
> From your heart acknowledge all wrongdoing and downfalls, and, confessing them,
> With the four powers complete, recite the six-syllable mantra.

In past lives, and in this life until now, we have brought harm to others countless times by lying to them, cheating them, stealing from them, bringing ruin upon them, assaulting them, killing them, and all kinds of other wrongdoing. This accumulated negativity is what has kept us trapped in saṃsāra, and it is now the chief hindrance to our progress on the path. It sustains the two kinds of obscuration which fall between us and the experience of the Buddha-nature: obscuration by emotions and obscuration of what can be known.

Our situation is not completely hopeless, however. As the Kadampa masters used to say, "The only good thing about wrongdoing is that it can be purified." Negative actions are compounded phenomena, so they must be impermanent; therefore, as the Buddha said, there can be no fault so serious that it cannot be purified by the four powers.

These four powers are the means through which purification of all wrongdoing can be effected. The first power is the power of support. Support here refers to the person or deity to whom we acknowledge and confess our faults, and who thus becomes the support for our purification. In this case, the support is Chenrezi, the manifestation of the wisdom of all Buddhas and Bodhisattvas. In other practices, the support might be Vajrasattva, for instance, or the Thirty-Five Buddhas of Confession, or the Buddha Vairochana, the sound of whose name alone is enough to liberate all beings from the lower realms; but of the many deities who may fulfill this capacity, all are manifestations of Chenrezi, the quintessential support for purification.

The second power is the power of regret. Regret arises naturally when we realize that all the suffering we have experienced until now in all our numerous rebirths in saṃsāra has been caused by our own wrongdoing—the five sins with immediate effect, the ten nonvirtuous actions, and the transgressions of the vows of the three vehicles.[41] We have all had so many countless lives, and if you were to heap together in one place all the bodies you have had, even just the bodies of all your rebirths as an insect would make a mound higher than Mount Meru. If you collected all the tears of sorrow and anguish you have shed in past lives, they would make an ocean larger than any in this universe. Many other such similes can be found in the *Sublime Dharma of Clear Recollection.*[42] All the suffering of all those endless rebirths was purely the result of your own harmful actions, such as lying or killing. As long as you remain unaware of the consequences your actions will bring, you will just go on behaving like a madman; but once you see clearly how all your past wrongdoing is what has kept you wandering in the interminable suffering of saṃsāric existence, you are bound to be stricken with deep remorse about all the negative actions you have committed, completely losing any urge to repeat them. With strong, sincere regret, you should confess all your faults, with nothing held back.

But regret by itself is not enough; the negative actions of the past still have to be purified. This is done with the third power, the power of the antidote. All negative actions committed with body, speech, and mind must be counteracted with their antidotes: positive actions of body, speech, and mind. To put this into practice, with your body do prostrations, honor holy sites by circumambulating them, and serve other people and the teachings; with your speech recite the maṇi; and with your mind, thinking how without the radiance of his compassion you would just sink deeper and deeper into saṃsāra, pray one-pointedly with great devotion to Chenrezi to dispel all your obscurations and negativity. In answer to your fervent prayer, visualize wisdom nectar flowing from Chenrezi's body and pouring into you and all sentient beings through the crown of the head. It fills your body and theirs, and completely washes away all obscurations, wrongdoing, and negativity, until at the end no trace is left; your body has become completely pure and as transparent as crystal. Chenrezi smiles radiantly and says, "Noble child, all your faults are purified." Melting into light, he dissolves into you. Feeling that Chenrezi's mind and yours have become one, remain for a while in a state of luminous voidness, beyond any concept.

The fourth power is the power of resolve, the determination never to repeat those harmful actions again, even at the cost of your life. Until now you might have been blind to the fact that wrongdoing is what causes suffering, but from now on you have no excuse not to change your ways. Nor is it right to think that since negative actions can be purified so easily, they do not matter very much; you have to make a resolute decision, from the very core of your being, that whatever happens you will never do any action that contradicts the Dharma. This will require constant mindfulness and diligence. The fourth power also includes the resolution to be pure in your body, speech, and mind, like Chenrezi. As you recite the six-syllable mantra, your negativity and obscurations will vanish, and all the qualities inherent in the enlightened state will begin to shine, like the sun emerging from behind the clouds.

Offering

27. The mind, holding on to an "I," clings to
    everything—this is the cause of saṃsāra;
So, as offerings to the exalted in nirvāṇa and
    charity to the lowly in saṃsāra,
Give everything—body, possessions, and
    virtue—and dedicate the merit to all;
Casting all attachments far away, recite the
    six-syllable mantra.

Through purification, you have cleared away the hindrances on the path to enlightenment, but in order to travel along this path you must now also gather the necessary provisions to sustain you on your journey. This gathering of provisions is the accumulation of merit and wisdom. The accumulation of merit, accomplished through virtuous actions and the making of offerings, will lead to the attainment of the Rūpakāya, the body of form; the accumulation of wisdom, accomplished by performing these virtuous deeds with a mind free from clinging, will lead to the attainment of the Dharmakāya, the absolute body. Both accumulations should be accomplished with the thought of benefiting others.

It is of crucial importance to understand that holding on to the idea of there being an "I," a truly existing self, is the fundamental cause of our wandering in the three realms of existence. Once this mistaken belief in an ego has taken root, we start clinging to *my* body, *my* mind, *my* name, *my* possessions, *my* family, and so forth; it is these notions that then make us crave pleasure and abhor pain. The result is an unceasing succession of alternating attraction and repulsion, and from these underlying urges arise the conflicting emotions that disturb our minds without respite.

In countless past lives, we have had plenty of wealth and

possessions; but we were so fearful of losing or using up what we had that we were incapable of being generous, in the form of either offerings to the Three Jewels or charity to others. There are even some very rich people who wear worn-out clothes and eat only the most meager meals, out of miserliness; this shows how blind they are to impermanence, for the time is bound to come—certainly when they die and quite possibly before—when they will lose everything they possess; and then, not only will they be unable to take any of their wealth with them, they may well end up being reborn in an existence where even the words "food" and "drink" are never heard for years on end. Although it is true that your possessions are no more real than treasure found in a dream, or than a mirage city shimmering on the horizon, by offering them to Chenrezi and the Three Jewels you will accumulate dreamlike merit which will lead you to dreamlike happiness, long life, and prosperity, and eventually to liberation. To accumulate true merit, make all your offerings and gifts with great devotion and without any pride whatsoever.

Out of all our belongings, it is our body that we cherish most; we can hardly even bear having it subjected to the prick of a thorn or the scorch of a tiny spark. To reverse this habit of clinging to your own physical comfort and possessions, offer your body to the Buddha as a servant and offer all your possessions as a vast cloud of offerings to all Buddhas and Bodhisattvas—that is the really meaningful way to use them. Furthermore, with your imagination, offer all that is beautiful in the universe: delicate flowers, cool gardens and forests, the finest music, wonderful fragrances, perfect foods, lights of all kinds, the most precious and exquisite jewels. Foremost among all these offerings is the sublime offering of the maṇḍala of the whole universe: Mount Meru and the four continents, the mountain of jewels, the wish-granting tree, and so forth—in short, the whole world-system filled with the inexhaustible wealth of gods and men. Present this infinite offering both to those who dwell in nirvāṇa, the Buddhas and Bodhisattvas, and to those in saṃsāra, all the beings of the six realms.

In addition to all these offerings, there is also described in the sūtras and tantras, as a further antidote to the ego-clinging that lies at the very root of saṃsāra, the very profound practice of visualizing your body being transformed into ambrosia and then being offered to the four classes of guests. Of these four, the first are those especially worthy of respect and devotion, the Three Jewels. The second are those whose qualities make them also worthy of offering, the Dharma-protectors. The third are those in need of compassion, all sentient beings of the six realms; for them, visualize that your offering of ambrosia is transformed into whatever can assuage their suffering—food for the hungry, medicine for the sick, clothing for those who are cold, and shelter for the homeless. The fourth class of guests are those to whom you owe karmic debts from both this and past lives, and who therefore make themselves felt as negative forces, creating obstacles and confusion, and preventing you from practicing; by making offerings to them in the form of whatever they most wish, your debts to them will be cleared.

The six-syllable mantra, too, can be recited as an offering to the Three Jewels and to all sentient beings; it has the power to bring infinite benefit. Even the most ruthlessly cruel and arrogant beings, completely lacking the slightest inclination toward the Dharma, can be tamed and helped with this mantra, for it is the source of the bodhichitta, whose infinite power of compassion always succeeds where force and violence fail.

Through these practices, whose essence is generosity and concern for others, you can free yourself from the ego-centered grasping mind, the very basis of saṃsāra. Making offerings and developing compassion for all sentient beings, you will eventually be able to give up any attachment to yourself whatsoever. This is the supreme offering, the true pāramitā of generosity, generosity "gone beyond"; for ordinary generosity has been sublimated into wisdom and compassion.

The ultimate generosity is illustrated by the following story.

> Once there was a great king, renowned for his immense compassion. Day after day, in the highest room in his palace, he used to meditate on loving kindness. The power of his compassion was such that no one, however hard he tried, could kill any living being in his kingdom. One morning, a dove flew in through the open window and collapsed upon the king's lap, breathless and terrified, pursued only a few seconds later by a hawk, who swooped into the room and, alighting near the king, said to him, "This dove is mine. I need meat for myself and my hungry nestlings."
>
> The king thought to himself, "There is no way I can give the mother hawk this dove; and there is no other meat I can get for her. But if I don't do something, she and her nestlings will all die." Hitting at last upon an answer to his dilemma, the king resolved to give the hawk some of his own flesh.
>
> "How much meat do you need?" he asked her.
>
> The hawk replied, "My own body-weight."
>
> The king took a balance and placed the hawk on one of its scales. With a sharp knife, he began to cut flesh from his right thigh, placing it on the other scale. But the balance didn't move at all. He cut flesh from his left thigh and placed that, too, on the scale, but it still didn't move. Then he cut flesh from all over his body and heaped it all on to the scale—but even then the balance stayed as it had been from the first. Finally he just sat on the scale, offering his whole body.
>
> At that very moment the dove and the hawk, two celestial beings who had come to test the king's compassion, reassumed their usual forms. "It is indeed true that you are a most compassionate being!" they said. At this,

> the king was at once miraculously healed of his wounds.
> In a future life he was to become the Buddha Shākyamuni.

At present we do not have the ability to offer our own heads, limbs, and flesh, as the great Bodhisattvas did, and in fact at our level it would be wrong to attempt such offerings; so we begin by offering our body mentally. Through this and all the other offering practices, as you gradually diminish your attachments, your mind will become more and more sublime and vast. Eventually, you will realize the empty nature of the ego; you will then be capable of perfecting the accumulation of wisdom, by making the most perfect offering of all—the realization of the void nature of all phenomena.

Guru Yoga

We now come to the very quintessence of the path, the practice of Guru Yoga, through which wisdom will arise naturally and effortlessly in our being.

> 28. The noble teacher has the nature of all Buddhas,
> And of all Buddhas, it is he who is the kindest.
> Seeing the teacher as inseparable from Chenrezi,
> With fervent devotion, recite the six-syllable mantra.

Your root teacher's qualities and abilities are equal to those of all the Buddhas of the past in every respect but one: the kindness he shows to you is even greater. How can this be so? Because it is he who is prepared to actually point out to you the path to liberation. Deeply appreciating this unique kindness, you should always venerate your spiritual master as the Buddha himself.

All the Buddhas of the past, present, and future have achieved and will achieve enlightenment by relying upon a spiritual teacher. The most profound of all teachings, the Mahāmudrā and the Great Perfection, are realized through devotion rather than through the fabrications of the intellect. With unwavering and single-minded devotion, see the teacher as the Buddha himself and everything he does as perfect; then his blessings, the wisdom of all the Buddhas' minds, will flow effortlessly into your being. Practice in accordance with his instructions, and, as all the clouds of doubt and hesitation are cleared away, the sun of his compassion will shine through, warming you with happiness.

The Chakravartin, the legendary universal monarch, derives his power over the four continents from the fabulous wheel which accompanies him wherever he goes. In the same way, if you keep your devotion always with you, it will bring you the power to progress effortlessly toward liberation. As Lord Buddha said, "I am always there for whoever has devotion." Just as a lake reflects the moon all the more brilliantly when its surface is clear and still, so the blessings of the teacher flow most powerfully when your faith is strong and clear.

It is through the blessings of the teacher that enlightenment can be achieved most swiftly. As the tantras say:

> The teacher is Buddha, the teacher is Dharma,
> the teacher is Saṇgha;
> The teacher embodies the wisdom of all Buddhas.

With this in mind, pray to your teacher as Chenrezi himself. It is also said:

> The teacher's mind is unchanging Dharmakāya,
> The teacher's speech is unceasing Sambhogakāya,
> The teacher's body is the all-embracing compassion
> of Nirmāṇakāya;
> Pray to the teacher, the natural presence of the
> four kāyas.

To pray to the teacher as inseparable from Chenrezi is the very essence of Guru Yoga. The literal meaning of Guru Yoga is "union with the teacher's nature." To blend your mind with the teacher's mind is the most profound of all practices and the shortest path to realization. It is the life-force of the path and the one practice that includes all others. It was through relying on a spiritual teacher that all the Bodhisattvas of the past generated the mind of enlightenment and reached perfection. The Bodhisattva Taktu-ngu, the "Ever-Weeping One,"[43] for example, was willing to give anything, even his own flesh and blood, in order to be accepted by his teacher; and the Bodhisattva Shönnu Norsang, "Youthful Excellent Wealth," followed no fewer than 143 spiritual masters.

It is important, therefore, to pray to your teacher at all times and in all circumstances, from the depths of your heart and from the very marrow of your bones. When sitting down, visualize him above your head and pray to him; when walking, visualize him above your right shoulder as if you were circumambulating him; when eating, visualize him in your throat, and imagining that your food is transformed into the purest ambrosia, offer it to him. When going to sleep, visualize him in your heart, seated upon a four-petaled red lotus, radiating light which fills the whole universe. All the pleasures you experience, all the beautiful sights and sounds, all the joys in your life, multiply them infinitely in your mind and offer them to him. When your circumstances are happy and everything is going well, think how it is all due to his kindness, and enjoy what you have with no more attachment than for a dream or an illusion. When you are weighed down by sickness, sorrow or ill treatment, reflect on how this is in fact your teacher's kindness, too, for it is through such difficulties that you have the chance to purify your past wrongdoing and karmic debts; and make the wish that all beings' suffering be added to your own, so that they no longer need to suffer.

If you can see even a demon as Chenrezi, your clinging to the reality of negative forces will dissolve, and such forces will no longer be able to create obstacles to your life or practice. When lightning strikes, rocks collapse, or wild beasts threaten, if your mind is filled with the thought of Chenrezi and you rely totally upon him, you will be completely free from fear. At the time of your death, too, if you think only of Chenrezi you will have nothing to fear from the terrifying apparitions of the bardo. But if you are overwhelmed by fear, hesitating between running away or hiding somewhere, you will be in constant anguish all your life, and at death you will be unable to overcome the delusory fears of the bardo.

All the sublime practices of the sūtras and tantras can be condensed into devotion to the teacher, and all of them are included in the practice of reciting the maṇi. Remembering that devotion to the teacher is the source of all realization, and that the essence of Guru Yoga—to merge your mind with Chenrezi's nature—is the most profound of all practices, recite the six-syllable mantra.

The Path of the Tantras

Having described the essential points of the path of the sūtras, Patrul Rinpoche now comes to the path of the tantras, which is also often called the path of the secret mantra, or the adamantine vehicle, the Vajrayāna. It is important to remember that the practice of the Vajrayāna is based on the Sūtrayāna, with which it must never conflict.

Empowerment

Before beginning to practice the Vajrayāna path, you need to receive an initiation, or empowerment, which gives you permission to receive the Vajrayāna teachings and to practice them, and which makes sure that your understanding of the practice matures properly until you can harvest the fruit. To practice the Vajrayāna without having received an empowerment would be like trying to press oil from stones.

29. Purifying the obscurations, initiating the practice
 of the path and actualizing the four kāyas,
The essence of the four empowerments is the
 teacher Chenrezi;
If you recognize your own mind as the teacher,
 all four empowerments are complete;
Receiving innate empowerment by yourself,
 recite the six-syllable mantra.

Before pouring into a container some very precious liquid, you would surely first make sure that the container had been thoroughly washed. In the same way, to ensure that you are a proper receptacle for the precious teachings it is important, before receiving them, to be cleansed by receiving an empowerment.

Empowerment (in Tibetan *wang* and in Sanskrit *abhiṣheka*) authorizes you to hear, study, and practice the teachings of the Vajrayāna. Specifically, it confers permission to practice the various stages of the path: the development stage, in which you visualize the deities and recite mantras; the completion stage, in which you practice the inner yogas; and the Mahāmudrā and Great Perfection, in which you encounter the absolute nature of awareness.

Although there are many levels of empowerment, the basis of all of them are the four fundamental empowerments corresponding to the four obscurations to be purified, the four processes through which the purification takes place, and the four aspects of accomplishment with result.

The vase empowerment purifies the body; the secret empowerment purifies the speech; the wisdom empowerment purifies the mind; and the symbolic empowerment purifies the subtle defilements of body, speech, and mind together. These four empowerments are received respectively from the body, the speech, the mind, and the indestructible adamantine wisdom of the teacher, here in the form of Chenrezi. The fruit of these four empowerments is the actualization of the four kāyas.

Through empowerment you will realize the true nature of all phenomena to be primordial purity. Now, why is it that we and all beings have until now been tormented by all the countless forms of suffering in the six realms of saṃsāra? It is simply because we have failed to perceive everything as primordially pure. Primordial purity really is the true state of all phenomena, and our usual impure perceptions are totally false, delusions without the slightest grain of truth—like mistaking a piece of rope for a snake or thinking a mirage is really the shimmer of water in the distance.

So the function of the four empowerments is to make you aware of the natural purity of everything. Through the blessing of Chenrezi's body, you will perceive the whole universe as Chenrezi's Buddhafield, the Potala Mountain. Through the blessing of Chenrezi's speech, you will perceive all the sounds in the universe—the sounds of water, fire, wind, the cries of animals, human voices—as the reverberation of the maṇi. Through the blessing of Chenrezi's mind, you will experience all thoughts as the display of awareness. Through the blessing of Chenrezi's body, speech, and mind together, you will realize that in reality body, speech, and mind are not three separate entities but are Chenrezi's one nature, voidness and compassion inseparable.

Having first received an empowerment from a qualified teacher, you must then reactivate the empowerment yourself over and over again, each time deepening your understanding, rekindling the blessings of the teacher, and repairing any breaches of samaya that may have occurred. To reactivate the vase empowerment, visualize Chenrezi clearly as the all-pervading lord of the infinite maṇḍalas and pray to him with yearning faith. To reactivate the secret empowerment, recite the maṇi with fervent devotion. To reactivate the wisdom empowerment, invoke with your devotion the blessings of Chenrezi's perfect, nonconceptual compassion in the form of rays of light emanating from his heart and dissolving into your heart. To reactivate the symbolic empowerment, pray to Chenrezi with immense, heartfelt respect, invoking his adamantine wisdom, which, in the form of five-colored rays of light radiating from all of his body, dissolves throughout your body. In this way, as you receive the four empowerments, the four obscurations[44] are cleared away and the four kāyas actualized.

Empowerment can also be considered according to ground, path, and fruit. The tathāgatagarbha, the Buddha-nature, has always been present within you: this itself is the ground empowerment. When at the time of initiation the inherent Buddha-nature is directly pointed out by the teacher and is subsequently realized gradually by the student, this is the path empowerment. Methods for this gradual process include the visualization of maṇḍalas[45] and deities, the recitation of mantras, and so forth; in this particular practice you visualize Chenrezi above your head, recite the six-syllable mantra, and again and again receive from him the four empowerments. The path empowerment leads to the fruit empowerment, which is simply the complete realization of your inherent Buddha-nature.

The blessings of the four empowerments and their power to purify obscurations should be maintained and increased by the practices of the corresponding four paths. These are the subject of the remaining verses of this section.

Pure Perception

30. Saṃsāra is nothing other than how things appear
to you;
If you recognize everything as the deity, the good
of others is consummated.
Seeing the purity of everything confers the four
empowerments on all beings at once;
Dredging the depths of saṃsāra, recite the six-
syllable mantra.

For beings of average faculties, the path is perfect renunciation. For great beings, the path is perfect compassion. For beings of the highest faculties, the path is the perception of perfect, primordial purity. It is with this pure perception of the Vajrayāna that we are here concerned.

What, then, is meant by pure perception? The way we usually experience the outer world, our bodies, and our feelings is impure, in the sense that we perceive them as ordinary, substantially existing entities. From this erroneous perception come the negative emotions which perpetuate suffering. However, take a closer look at all these appearances; you will find that they have no true existence. From a relative point of view they appear as a result of various causes and conditions, like a mirage or a dream, but in reality nothing that arises from causes and conditions has any true existence whatsoever. In fact, there is not even anything to appear. As it is said, "He who realizes voidness is the true sage."

If you continue investigating, you will find that there is nothing anywhere, not even a single atom, that has a verifiable existence. Now, to see things otherwise, as truly existing, is the deluded perception underlying saṃsāra—but even that deluded perception itself has never actually left the realm of voidness. Ignorance, therefore, is no more than a transient veil devoid of intrinsic existence. When you recognize this, there is no impure perception; there is only the limitless display of the Buddha's body, speech, mind, and wisdom. Then there is no longer any need to try to get rid of the three worlds of saṃsāra or to suppress suffering, because neither saṃsāra nor suffering actually even exist. Once you realize that saṃsāra is as void as a mirage, all the karmic patterns and negative emotions that lie at its root are severed.

Voidness, however, is not just nothingness or empty space, for as the Prajñāpāramitā says, "Form is voidness, voidness is form; voidness is no other than form, and form is no other than voidness." So voidness is inseparable from the display of the kāyas and wisdoms. In this sense, all appearances are Chenrezi's body, all sounds are his mantra, and all thoughts are the bliss-void unity of compassion and voidness. When you realize this true voidness of phenomena, you will spontaneously feel an all-embracing, nonconceptual compassion for all beings who are immersed in saṃsāra's ocean of suffering because they cling to the notion of an ego.

This troublesome ego which is so concerned about itself has

in reality never begun to exist, it does not exist anywhere now, and so it cannot cease to exist. Not the slightest trace of it can be found. When you recognize the void nature, therefore, any notion of there being an ego to dissolve vanishes, and at the same time the energy to bring about the good of others dawns, uncontrived and effortless. Here you will see the true face of Chenrezi, voidness and compassion united. And here begin the ten successive levels of the Bodhisattvas, who are able to extend an instant into a whole epoch and condense an epoch into an instant. They are filled with spontaneous, nonconceptual compassion, and whatever they do, even a simple gesture of their hands, brings benefit to beings. They are never fooled by appearances, just as a magician is never fooled by his own tricks, for they know that appearances have no true existence, and they know that failing to recognize that fact is delusion. They bestow all the common and supreme accomplishments. Working tirelessly for the benefit of all living creatures, they dredge the very depths of saṃsāra.

Praying fervently to Chenrezi, visualize infinite rays of light emanating from his body, dispelling the suffering and obscurations of all living creatures and conferring upon them the four empowerments. All male beings become Chenrezi, all females Jetsun Drölma, and the whole universe becomes their Buddhafield. To practice in this way brings benefit to all beings.

All phenomena of saṃsāra and nirvāṇa are projections of your mind. So, too, is Chenrezi. To merge all practices into one, remain in the state where emptiness and appearances are of one single essence, and recite the maṇi.

The Development Stage

The path of secret mantra is divided into the development and completion stages. The development stage includes the yogas of the wisdom aspects of body, speech, and mind—vajra body, vajra speech, and vajra mind; its purpose is to realize the primordial purity of all phenomena. The completion stage leads to the nonconceptual realization of the nature of mind.

Vajra Body

> 31. The mind cannot cope with all the many visualization practices;
> To meditate on one Sugata is to meditate on them all.
> Whatever appears, appearances are the form of the Great Compassionate One;
> In the realm of the deity's body, apparent yet void, recite the six-syllable mantra.

The central practice of the development stage is to visualize yourself and all other beings as deities, and the universe as a maṇḍala or a Buddha-field. People these days, with their limited intellect, short lifespan, and feeble diligence, would find it difficult to master all the elaborate visualizations found in the tantras. To attempt all these complex practices is unnecessary, however, for by thoroughly mastering a practice focused upon a single Buddha you can discover the wisdom and compassion of them all.

For the present practice, you may either visualize yourself as Chenrezi or visualize Chenrezi above your head, thinking of him as no different from your root teacher, the teacher for whom you feel the greatest devotion. He is white in color—the dazzling white of a snow peak reflecting a hundred thousand suns, dispelling the darkness of the whole universe. He has one head, symbolizing the oneness of the absolute nature; four arms, symbolizing loving-kindness, compassion, rejoicing, and equanimity; two legs crossed in the vajra posture, symbolizing the sameness of saṃsāra and nirvāṇa; he is sitting on a thousand-petaled lotus, symbolizing compassion, and a moon disc, symbolizing voidness.

One pair of hands are together at his heart and hold a jewel, which represents the bodhichitta, the wish-granting gem which bestows the supreme and ordinary siddhis. Of the other pair of hands, one holds out a crystal rosary to his right, and the other a white lotus to his left; the rosary symbolizes his unceasing compassion extending like an unbroken thread through the heart of every being, and the lotus the unchanging purity of his wisdom blooming above the mud of saṃsāra. The jewel also symbolizes wisdom-bliss as the means, while the lotus symbolizes wisdom-voidness as the realization. His beautiful body, bearing all the major and minor marks of a Buddha, is clad in the jewels and silks of the Sambhogakāya.

The purpose of the visualization practices of the development stage, such as this one, is to develop pure perception—that is, to see yourself and all beings as wisdom deities and your environment as a Buddha-field, to hear all sounds as mantras, and to understand all thoughts as the display of awareness. This pure perception is not some artificial idea of purity that you try to superimpose upon phenomena; it is, rather, the recognition that all phenomena are truly and inherently pure. It is accomplished through various techniques of meditation which are gradually perfected. At first you may not be able to visualize Chenrezi as a whole very clearly, so start by visualizing his face: the black and white of his two eyes gazing compassionately upon all beings, his perfectly arched eyebrows, the curve of his nose, and his radiant smile. Then slowly extend the visualization to his whole head—its perfect shape and its ornaments, the golden crown and earrings. Gradually, move down to visualize the rest of his body and the various ornaments, the three rows of necklaces, the antelope skin over his left shoulder and covering his left breast, the jeweled bracelets and anklets, the colorful silken scarves, the white shawl embroidered with gold, and the lower garment of five colors. Visualizing each detail slowly in this way, one by one, you will gradually be able to maintain the overall visualization.

Then, in each pore of Chenrezi's body, visualize a Buddha-field, and in each of these billions of Buddha-fields a Buddha turning the wheel of Dharma for his retinue of Shrāvakas, Pratyekabuddhas, and Bodhisattvas. These Buddhas' teaching on the view, meditation, and action of the Mahāyāna is based on the sublime Dharma of the six-syllable mantra, and their ability to teach is such that for kalpas on end they can expound the meaning of even a single syllable, OṂ for instance, without ever exhausting the subject. Nothing in these Buddha-fields is impure. There is no hatred of enemies or attachment to friends. All males are Chenrezi and all females Jetsun Drölma. All these Buddha-fields are the display of Chenrezi's net of magical emanations, the expression of emptiness and compassion inseparable.

As well as visualizing your body as the vajra body of Chenrezi, you also have to see the whole environment outside as transformed into Chenrezi's Pure Land, the Potala Mountain in the Blissful Land of Sukhāvatī, graced with such marvels as the hill of jewels, the river of nectar, and the wish-granting tree; clouds of offerings fill the sky, the mantra OṂ MAṆI PADME HŪṂ resounds everywhere, and "suffering" is a word that is never even heard.

When you visualize the deity's vajra body, you should not think of it as something solid made of flesh, bones, and blood but as like a rainbow, brilliant, colorful, and clear, yet without any substance. This is the void aspect of Chenrezi's nature, which has no impure or solid constituents; Chenrezi is completely unsullied by the five aggregates,[46] which together are what give rise to the idea of an ego.

At first, however diligently you try, you may well find it difficult to master all the details of the visualization. If that is the case, simply develop a clear conviction that you are Chenrezi himself—not as the result of some mental fabrication but inherently so. If you visualize Chenrezi above your head, simply be confident that he is there and be clearly aware of his presence. As time goes on, by focusing on each detail again and again, you will gradually become familiar with the visualization until it becomes quite natural, just as all the details of a place where you have lived for a long time readily appear in your mind.

When the visualization of Chenrezi becomes clear and stable, visualize light rays radiating out from his body in each of the ten directions,[47] making offerings to all the Buddhas and Bodhisattvas in the innumerable Buddha-fields. These rays of light return, carrying the blessings of all the enlightened ones, and dissolve back into Chenrezi, who becomes even more brilliant and resplendent. Once again, he emanates rays of light, which this time reach out to all beings, dispelling their suffering, establishing them in the wisdom of great bliss, and transforming them into male and female Bodhisattvas and the whole universe into a perfect Buddha-field.

While you are meditating on Chenrezi, ordinary thoughts will come to a standstill and the mind will settle in tranquility. If you then look at the nature of mind, it will begin to become clear to you that the deity is essentially one with voidness. This understanding will then expand into the realization that all appearances are void in nature and therefore perfectly pure. To maintain this realization at all times is known as the development stage of infinite purity.

Vajra Speech

32. Recitations, sādhanas, and powerful spells are just
    complications;
    The all-inclusive six-syllable mantra is the very
    sound of the Dharma.

All sounds have never been other than the speech of Sublime Chenrezi;
Recognizing them as mantra, resounding yet void, recite the six-syllable mantra.

One of the principal elements in Vajrayāna practice is mantra. Mantras are Sanskrit formulas which, in the realm of sound, have an importance equivalent to that of visualized deities in the realm of form. Mantras are of many different kinds, including awareness mantras, secret mantras, and dhāraṇīs; there are also mantras of approach, mantras of achievement, and mantras for accomplishing the four activities.

There is no mantra however, that can be considered superior to the maṇi, which includes not only all the functions but also all the power and blessings of all other mantras. The learned sages of the past, like the great Karma Chagme,[48] for example, were unable to find anywhere in the scriptures a mantra more beneficial, quintessential, or easier to practice than the maṇi; so it was this mantra that they took as their main practice. Even just hearing the maṇi can be enough to free beings from saṃsāra. For example, the story goes that there were once five hundred worms struggling for existence in a foul and terrible pit. Chenrezi, feeling compassion for their suffering, took the form of a golden bee and flew over the pit, buzzing the maṇi. The worms, hearing the sound of the six syllables, were completely freed from their sufferings and took rebirth in a celestial realm.

The maṇi is not just a string of ordinary words. It contains all the blessings and compassion of Chenrezi; in fact, it is Chenrezi himself in the form of sound. As we are now, our karmic obscurations prevent us from being able to actually meet Chenrezi in his Buddha-field; but what we can do is listen to his mantra, recite it, read it, and write it beautifully in golden letters. Since there is no difference between the deity himself and the mantra which is his essence, these activities bring great benefit.

The six syllables are the expression of the six pāramitās of Chenrezi, and as he himself said, whoever recites the six-syllable mantra will perfect the six pāramitās and purify all karmic obscurations.

In order to practice the recitation of this mantra, first visualize Chenrezi as described before, as clearly and vividly as possible. In Chenrezi's heart, visualize a six-petaled lotus, upon which is a full-moon disc. In the center of the moon disc stands the syllable HRĪḤ, surrounded by the six syllables OṂ MA ṆI PAD ME HŪṂ arranged clockwise in a circle like a string of pearls, radiating streams of light which carry offerings to the Blissful Paradise of Sukhāvatī, to the Paradise Beautiful to Behold, and to all the infinite other Buddha-fields. Each ray of light carries a multitude of offerings, such as the eight auspicious symbols, the eight precious substances, the seven emblems of royalty, wish-granting trees, and precious vessels, and makes huge clouds of offerings to the Buddhas and Bodhisattvas of each Buddha-field, filling the whole sky. By accepting your offerings, the Buddhas help you to accumulate merit and wisdom.

All these rays of light then return, carrying in the form of precious nectar the blessings of the body, speech, and mind of all the Buddhas, along with their wisdom, power, and love, and dissolve into the mantra in Chenrezi's heart. Chenrezi becomes even more radiant and resplendent, like gold bathed in saffron water.

Again, boundless rays of light emanate from the mantra circle, this time dispelling the suffering of all sentient beings in the six realms: the searing heat and biting cold of the hells; the insatiable hunger and thirst of tortured spirits; the cruel stupidity, slavery, and abuse of the animal realm; the human sufferings of birth, old age, sickness, and death; the jealousy and feuding of demigods; and the anguish experienced by the gods when finally, from their exquisite worlds of pleasure and absorption, they fall headlong to the depths of the lower realms. All this misery is dispelled by the radiant light streaming out from the mantra, just as the morning sun melts away frost on a winter meadow. All beings are transformed into Chenrezi; first your immediate environment, and then the whole universe, become the paradise of the Potala Mountain.

When the welfare of all beings has been achieved in this way, gather and absorb the light rays back into yourself, Chenrezi. Each pore of your body contains an infinity of Buddha-fields, each of which resounds with the six-syllable mantra. Its vibration fills the whole of space, like the buzzing of a million bees swarming out from a hive that has been broken open. The sound of the mantra dispels ignorance and subdues all negative forces. It awakens the Shrāvakas from their meditative absorption and brings them to the Mahāyāna path; it makes offerings to the Bodhisattvas, exhorting them to continue working for the benefit of beings; and it enjoins the Dharma-protectors to safeguard the teachings and increase the happiness and prosperity of all.

The sounds of wind and running rivers, the crackling of fire, the cries of animals, the songs of birds, human voices—all the sounds of the universe—are the vibration of the six-syllable mantra, the self-arisen sound of the Dharma, sound yet void, the resonance of the unborn Dharmakāya. Through recitation, practicing the yoga of vajra speech, you will effortlessly attain the ordinary and supreme accomplishments.[49]

Vajra Mind

33. As thoughts and the two obscurations are pacified,
    experience and realization increase;
    As your perceptions come under control, enemies
    and obstructing influences are subjugated.
    It is Chenrezi who bestows in this very life the
    supreme and common siddhis;
    As the four activities are accomplished by themselves, recite the six-syllable mantra.

There are no entities, of any kind, that truly and permanently exist. All the phenomena of both saṃsāra and nirvāṇa—even appearances seen as the deity and sounds heard as mantra—are projections of the mind. If you search for the nature of this mind, you will find that, as it is said in the *Prajñāpāramitā:*

> Mind,
> Mind does not exist,
> Its expression is clarity.[50]

What we normally call the mind is the deluded mind, a turbulent vortex of thoughts whipped up by attachment, anger, and ignorance. This mind, unlike enlightened awareness, is always being carried away by one delusion after another. Thoughts of hatred or attachment suddenly arise without warning, triggered off by such circumstances as an unexpected meeting with an enemy or a friend, and unless they are immediately overpowered with the proper antidote they quickly take root and proliferate, reinforcing the habitual predominance of hatred or attachment in the mind and adding more and more karmic patterns.

Yet, however strong these thoughts may seem, they are just thoughts and will eventually dissolve back into emptiness. Once you recognize the intrinsic nature of the mind, these thoughts that seem to appear and disappear all the time can no longer fool you. Just as clouds form, last for a while, and then dissolve back into the empty sky, so deluded thoughts arise, remain for a while, and then vanish in the voidness of mind; in reality nothing at all has happened.

When sunlight falls on a crystal, lights of all colors of the rainbow appear; yet they have no substance that you can grasp. Likewise, all thoughts in their infinite variety—devotion, compassion, harmfulness, desire—are utterly without substance. This is the mind of Chenrezi. There is no thought that is something other than voidness; if you recognize the void nature of thoughts at the very moment they arise, they will dissolve. Attachment and hatred will never be able to disturb the mind. Deluded emotions will collapse by themselves. No negative actions will be accumulated, so no suffering will follow. This is the culmination of pacification, the first of the four activities.

If you practice the yogas of body, speech, and mind without falling prey to thoughts, at this point Chenrezi's compassion and your own innate Buddha-nature will begin to meet and merge into one. Meditative experiences will increase, along with devotion and compassion, just as the sun's rays increase in power when focused through a magnifying glass. This is the culmination of increasing, or enriching, the second activity.

Once you see that all phenomena of both saṃsāra and nirvāṇa are just fabrications of mind and that the nature of mind is void, then transmuting impure perception into pure perception is not a problem—all phenomena are simply revealed as primordially pure. This realization brings you, in general, unlimited control over all phenomena and, in particular, the ten powers of supreme beings—power over matter, power over life, power over karma, and so forth.[51] It is said, "By mastering one's own perception, one can master all phenomena." Once you are free from the power of deluded thoughts you will be able to transform the elements at will and master the inexhaustible sky treasure.[52] During a terrible famine in India, the great master Nāgārjuna transmuted iron into gold, with which he was able not only to sustain the whole saṅgha throughout the famine but also to build many new temples.[53] All the miracles with which the eighty-four mahāsiddhas demonstrated their power over appearances were made possible by their realization of voidness and their freedom from delusion. Finally comes mastery of enlightenment itself—the culmination of power, the third activity.

Once the deluded mind has been subjugated, there is nowhere

left to harbor harmful spirits or negative forces; and once your being is permeated by bodhichitta, what you might formerly have perceived as evil and obstructive forces you then see as manifestations of your teacher, through which you can strengthen loving-kindness and compassion. In this way, suffering fades away, and you use negative forces, obstacles, and difficulties to make progress in your practice. This is the culmination of subjugation, the fourth activity.

Through the practice of the development stage—visualizing Chenrezi and reciting his mantra—you recognize his wisdom. From this spark of recognition, wisdom grows like a fire spreading through a dry forest. This is the essence of the completion stage. Through this practice, the mind is tamed and the four activities are accomplished of their own accord. Obscurations and evil deeds, sickness and suffering, are pacified; life span, merit, prosperity, and wisdom increase; people, thoughts, and inner energies are brought under your power without struggle; and all negative forces, enmities, obstacles, and the inner demons—the emotions—are subjugated.

Postmeditation

In order to experience fully the profound meaning of the Vajrayāna, it is important to maintain the practice at all times, not only during actual meditation sessions. Practice for meditation sessions and practice for periods between such sessions can be considered separately. The purpose of the meditation practice itself, as we have seen, is to gain stability in the perception of all appearances as the deity's form, all sounds as his mantra, and all thoughts as the Dharmakāya, thus recognizing the absolute nature of mind, void and luminous. Now, in periods between meditation sessions, whatever you are doing you must maintain this recognition without relapsing into ordinary habits, so that you can develop the understanding acquired during meditation. In this way all of your activities will be linked with the view, meditation, and action of the Vajrayāna.

34. Offer the torma of whatever arises to the guests
of immediate liberation;
Mold the clay of whatever appears into the tsa-tsa
of void appearance;
Offer the prostration of nonduality to the Lord
of Mind Nature.
Consummating these Dharma activities, recite
the six-syllable mantra.

Between meditation periods, make sure that everything you do is in harmony with the Dharma. This will help to deepen your understanding of the view. If, as soon as you finish meditating and start something else, you just let your thoughts go on proliferating until you get completely carried away by delusion, your meditation will make no progress and you will find yourself constantly struggling against all sorts of obstacles—heavy dullness or wild, frenetic states of mind, for example. So whenever you have the time free, do prostrations, circumambulate holy places, make torma offerings, or mold tsa-tsa; in short, do only what is truly meaningful.

Ritual offerings of torma[54] are offered to four kinds of recipients, usually known as "guests": those worthy of respect, the Three Jewels and the protectors of the Dharma; and those who need your compassion, all sentient beings and obstructing spirits to whom you owe karmic debts. To offer tormas properly, having blessed them with dhāraṇīs and mantras, brings boundless benefit. There are also instructions on the offering of water tormas. A torma offered to the Three Jewels accomplishes the two accumulations; offered to the Dharma-protectors it pleases them and enjoins them to action; offered to all beings it relieves them from their various sufferings and soothes spirits tortured by hunger and thirst; and offered to our karmic creditors it repays the debts we have contracted in all our past lives, freeing us from sickness, evil influences, and obstacles of all kinds.

A tsa-tsa is a small stūpa[55] generally molded out of clay that symbolizes the absolute aspect of a Buddha's mind, the Dharmakāya. The great paṇḍita Atīsha used to make three tsa-tsas every day with his own hands, and he considered this a very beneficial activity. If you have no time to make tsa-tsas of clay, there are instructions on how to make them using the four elements of earth, water, fire, and air. Offering tsa-tsas is another way to accomplish the two accumulations.

If you cannot make material offerings, you can always offer mentally all the beauty of the universe, the sun and moon, flowers, perfumes, the songs of birds; and instead of offering a material torma, realizing the mind as Chenrezi, visualize your body as pure wisdom nectar and offer it to the four classes of guests mentioned above.

Whether Chenrezi is the deity to whom you make offerings, the subject of your meditation, or the focus of your prostrations and devotion, immeasurable benefit will result. However, as we have seen before, all phenomena are projections of the mind; the person making offerings, the deity to whom offerings are made, and the offerings themselves do not exist in any way as concrete realities. So when a great Bodhisattva practices generosity and the other pāramitās, he knows that all these activities are no more real than a magical illusion or a dream. He makes vast offerings and accumulates infinite merit, but all the time he remains totally free of attachment, pride, and condescension.

35. Overcome your enemy, hatred, with the weapon
    of love;
    Protect your family, the beings of the six realms,
    with the skillful means of compassion;
    Harvest from the field of devotion the crop of
    experience and realization.
    Consummating your life's work, recite the six-
    syllable mantra.

According to ordinary values, overcoming your enemies, protecting your family, and growing rich and prosperous are what constitute a satisfying and well-led life. But as Buddhists we should try to overcome our own aggression rather than our enemies, to take care of our own patience rather than our family, and to invest more in love and kindness than in material prosperity.

It is said that there is no greater evil than hatred and no greater virtue than patience. While a single moment of anger destroys countless aeons of merit and leads to unmitigated suffering in the hell realms, patience toward those who harm you and the sincere wish to bring them happiness will bring you swiftly onto the path taken by all the Buddhas.

There is no better way to deal with enemies than to feel great love for them, realizing that in former lives they have been your loving parents. There is no better way to nurture your family and look after others than to practice the Dharma and dedicate to all beings the merit you thereby obtain. There is no better or more bountiful harvest than the one you sow in the soil of your faith and endeavor so that it ripens into the richness of merit and wisdom.

"Evil is only subdued by compassion," goes the saying. So, faced with all the troubles of this world, recite the maṇi, praying that all human and nonhuman beings who, overwhelmed by hatred, want only to harm, kill, and destroy, may be touched by compassion and give birth to the sublime thought of enlightenment.

The power of love to conquer aggression is illustrated by Lord Buddha's encounter with Māra. On the eve of his enlightenment, as the Buddha sat under the bodhi tree at Vajrāsana, the Diamond Throne of India, the demon hosts of Māra's armies surrounded him like a huge black cloud. Raging with malice and envy, they shouted insults and hurled weapons, but the Buddha remained serene and filled with such loving-kindness that their insults turned into beautiful melodies and their vicious missiles became a rain of flowers. With the weapon of loving-kindness you will always be able to vanquish malevolence, and having to face hostility and aggression will only enhance your bodhichitta.

To be kindhearted means to be continually thinking how wonderful it would be if people could be free of their suffering and enjoy happiness. It also means devoting both words and actions to trying to actually make that happen. Once, when the glorious Lord Atīsha was suffering from a painful affliction of one of his hands, he put it on Dromtönpa's lap, saying, "Please bless my hand—you are very kindhearted, and that by itself is enough to relieve the pain."

There are innumerable beings wandering in saṃsāra, completely lost and all in desperate need of your help. Since they have all been your loving parents at one time or another in the past, you must help them. But how? Even if you could provide all of them with money and comfort, that would only bring them an incomplete and short-lived respite from their suffering. Reflect deeply; of all the possible ways to help them, there could be no gift more beneficial than the gift of the Dharma, for that is something that will not only help them in this life but also free them from future rebirths in the lower realms and finally lead them to enlightenment.

The greater the number of beings you include in your good intentions, the greater the merit. If, in whatever you do, you aspire to accomplish the present welfare and ultimate bliss of all beings, following Chenrezi's example, then that can truly be called "consummating your life's work."

36. Cremate that old corpse of clinging to things as
    real in the fire of nonattachment;
  Conduct the weekly funeral ceremonies of ordinary
    life by practicing the essence of Dharma;

As the smoke-offering to provide for the departed,
dedicate your accumulated merit for all their
future lives.
Consummating all positive actions done for the
sake of the dead, recite the six-syllable mantra.

In Tibet, when someone dies, it is customary to cremate the body and to perform ceremonies every week for seven weeks, making offerings for the deceased. As a Dharma practitioner, however, the most beneficial thing you can do when someone has died is to meditate on the essential meaning of the Dharma and dedicate the merit to the dead person.

This essential meaning, the very heart of the Dharma, is the nonexistence of a self in anything. The tree of saṃsāra is rooted in the belief that there is a self, in clinging to things as real, in ego-clinging; once this clinging is consumed by the fire of wisdom, the whole tree and all its branches of delusion, luxuriant with the foliage of attachment and hatred, are bound to be burned up too.

Without this understanding, performing rituals just for money or show will only serve to delay your practice and can eventually become a serious obstacle. Realizing that wealth and influence are essentially empty goals, keep to a flawless way of life, devoted entirely to practice. Have no more attachment to this life than to a corpse. Life is precarious, a bubble which could burst at any moment—there is no way of knowing for sure which will come first, tomorrow morning or death. In fact, every time you breathe out, it is not at all certain that you will breathe in again.

Just as the rituals for the dead are observed regularly every week during the funeral period, there are two practices that should be observed regularly every morning and evening of your life. Every morning, generate bodhichitta and pray that throughout the day you will never forget to think of the welfare of others. Every evening, remember all that you have thought and done during the day and determine how much was motivated by compassion and how much by selfishness; it is important to look at your most subtle attitudes and intentions before deciding what you should or should not have done. Never think that any tiny act is insignificant just because it is so small, for the least negative action can set off a devastating chain of consequences, in the same way that a single minute spark can set fire to an entire forest. Conversely, just as a slight trickle of water quickly fills a large pitcher, when one small positive action is added to many others the accumulated effect soon becomes substantial. Acknowledging your failings in this way, and regretting them sincerely, resolve from now on to eliminate selfish thoughts and acts; and at the same time dedicate the merit of your positive actions to all sentient beings, resolving to develop more and more compassion. Through this process of constant awareness and critical appraisal of your actions, they will gradually become more and more positive.

A great sage of the past, the wise Drakhen, feeling determined to rid himself of all defects, took up the habit of setting aside a black pebble for every negative thought he had during the day and a white one for every wholesome thought. At the end of the day he counted how many black and how many white pebbles he had collected. At first, the day's pebbles were all black; but after a while, through constant vigilance, he began to finish each day with equal piles of white and black. Finally, when he had thoroughly trained his mind, there were only white pebbles. Like him, you should persevere until there is not a single action left which is contrary to the teachings. Never forget that to purify yourself in this way it is important to maintain the intention to help all beings.

If we persist for long enough, we can learn to do anything. Once a rich man came to see Lord Buddha, suffering from such miserliness that he was unable to give away even the tiniest thing. To accustom him to generosity, the Buddha taught him to consider his right hand as himself and his left hand as someone else, and to think that he was making gifts while passing small objects from one hand to the other. When the miser had slowly become used to the idea of giving in this way, Lord Buddha told him to make small presents, such as fruit, grain, and the like, to his wife and children. Then the Buddha told him to give charity, first to the poorest of his neighbors and then to others more distant. Eventually, he became capable of giving away all his riches, clothes, and food to the poor of the whole province, and at that point the Buddha told him that he had achieved true generosity.

The same sort of training can be applied to develop or eliminate any kind of positive or negative thought. Devotion, for instance, can be cultivated in this way until, your mind filled only with thoughts of your teacher, you spontaneously feel that whatever happens to you is completely in his hands. Even at the memory of his presence—his voice, his gestures—your eyes flow with tears. When this true devotion arises, look at it and recognize the primordial nature of mind, devoid of form and characteristics.

37. Put your child, devotion, at the doorway of your
practice;
Give your son, renunciation, mastery over the
household of ordinary life;
Wed your daughter, compassion, to the
bridegroom of the three worlds.
Consummating your duty to the living, recite the
six-syllable mantra.

Ordinary people try to bring up their children as best they can. They seek good marriages for them, transfer to them their wealth and family property, and show them how to look after their relatives and friends and overcome their adversaries, just as their ancestors have done for generations. But the success that parents always wish for their children is only temporary and will ultimately prove harmful. As a Dharma practitioner, what you should aspire to is, rather, that the child of unshakable devotion be born in your heart and successfully manage the household of your practice.

The fear that their homes might become barren and their family lines extinct motivates most people to have children and to get them married off as soon as possible. As a Dharma practitioner, it is fear that your practice will die out and your life will be wasted that should motivate you to give birth to the son of renunciation in your mind, so that he can assume authority over the household of ordinary life. Renunciation is born when you know that there is ultimately no satisfaction in saṃsāric life. Since ordinary joys are short-lived dreams, there is no reason to long for success or to fear failure. If you happen to grow rich, there is no reason to feel attached or proud; simply use your wealth positively and meaningfully. Whatever power you gain, use it to serve the Three Jewels and the great teachers, and whatever land you own, make it available for the benefit of the saṅgha; in short, whatever you acquire, use it to preserve the Dharma and to benefit others. Used in this way, your dreamlike wealth and influence will bring you more and more dreamlike merit, which in turn will bring you closer and closer to the threshold of dreamlike enlightenment.

Parents normally want to make sure their daughter marries someone of good family with wealth and status. Similarly, out of great love and tenderness for sentient beings, you should wed your daughter of accumulated merits without any hesitation to the bridegroom of the well-being of others. If you have the precious attitude of bodhichitta, you cannot help but lead a truly meaningful life; so reinforce all your actions with compassion, purify your defilements, dedicate your merit to all beings, and recite the six-syllable mantra.

The Completion Stage

The Nature of Mind

38. Whatever appears is delusion and has no true existence;
Saṃsāra and nirvāṇa are just thoughts and nothing more.
If you can liberate thoughts as they arise, that includes all stages of the path;
Applying the essential instruction for liberating thoughts, recite the six-syllable mantra.

We now come to the teachings on one of a number of practices belonging to the Great Perfection: the practice of the completion stage, beyond any conceptualization whatsoever.

The *Samādhirāja-sūtra* says, "We should understand that, in the unborn ground, none of all the many things we perceive—our bodies, houses, carts, and so forth—has any true existence." If you examine anything closely, you will not be able to find any point at which it has come into being, any point where it continues to exist, or any point at which it ceases to be. It is only because of the transient conjunction of a set of causes and conditions that a particular phenomenon arises, just as the combination of the sun's rays and a summer shower produces a rainbow. If you can develop the complete certainty that this whole unceasing display of illusory appearances is void in nature, that in itself would be the ultimate completion stage.

We ordinary beings are convinced that all the phenomena of both saṃsāra and nirvāṇa first come into being, then exist in some way for some time, and eventually cease to exist. But if we conduct a thorough investigation into things, using the logic of the Madhyamaka, we fail to find even the tiniest particle of existence in any of these phenomena. Once we understand that, it is easy to let go of saṃsāra and to be free from attraction to nirvāṇa, for both are no more than projections of the dualistic mind. Seen with the eyes of a Buddha, even the accumulation of merit and the practice of the pāramitās are devoid of any intrinsic reality.

However much we might prefer to believe that things are permanent, they are not. Yesterday's happiness turns into today's sadness, today's tears into tomorrow's laughter. As their different causes and conditions take effect, emotions, good and bad actions, happiness and suffering, all seem to take form. Yet an enlightened being looking at the world of illusion, which seems so real to us, sees it as no more substantial than a mirage, or a kingdom conquered in last night's dream. It is because we believe so strongly in the true and tangible existence of the material world that we feel such strong attraction and aversion to things. Without this belief, our minds would not be subject to all these delusions and there would be no saṃsāra.

The ordinary mind is as capricious as a restless monkey, instantly happy as soon as we give him a morsel of food and suddenly furious the moment we raise a stick at him. Every instant, the mind moves on to something new. One moment we may be thinking of the guru with great devotion, the next we are craving for some desirable object. These trains of thought and states of mind are constantly changing, like the shapes of clouds in the wind, but we nevertheless attach great importance to them. An old man watching children at play knows very well that whatever is going on is not at all important and feels neither elated nor upset at what happens in their game. The children, however, take it very seriously. Like them, whenever we experience suffering, instead of seeing it as the dreamlike result of our past negative actions and making it an opportunity to take others' suffering upon ourselves, we feel upset and depressed. We say to ourselves that, as someone who has done so much practice, we really don't deserve such misery, and we begin to feel dubious about the blessings of our teacher and the Three

Jewels. Such an attitude can only amplify our difficulties.

Mind is what creates both saṃsāra and nirvāṇa. Yet there is nothing much to it—it is just thoughts. Once you recognize thoughts as void, the mind will no longer have the power to deceive you. But as long as you take your deluded thoughts as real, they will continue to torment you mercilessly, as they have been doing throughout countless past lives. To gain control over the mind, you need to be aware of what to do and what to avoid, and you also need to be very alert and vigilant, constantly examining your thoughts, words, and actions.

The mind inhabits the body like a visitor in a house. Whatever the body encounters, it is the mind that sees, hears, smells, tastes, or feels it. Once the mind has gone, the body is just a corpse. It doesn't care whether what is placed in front of it is beautiful or ugly. It doesn't care whether it is praised or insulted. It feels no pleasure when it is wrapped in brocade, no pain when it is burned. By itself, the body is an object not essentially different from a lump of earth or stone. And when body and mind separate, speech, which has been somewhere in between, disappears too, like a vanishing echo. Of body, speech, and mind, mind is what counts, and it is to mind that the Dharma must be applied.

When you recognize the void nature of the mind, grasping falls away and you are no longer taken in by your deluded thoughts. When a Bodhisattva helps others, he has no idea of getting something in return or of being praised for his generosity; he has no attachment whatsoever to his virtue. This is the absolute Chenrezi, compassion and voidness itself.

39. Your own mind, aware and void inseparably, is
    Dharmakāya.
  Leave everything as it is in fundamental simplicity,
    and clarity will arise by itself.

Only by doing nothing will you do all there is to
be done;
Leaving everything in naked void-awareness, recite
the six-syllable mantra.

It is no good looking anywhere outside you for the ultimate nature of mind—it is within. When we speak of the "mind," it is important to know whether we are talking about the ordinary mind, referring to the innumerable chains of thoughts that create and maintain our state of delusion, or, as here, about the nature of mind at the source of all those thoughts—the clear, void state of awareness completely free of delusion.

To illustrate this distinction, Lord Buddha taught that there are two ways to meditate—like a dog and like a lion. If you throw a stick at a dog, he will chase after the stick; but if you throw a stick at a lion, the lion will chase after you. You can throw as many sticks as you like at a dog, but at a lion only one. When you are completely barraged with thoughts, chasing after each one in turn with its antidote is an endless task. That is like the dog. It is better, like the lion, to look for the source of those thoughts, void awareness, on whose surface thoughts move like ripples on the surface of a lake, but whose depth is the unchanging state of utter simplicity. Resting in the unwavering continuity of that state, recite the six-syllable mantra.

The Four Yogas

The Buddhist path can be described comprehensively according to two systems: the cause vehicle and the result vehicle. Where the first, which includes both the Hīnayāna and the general Mahāyāna, speaks of the five paths, the second, the Mantrayāna, speaks of the four yogas: one-pointedness, simplicity, one taste, and nonmeditation.[56] The teaching of the four yogas focuses on the union of the development and completion stages.

ONE-POINTEDNESS

> 40. Let stillness cut the momentum of moving thoughts;
> Within movement see the very nature of stillness.
> Where stillness and movement are one, maintain the natural mind;
> In the experience of one-pointedness, recite the six-syllable mantra.

The mind has, in general, two aspects, stillness and movement. Sometimes, the mind is quiet and free from thoughts, like a calm pool; this is stillness. Eventually, thoughts are bound to arise in it; this is movement. In truth, however, although in a sense there is a movement of thoughts within the stillness, there is actually no difference between these two states—just as the nature of stillness is voidness, the nature of movement is also voidness. Stillness and movement are merely two names for the one mind.

Most of the time we are unaware of our state of mind and pay no attention to whether the mind is still or moving. While you are meditating, a thought might arise in your mind—the idea of going shopping, for instance. If you are aware of the thought and just let it dissolve by itself, then that is the end of it. But if you remain unaware of what is happening and let that thought grow and develop, it will lead on to a second thought, the thought of having a break from your practice, and in no time at all you will find yourself actually getting up and going out to the market. Soon many more thoughts and ideas will arise—how you are going to buy this, sell that, and so forth. By this point you will be a very long way away from the recitation of the *maṇi.*

It is completely natural that thoughts keep on arising. The point is not to try to stop them, which would be impossible anyway, but to liberate them. This is done by remaining in a state of simplicity, which lets thoughts arise and vanish again without stringing onto them any further thoughts. When you no longer perpetuate the movement of thoughts, they dissolve by themselves without leaving any trace. When you no longer spoil the state of stillness with mental fabrications, you can maintain the natural serenity of mind without any effort. Sometimes, let your thoughts flow, and watch the unchanging nature behind them. Sometimes, abruptly cutting the flow of thoughts, look at naked awareness.

Innumerable thoughts and memories, stirred up by the tendencies to which we have become habituated, arise in the mind. One after the other, each thought seems to vanish into the past, only to be replaced as the next, in its turn, becomes fleetingly present to the mind before itself giving way to future thoughts. Each thought tends to pick up the momentum of the one before it, so that the influence of a string of thoughts grows as time passes; this is called "the chain of delusion." Just as what we call a rosary is in fact a string of single beads, so also what we usually call the mind is really a succession of momentary thoughts; a trickle of thoughts makes the stream of consciousness, the mind-stream, and the mind-stream leads on to the ocean of existence. Our belief that the mind is a real entity is a conclusion based on insufficient investigation. We believe a river we see today to be the same river we saw yesterday, but in reality a river never stays the same even for a second—the water that made up yesterday's river will surely be part of the ocean by now. The same is true for the countless thoughts that run through our "mind" from morning to evening. Our mind-stream is just a succession of instantaneous thoughts; there is no separate entity that you can point out as being a mind.

Now, if we investigate the thought process according to the logic of the Madhyamaka, it becomes evident that past thoughts are already dead, like a corpse. Future thoughts have not yet been born. As to present thoughts, they cannot be said to have any properties such as location, color, or shape; they leave no traces; and indeed they are nowhere to be found. In fact, there could be no possible point of contact between past, present, and future thoughts; if there was any real continuity between, for instance, a past thought and a present thought, that would necessarily mean either that the past thought is present or that the present thought is past. If the past really could extend to the present in this way, it would also follow that the future must already be present. But nevertheless, ignorant of the true nature of thoughts, we maintain the habit of seeing them as being continuously linked, one after another; this is the root of delusion, and this is what allows us to be more and more dominated by our thoughts and emotions, until total confusion reigns.

It is of vital importance to be aware of the arising of thoughts and to still the waves of thoughts that assail you. Anger, for instance, is an extremely destructive tendency which spoils all the good qualities you may otherwise have. No one enjoys the company of an angry person. There is nothing inherently very frightening about the appearance of snakes, but because they are generally very aggressive, the mere sight of them inspires fear and loathing. Whether in a human or a snake, such a preponderance of anger is nothing more than the outcome of an unchecked accumulation of negative thoughts. If at the very moment an angry thought arises, you recognize it for what it is and understand how negative it is, your anger will calm down of its own accord and you will always be able to stay on good terms with everyone. On the other hand, if you let that first angry thought give rise to a second angry thought, in no time at all your anger will be completely out of control, and you will be ready even to risk your life to destroy your adversary.

Always remember, therefore, that a thought is merely the experience of many factors and fleeting circumstances coming together. Whether the thought is good or bad, it has no true existence. As soon as a thought arises, if you recognize its void nature, it will be powerless to produce a second thought, and the chain of delusion will cease there and then. As we have said, this does not mean that you should try to suppress the natural creativity of your mind, or that you should try to stop each thought with a particular antidote. It is enough simply to recognize the emptiness of thoughts and to then let them rest in the relaxed mind. The innate nature of mind, pristine and unchanging, will then remain vivid and stable.

Of the two aspects of meditation practice, tranquility and insight,[57] tranquility provides the foundation upon which insight, or vast perspective, can open out on the nature of mind and thus enable you to liberate your negative emotions. If the foundation, tranquility, is unsound, insight will be unstable too, and your deluded thoughts will be difficult to control. It is therefore essential to develop the yoga of one-pointedness, remaining in unwavering awareness.

SIMPLICITY

> 41. By examining relative truth, establish absolute
>   truth;
> Within absolute truth, see how relative truth arises.
> Where the two truths are inseparable, beyond
>   intellect, is the state of simplicity;
> In the view free of all elaboration, recite the six-
>   syllable mantra.

In conventional, relative truth, we might accept that the phenomenal world can be broken down into indivisible particles; but the logic of the Madhyamaka shows that such particles could never have any independent or permanent existence. This being so, how can we say that material objects truly exist? Similarly, although we can try to dissect the mind into indivisible instants of consciousness, we find that these, too, must ultimately be devoid of any tangible existence.

To recognize the continuity and all-pervasiveness of this void nature, this absence of any true existence, is to recognize absolute truth. This is the natural state of mind, untouched by any obscuration, in which all phenomena are seen as the Buddhas see them, as dreams or magical illusions. Here, thoughts do not give rise to negative emotions or the accumulation of karma, favorable circumstances engender neither pride nor attachment, and adverse circumstances are quickly transformed into the path of enlightenment—for example, an encounter with someone who irritates you, instead of causing anger, helps you to generate compassion and becomes a chance to recognize the absolute truth which is inseparable from the bodhichitta. If you are unable to give up your attachment to things, it is simply because you fail to recognize their void nature. Once you have realized this void nature, you will no longer feel proud of dreamlike success or depressed by dreamlike failure.

Some people find themselves surrounded by beauty, comfort, natural abundance, and safety, whereas others may have to live in harsh, barren, impoverished, and dangerous environments. Now, this is the result neither of chance nor of some grand design. To have been born in a pleasant place is the result of generosity, helpfulness, and virtue in former lives, while adverse living conditions are the consequence of harm brought to others in previous lives by attacking them, imprisoning them, and so forth. Phenomena are not the work of a creator; they are simply what manifests as the combined result of many causes and circumstances. In the same way that, as the result of sunlight shining through rain, a rainbow appears in the sky, so also, as the result of a great number of actions in your past lives, in this life you are either happy, healthy, prosperous, and loved by all or unhappy, poor, beset by sickness, and despised. Indeed, every detail of the universe and the beings it contains is nothing more than the result of many interdependent factors momentarily coming together; this is why all phenomena are so impermanent and undergo such constant change.

So when you examine anything deeply, you always arrive at voidness, and only voidness; voidness is the ultimate nature of everything. As beginners who may be on the path of accumulation or the path of union,[58] we ordinary beings have not had the actual realization of voidness. We know that smoke indicates the presence of fire but is not the fire itself; nevertheless, by following the smoke we can find the fire. Likewise, it is important to understand that the view of voidness is not the same as the actual experience of voidness; but by following the view and becoming familiar with it, we will arrive at the actual realization of voidness itself, free from any concepts or theories. This is the ultimate understanding of the Madhyamaka, the inseparability of the two truths, the union of appearances and voidness.

The void nature of all phenomena is the absolute truth, and the way they appear is relative truth. By examining relative truth you will come to realize absolute truth, since absolute truth is the ultimate nature of everything. If the whole world—all its continents, all its mountains and forests—were to be destroyed and to completely disappear, only all-pervading empty space would be left. Something quite similar happens when you truly realize what relative phenomena are, that they do not exist as solid entities: nothing remains but all-pervading voidness. But as long as you still believe in the solid, tangible existence of relative truth, you will never be able to realize absolute truth. Once you realize absolute truth, you will see what appears within it—the whole, infinite display of relative phenomena—as no more than an illusion or a dream, to which you will feel no attachment. To realize that appearance and voidness are one is what is called simplicity, or freedom from all conceptual limitations, freedom from all elaboration.

The two truths are not two distinct entities, like the horns of a cow; they are simply the "appearing" and "void" aspects of the natural state. Having first understood the view intellectually, develop first-hand experience and confidence in the oneness of appearance and voidness. This realization of the inseparability of the two truths is a profound experience, completely beyond any intellectual concept. This is the yoga of simplicity. Maintaining this view, recite the six-syllable mantra.

ONE TASTE

> 42. From appearances, cut away the clinging of mind;
> From mind, demolish the lair of fictitious appearances;
> Where mind and appearances are one is infinite openness;
> In the realization of one taste, recite the six-syllable mantra.

The way objective phenomena appear to us subjectively is a function of the mind. Things seem to us either pure or impure, good or bad, attractive or repellent, depending solely on the way our own minds perceive them. As Shāntideva said, speaking of the hell realms:

> Who made this ground of blazing iron?
> Whence came these banks of fire?
> All such things
> Arise from the negative mind.

In fact, when your organs of sense encounter an object, the only part the object itself plays is to initiate the process of perception in your consciousness. From then on, as your mind reacts to the object, influenced by all your accumulated habits and past experiences, the whole process is entirely subjective. So, when your mind is full of anger, the whole world seems to be a hell realm. When your mind is peaceful, free from any clinging or fixation, and whatever you do is in accordance with the teachings, you experience everything as primordially pure. While a Buddha sees the hells as a paradise, deluded beings see a paradise as the hells.

Our perceptions are colored by delusions in the same way that the vision of a person with jaundice is colored by the bile in his eyes, making him see a white conch as yellow. It is clinging that makes the mind project its delusions onto appearances. As soon as the mind perceives something, it clings to that perception; then it appraises the object as being desirable, offensive, or neutral; finally, taking action on the basis of this distorted perception with desire, aversion, or indifference, it accumulates karma.

To cut through the mind's clinging, it is important to understand that all appearances are void, like the water you might see in a mirage. Beautiful forms are of no benefit to the mind, nor can ugly forms harm it in any way. Sever the ties of hope and fear, attraction and repulsion, and remain in equanimity in the understanding that all phenomena are nothing more than projections of your own mind.

Once you recognize the true nature of mind, this whole fiction of relative appearances and your attachment to them will simply cave in. Good and bad, pure and impure, lose their compelling flavors and melt into one taste. You will reach the realization of Jetsun Milarepa, making no distinction between iron and gold. When Gampopa offered him gold and tea, Milarepa said: "I am an old man with no need for gold and no stove to boil tea." Resting in this view, recite the six-syllable mantra.

NONMEDITATION

43. In the nature of mind, the simplicity of void
 awareness, everything is freed;
Thoughts, the spontaneous creativity of awareness,
 are purified in their own sphere.
Mind and awareness are one in the single essence.
In the nonmeditation of Dharmakāya, recite the
 six-syllable mantra.

The ultimate nature of mind is primordial awareness, from which thoughts emanate like light radiating from the sun. Once this nature of mind is recognized, delusion vanishes like clouds dissolving in the sky. The nature of mind free from delusion is without birth, existence, or cessation. In the terminology of the Mantrayāna, it is called primordial continuous mind,[59] or ever-present simplicity. It is also described in the sūtras; for example, the *Prajñāpāramitā* says:

> Mind,
> Mind does not exist,
> Its expression is clarity.[60]

When you examine the still mind, the moving mind, and the mind that can recognize stillness and movement, however long you search for "mind" you will find nothing but voidness: mind has no form, no color, and no substance. This is the void aspect of the mind. Yet the mind can know things and perceive an infinite variety of phenomena. This is the clarity aspect of mind. The inseparability of these two aspects, voidness and clarity, is the primordial continuous mind.

At the moment, the natural clarity of your mind is obscured by delusions. But as this obscuration clears you will begin to uncover the radiance of awareness, until you reach the point where, just as a drawing on water disappears the moment it is made, your thoughts are liberated the moment they arise. To experience mind in this way is to encounter the very source of Buddhahood, the practice of the fourth empowerment. When the nature of mind is recognized it is called nirvāṇa; when it is obscured by delusion it is called saṃsāra. Yet neither saṃsāra nor nirvāṇa has ever departed from the continuum of the absolute. When realization of awareness reaches its full extent, the ramparts of delusion will have been breached and the citadel of Dharmakāya beyond meditation can be seized once and for all. Here there is no longer any distinction between meditation and postmeditation, and experience is effortlessly stabilized; this is nonmeditation. In the limitless expanse of Dharmakāya, recite the six-syllable mantra.

To summarize, the yoga of one-pointedness emphasizes taming the mind, and that of simplicity establishes insight. These two are united in the experience of one taste, and when this experience becomes unshakable, it is the yoga of nonmeditation.

The four yogas of the Mantrayāna correspond to the five paths of the sūtra system. It is therefore important to keep the view, meditation, and action of both the sūtras and the tantras together. All the different levels of teaching have but one goal, to cut through the obscuring emotions; so they are in perfect agreement with each other. The many different streams of teachings, reflecting the needs of different students and the wisdom of different teachers, are really but a single river.

The peerless physician of Takpo, the holy Gampopa, first served a Kadampa master and practiced the Mahāyāna path. Later, at the feet of Jetsun Milarepa, he practiced the tantric systems of Mahāmudrā and of the inner heat and the rest of the six yogas of Nāropa, becoming one of the fathers of the Kagyu lineage. The great Kadampa teachers, famous for their practice of the sūtra system, also instructed their students in the completion phase of Mahāmudrā, and in the six yogas too, skillfully blending together all these practices. Never forget that the main point is not whether our practice belongs to the sūtras or tantras, or whether it is of this or that level, but that it serves as an effective antidote to attachment and the obscuring emotions.

Transformation of the Senses, Emotions, and Aggregates

Of all the countless teachings on many levels that make up the path of secret mantra, the essence is to see all appearances as the body of the deity, to hear all sound as mantra, and to recognize all thoughts as the Dharmakāya. In this way, the six sense perceptions, the five poisonous emotions, and the five aggregates are transformed into their wisdom counterparts, and the body, speech, and mind are realized as the vajra maṇḍala, the self-existing maṇḍala of primordial purity.

THE SIX SENSE OBJECTS

Forms

44. To recognize as the deity whatever forms appear is
the crucial point of the development stage;
Clinging to appearance as beautiful or ugly is liberated into its own nature.
Free of clinging, mind as it appears is the body of
Supreme Chenrezi.
In the self-liberation of visual experiences, recite
the six-syllable mantra.

Mind by itself is intangible, like empty space, and can only engage in any activity, whether leading to saṃsāra or nirvāṇa, through the medium of the body. Even in the bardo, we have a dreamlike body which allows us to experience the various stages of the passage from one existence to the next. While mind and body are united, the phenomenal world can be perceived through the organs of sense and their corresponding consciousnesses. The function of these sense-consciousnesses is simply to perceive their corresponding objects—forms, sounds, smells, and the rest—without adding anything. But the mind then elaborates on these perceptions, thinking, "This is beautiful," "That is ugly," "This might harm me," "That will bring me pleasure." It is not the form of the external object, nor the eye, nor the visual consciousness that produces these subjective elaborations, which in the end lead to the accumulation of karma; it is the mind. A beautiful object has no intrinsic quality that is good for the mind, nor an ugly object any intrinsic power to harm it. Beautiful and ugly are just projections of the mind. The ability to cause happiness or suffering is not a property of the outer object itself. For example, the sight of a particular man can cause happiness to one person and suffering to another. It is the mind that attributes such qualities to the perceived object.

When in this way an object encountered by one of the sense organs is perceived by the sixth sense, mind, as either pleasurable or offensive, this distorted perception is brought about by grasping. Here is the very basis of saṃsāra. But if there is no grasping, the perception is liberated into wisdom. This is the experience of the purity of nirvāṇa, where it is no longer necessary to reject pleasurable sensations. It is in order to be free of grasping that you should train in recognizing all appearances as Buddha-fields and all beings as deities. To see things in this way transforms your perception of the world into primordial purity and allows you to realize all the qualities of the Buddha-fields.

As you examine carefully the nature of all the infinite and varied phenomena in the universe and all the beings it contains, you find that nothing has ever left the continuity of voidness. It is said, "The truth of voidness is the truth of everything." Voidness, in fact, is what makes it possible for infinite phenomena to appear. The phenomenal world we perceive, being the spontaneous display of voidness, is the Buddha-field, and all male and female beings are Chenrezi and Tārā. This is the very basis of the Mantrayāna.

As we are now, we feel attracted to what is beautiful and repelled by anything ugly; we feel happy when we see a friend and upset when we see someone we dislike. These subjective reactions are all produced by the mind's clinging to objects. When we are able to see even negative forces as the display of Chenrezi's wisdom, that clinging is purified and no negative forces are able to disturb our life or practice. When we perceive all phenomena as primordially pure, as the display of deities, mantras, and wisdom, all sense perceptions can be used as the path. When we see that everything arises out of voidness as the manifestation of Chenrezi, and thus recognize the expanse of infinite purity, we then no longer discriminate between good and bad, pure and impure; it is all the display of Chenrezi. Friends are Chenrezi, enemies are Chenrezi, all are one as Chenrezi.

When this experience arises, be careful not to hold on to it or feel proud about it. This vast purity is not the product of our meditation; it is the true nature of things. Gold is never fundamentally altered by being mixed with the other materials in gold ore, and through the processes of extraction and refining it merely becomes itself. In the same way, everything, the whole universe and all sentient beings, is primordially void. Phenomena are neither spoiled by the idea of impurity nor improved by the idea of purity. The true nature is, simply, always itself.

As the root text says, to train in experiencing all appearances as pure is the crucial point of the development stage. This normally implies the visualization of a deity, but if you cannot keep all the details of the visualization in mind, to see the world as a Buddha-field and sentient beings as having the nature of the deity is sufficient. Maintaining this experience, recite the six-syllable mantra.

Sounds

> 45. To recognize sounds as mantra is the crucial point of recitation practice;
> Clinging to sound as pleasant or unpleasant is liberated into its own nature.
> Free of grasping, the spontaneous sound of saṃsāra and nirvāṇa is the voice of the six syllables.
> In the self-liberation of hearing, recite the six-syllable mantra.

Usually, to listen to words of praise, good news, or beautiful music gives us pleasure; while, on the other hand, to hear criticism, false accusations about ourselves, bad news about those we love, or loud, dissonant noises immediately makes us feel distressed or irritated. The capacity to create such moods is a property not of these various sounds themselves, but of the clinging mind. The Bodhisattva, who knows that the nature of mind is unborn, perceives all sounds, whether pleasant or unpleasant, as mantra. Praise does not make him feel proud, and harsh words, instead of inciting his anger, only increase his patience and compassion. If you perceive all sounds as mantra, good or bad news will no more disturb you than the wind can disturb a mountain. In fact, to get upset when you hear bad news is only to create suffering for yourself; it will neither bring the dead back to life nor restore stolen possessions.

Like all phenomena, sounds are the result of a combination of various causes and circumstances and do not exist as independent entities. The beautiful sound of a lute depends on the proper tuning of all its strings, and if one string is broken or out of tune the sound it produces is discordant and unpleasant. Examine any sound carefully and deeply; the natural sounds of the weather, wind, thunder, and the rustling of leaves, as well as animal calls, human speech and song, are all composed of the basic elements of sound, and the nature of these is voidness.

The seed-syllable A, which symbolizes the unborn nature, is considered to be the source of all sounds and to contain the essence of the wisdom Buddhas. In particular, from it arises the six-syllable mantra. While you recite the mantra, recognize all sounds as arising from voidness, as an infinite display of mantras—the speech of the Buddhas. Then, even a small number of recitations will bear fruit. This is the practice of bringing all sounds to the path.

Ordinary conversation, which is fundamentally the expression of attachment and hatred, will only cause the wheel of delusion to spin faster and faster. But the recitation of mantra will protect your mind and lead you to realize the wisdom nature of speech. Therefore, recite the maṇi at all times, until it becomes one with your breathing.

Smells

46. To recognize smells as unborn is the crucial point of the completion stage;
Clinging to odor as fragrant or foul is liberated into its own nature.
Free of grasping, all smells are the fragrant discipline of Supreme Chenrezi;
In the self-liberation of smelling, recite the six-syllable mantra.

We love to savor fragrant scents, and we hold our noses to ward off foul smells. Yet all smells, whether the subtle perfume of sandalwood or the stench of excrement, are void in nature; recognize them as pure and without essence, and offer them to the Buddhas as the fragrance of perfect discipline. Such an offering perfects the two accumulations of merit and wisdom. Since the Buddhas are not affected by dualistic perceptions, we, too, should give up all thoughts of like and dislike. When we do so, the perception of smells will be liberated into its own nature.

Flavors

47. To recognize flavors as a sacramental feast is the crucial point of offering.
Attachment to taste as delicious or disgusting is liberated into its own nature;
Free of grasping, food and drink are substances to delight Supreme Chenrezi;
In the self-liberation of taste, recite the six-syllable mantra.

We usually relish delicious, savory, or sweet flavors and dislike anything that tastes bitter, sour, burning, or pungent. In fact, it is only the mind that clings to tastes as being delicious or disgusting. Once the mind realizes that such attributes are unborn and devoid of any existence, the pure nature of every flavor can be recognized. Food and drink then become the wisdom offering of the gaṇachakra, the practice of the feast-offering.[61]

Through this practice you will accumulate merit, overcome your habitual craving for food and drink, and avoid falling into unsuitable ways of sustaining yourself. When all attachments are liberated into the primordial nature, that is the supreme offering.

Sensations

48. To recognize sensations as essential sameness is
 the crucial point of equal taste;
Feelings of repletion and hunger, hot and cold,
 are liberated into their own nature.
Free of grasping, all sensations and feelings are
 the deity's activity;
In the self-liberation of sensation, recite the six-
 syllable mantra.

We discriminate between the soft feel of silk and the roughness of jute, the smoothness of a cup and the sharp prick of a thorn. But like the other sense perceptions, these sensations are no more than daydreams.

Once you stop discriminating between pleasant and unpleasant sensations, leaving them as they are in the essential sameness of their void nature, the mind will no longer be always elated or dejected. This is the experience of equal taste, the supreme practice of bringing both joy and suffering to the path. To crave the feel of soft things and to find anything abrasive unbearable is just clinging. Let all attachment and repulsion subside in the void nature, and Buddha-activity will reveal itself spontaneously.

To summarize, clinging to sense perceptions is what keeps you wandering in saṃsāra, and this is why it is usually taught that you should abandon all pleasures of the senses. But if you have realized the void nature of illusory phenomena and are therefore truly free from clinging, all your sense perceptions can be brought to the path in order to increase your accumulation of merit and wisdom, and to bring progress to your meditative experiences and realization. Whatever you see, taste, smell, hear, or feel, think of it like the reflection of the moon in a clear lake, or a vivid rainbow in the sky—fascinating to the eye but fleeting and elusive, ungraspable and devoid of any tangible existence. Seen in this way, your perceptions will never be solidified by fixation or entangled by clinging.

Mind

> 49. To recognize all phenomena as void is the crucial point of the view;
> Belief in true and false is liberated into its own nature.
> Free of grasping, everything there is, all of saṃsāra and nirvāṇa, is the continuum of the Dharmakāya;
> In the self-liberation of thoughts, recite the six-syllable mantra.

The mind, dividing experience into subject and object, first identifies with the subject, "I," then with the idea of "mine" and starts to cling to *my* body, *my* mind, and *my* name. As our attachment to these three notions grows stronger and stronger, we become more and more exclusively concerned with our own well-being. All our striving for comfort, our intolerance of life's annoying circumstances, and our preoccupation with pleasure and pain, wealth and poverty, fame and obscurity, praise and blame, are due to this idea of "I."

We are usually so obsessed with ourselves that we hardly ever even think about the welfare of others—in fact, we are no more interested in others than a tiger is interested in eating grass. This is completely the opposite of the outlook of the Bodhisattva. The ego is really just a fabrication of thought, and when you realize that both the object grasped and the mind that grasps are void, it is easy to see that others are not different from yourself.

All the energy we normally put into looking after ourselves, Bodhisattvas put into looking after others. If a Bodhisattva sees that by plunging into the fires of hell he can help even a single being, he does it without an instant of hesitation. Bodhisattvas who have reached the eighth level[62] realize that saṃsāra and nirvāṇa are completely the same. This is the ultimate view. The great Sakyapa teacher Jetsun Trakpa Gyaltsen[63] received from Mañjushrī in a vision the famous instructions on "freedom from the four attachments." In the last verse, Mañjushrī said, "If there is clinging there is no view." Shāntideva, too, said, "Everything is like the sky—this is what I have to realize." This is the ultimate view of both sūtra and tantra.

The view of voidness has to be first understood, then experienced, and finally realized. It is from voidness that saṃsāra and nirvāṇa arise, and it is into voidness that they dissolve. Even while they appear to exist, they have actually never departed from voidness. So, if you recognize all phenomena as being void in nature, you will be able to cope with whatever happens, whether you experience pleasure or pain, without any clinging.

Seen through the eyes of voidness, true and false are dualistic notions which can exist only in relation to each other. Only if there is false can there also be true; but if false is void then true must be void too. In the view of voidness, therefore, there can be no true assertions whatsoever, no conditions, and no clinging. When a Bodhisattva is firmly established in this view, he has no attachment to the peace of nirvāṇa, and to accomplish the welfare of beings he is able to assume any form whatsoever. He has the unremitting confidence that enables him to work with sentient beings for endless kalpas, no matter how far they have gone astray. Never thinking of the enlightenment for which he strives as being for himself, his only concern is to help others toward that goal.

THE FIVE EMOTIONS

To realize the perfect view is to be totally free from the five poisons, the emotions which keep us enslaved in saṃsāra. As the five poisons disappear, the five corresponding wisdoms are revealed.

Hatred

> 50. Don't follow after the object of hatred; look at the angry mind.
> Anger, liberated by itself as it arises, is the clear void;
> The clear void is none other than mirrorlike wisdom.
> In the self-liberation of hatred, recite the six-syllable mantra.

How does saṃsāra come about? As we perceive everything around us with our five senses, all sorts of feelings of attraction and repugnance arise in our minds, and it is from these feelings that saṃsāra arises. The simple perception of things, in itself, is not what causes us to wander in saṃsāra; it is rather our reaction to these perceptions and the interpretations we place on them that keep the wheel of saṃsāra turning. Now, the extraordinary feature of the Mantrayāna is that, instead of perpetuating saṃsāra in this way, we can cultivate the perception of all phenomena as the pure display of wisdom.

When you feel hatred toward someone, your hatred and anger are not in any way something inherent either to that person as a whole or to any aspect of him. Your anger only exists in your own mind. As soon as you glimpse him, your thoughts dwell on all the times he brought harm to you in the past, how he might harm you in the future, or what he is doing to harm you now; even hearing his name upsets you. As you become fixated on these thoughts, full-blown hatred develops, and at that point you feel an irresistible urge to pick up a stone and throw it at him, or to grab something with which to strike him, thinking, "I'd really like to kill him!"

Anger might seem extremely strong, but where does it get the power to overwhelm you so easily? Is it some external force, something with arms and legs, weapons and armor? If not, then is it somewhere inside you? If so, where is it? Can you find it in your brain, in your heart, in your bones, or in any other part of you? Impossible though it is to locate, anger does seem to be present in a very concrete way, a strong clinging that freezes your mind into a state of solidity and brings a great deal of suffering both to yourself and to others. Just as clouds, too insubstantial to support your weight or be worn as clothing, can nevertheless darken the whole sky and cover the sun, so in the same way thoughts can obscure the pristine radiance of awareness. By recognizing the void, transparent nature of mind, let it return to its natural state of freedom. If you recognize the nature of anger as void, it loses all its power to harm and becomes mirrorlike wisdom; but if you fail to recognize its nature and give it free rein, it will be no less than the very source of the scorching and freezing torments of hell.

People usually think of the overpowering and destruction of an adversary as a positive accomplishment, but this is unquestionably not the viewpoint of the Buddhist teachings. When anger erupts, do not pursue it, but instead look at the nature of anger itself; it is just a void fabrication within the void expanse of the mind. For innumerable lives, enslaved by your own aggression, you have accumulated immeasurable negative karma. From now on be more prudent, remembering that anger is the seed from which all the torments of the hells can grow. Eradicate anger, and there can be no more hell realms. Instead of hating so-called enemies, therefore, the real target of your hatred should be hatred itself.

If you do not pursue angry feelings, if you do not alienate yourself from others with anger, if your anger is liberated into its true nature, then that is mirrorlike wisdom, a mirror in which others are reflected as yourself. Were an angry thought ever to arise in Chenrezi's mind, it would simply make his wisdom even more brilliant. Furthermore, when you understand clearly that anger cannot be inherent in an outer object and that the inner angry mind is devoid of any tangible existence, you will feel spontaneous compassion radiating out to all beings, especially to those tormented by the fires of anger.

Long ago, in one of the Lord Buddha's previous lives, when he was a Bodhisattva in the form of a snake, some cruel children caught him and tortured him to death. Had he wanted, the Bodhisattva could have annihilated them with a single glance; but as his heart was free from the slightest thought of anger, that was not what he did. Instead, he prayed that through the connection they were making with him by killing him, they would in future become his disciples and be led by him to enlightenment. This exemplary courage and patience was the result of his complete realization of voidness and compassion.

Anger is the mortal enemy of liberation, since one moment of anger destroys virtue accumulated over aeons. To eliminate anger is therefore one of the principal aims of a Bodhisattva. So, strenuously maintaining the discipline of patience, recite the six-syllable mantra. As it is said, "There is no greater wrong than anger, no greater discipline than patience."

Pride

51. Don't chase after the object of pride; look at the grasping mind.
    Self-importance, liberated by itself as it arises, is primordial voidness;

This primordial voidness is none other than the
wisdom of essential sameness.
In the self-liberation of pride, recite the six-syllable
mantra.

Whenever we acquire some admirable quality, some particular knowledge or skill, pride arises in no time and spoils that positive attribute, whatever it might be. Overwhelmed by self-importance, dazzled by our own beauty, intelligence, learning, and power, we are completely blind to all the genuine and perfect qualities of the great teachers. But in reality, even if ordinary people such as ourselves, lost in saṃsāra's delusions, sometimes happen to have a few good qualities, these are sure to be far outnumbered by faults; and compared to the immeasurable virtues of the great beings, our own are as minute as a speck of flour. Indeed, the virtues of which we feel so proud are very often defects in disguise.

So, whatever limited and unstable talents you may have, there is absolutely no reason to feel proud of them. As the saying goes, "Just as water never collects on top of a mountain peak, true worth never collects on top of the crag of pride." Pride stops you developing devotion, wisdom, or compassion; it closes you off from the teacher's blessings and impedes all progress on the path. So, to avoid the dangers of pride, it is important to examine yourself honestly.

If you analyze pride carefully, you will find that it is not inherent in whatever you feel proud of, but is produced by the grasping mind. If you always stick to a modest position and keep your mind humble, pride will vanish like morning mist. A mind free of the grip of pride remains always in Chenrezi's wisdom of essential sameness.

Desire

52. Don't hanker after the object of desire; look at the
craving mind.

Desire, liberated by itself as it arises, is bliss-void;
This bliss-void is none other than all-discriminating wisdom.
In the self-liberation of desire, recite the six-syllable mantra.

Whatever happiness you might expect from your parents, your children, your friends, your wealth, or your possessions, it will never last long, for in the end they will all be snatched away from you by death—if not before. It is useless to cling to them.

When you die, however much you have been admired, however rich and powerful you have become, none of it will be of any use. You will wander in the intermediate state between death and birth, accompanied only by your positive and negative karma. To amass wealth and possessions and then to protect and increase them is an endless, frustrating task.

The sight of gold and diamonds fascinates us, and we are quickly overcome by the compulsive desire to possess them. But even if we somehow manage to buy such costly and beautiful objects, our clinging, far from coming to an end, only increases. Worried that we might lose the precious jewelry we have acquired, we put it all in a safe and never even dare to bring it out and wear it. After a whole lifetime based on craving, our experience in the intermediate state can only be one of extreme fear and panic.

Working in trade, farming, or any business whose profits are at others' expense is bound to bring us more and more negative karma. Never satisfied with what we have, always trying to get what we want, for countless lifetimes we have completely worn ourselves out. Would it not be better to give it all up and instead learn how to be satisfied with just enough clothing to wear and just enough food to live on?

If you commit yourself to the practice and recite the six-syllable mantra with a mind free from clinging, you will find yourself less and less fascinated by life's ordinary pursuits, and you will no longer waste your life. Desire and attachment will subside into their own nature, which is none other than Chenrezi's all-discriminating wisdom.

Jealousy

> 53. Don't follow after the object of jealousy; look at the critical mind.
> Jealousy, liberated by itself as it arises, is void intellect;
> This void intellect is none other than all-accomplishing wisdom.
> In the self-liberation of jealousy, recite the six-syllable mantra.

An ordinary person feels jealous of anyone whose achievements are equal to, or greater than, his own. Here again, however, jealousy is not something inherent in the object of your jealousy; it is just a fabrication of the mind. Whenever a jealous thought arises, simply recognize it for what it is and rejoice with all your heart in the superior achievement of the other person.

Once you allow jealous thoughts to proliferate, they can develop an inordinate intensity. An example is the story of Devadatta's jealousy of his cousin Gautama. Even after Gautama became the Buddha, Devadatta tried repeatedly in all sorts of malicious ways to vie with him. His jealous deeds were such that eventually the earth opened beneath his feet, and he fell into the fires of hell; there, experiencing terrible torments, he repented, crying, "From the depths of my heart, I take refuge in you, Gautama!" Although in a future life he was to take rebirth as a Pratyekabuddha, in that life even the Buddha could not save him. Envy, therefore, is a very serious fault; never fall under its influence.

Just by feeling great joy in your heart at others' achievements—for example, at the vast offerings someone might be making to the Three Jewels—you will be accumulating the same merit as that person. Instead of being infatuated by your own achievements, instead of falling prey to jealousy, rejoice at the inestimable virtues of others, especially at the deeds of the supreme beings. This is none other than all-accomplishing wisdom itself.

Ignorance

> 54. Don't just take for granted ideas forged by
>   ignorance; look at the nature of ignorance itself.
> The hosts of thoughts, liberated by themselves as they
>   arise, are awareness-void;
> This awareness-void is none other than the wisdom of
>   the absolute expanse.
> In the self-liberation of ignorance, recite the six-
>   syllable mantra.

Ignorance here means ignorance of our own Buddha-nature. In this respect, we are as ignorant as a beggar with a precious jewel in his hand who, not recognizing how valuable it is, simply throws it away. It is because of ignorance that we are the slaves of our thoughts and cannot tell right from wrong. It is because of ignorance that we are blind to the law of cause and effect and refuse to believe that every action has a result. It is because of ignorance that we cannot accept the existence of past and future lives. It is because of ignorance that we have no confidence in the beneficial results of praying to the Three Jewels. It is because of ignorance that we do not recognize the truth of the Dharma. Ignorance is at the very root of the eighty-four thousand negative emotions, for as long as we fail to see that the true nature of everything is voidness, we insist on believing that things really exist; and this is the source of all deluded perceptions and all negative thoughts.

However, ignorance is not everlasting like the permanent

darkness of a cavern deep underground. Like any other phenomenon, it can only have arisen from voidness and therefore can have no true existence. Once you recognize the void nature of ignorance, it turns into the wisdom of the absolute expanse. This is the wisdom mind of Chenrezi, the Buddha-nature, the essence of the Tathāgatas, which is present in all beings. Only because of ignorance, as the Buddha demonstrated, do we believe our deluded perception instead of recognizing this, our own nature.

By establishing its void nature, recognize the dullness and delusion of ignorance as the absolute expanse itself. Then rest in that experience and practice the view, meditation, and action. This is the very heart essence of Chenrezi.

Whenever thoughts and emotions related to the five poisons arise, therefore, instead of allowing yourself to be carried away by them, just look at their nature; by doing so you will eventually come to recognize the five poisons as the five primordial wisdoms, which are the natural condition of the undeluded mind. At that point, your thoughts will be liberated as soon as they arise, and you will never lose sight of awareness, the absolute Chenrezi.

The absolute Chenrezi is none other than voidness, yet on the relative level Chenrezi assumes infinite forms to meet the needs of beings. All of these manifestations, with their various names, forms, and colors, are the display of his wisdom, the expression of the creativity of voidness and compassion. In particular, Chenrezi displays five main forms which correspond to the five aggregates and the five realms[64] of saṃsāra. The next five verses explain the transformation of the five aggregates, or skandhas, into these five aspects of Chenrezi.[65]

THE FIVE AGGREGATES

Form

55. Form is unborn, primordially void, like the sky;
The quintessence of this awareness-void is Chenrezi—
It is none other than the Sublime King of the Sky.
In the view of voidness, recite the six-syllable mantra.

We see a rainbow in the sky only because of the conjunction of sunlight and rain. In the same way, all the infinite variety of forms that we see only result from the ephemeral conjunction of a number of conditions; none of them, under scrutiny, can be found to have any substantial existence. For instance, we use the word *body* to refer to an ever-changing agglomeration of bones, flesh, and blood, yet in truth there is no such entity as a body.

It is the five skandhas that support the false concept of a substantially existing "I," the source of all suffering. But once we recognize the skandha of form to be void, it is none other than Chenrezi. The name given to this aspect of Chenrezi, King of the Sky, conveys the vast and all-pervasive way in which he takes form. In every single pore of his body infinite Buddha-fields appear without the pore enlarging or the Buddha-fields shrinking. However, Chenrezi's body is not flesh and blood but a display of his wisdom, void in nature. Recognizing this, recite the six-syllable mantra.

Feeling

56. Feeling is the lasso that binds mind and object together;
When you know it as nondual sameness, it is Chenrezi—
It is none other than the Sublime Bountiful Lasso.
In the realization of same taste, recite the six-syllable mantra.

It is the conjunction of the body with the mind that enables feelings of pleasant and unpleasant, happiness and suffering, to arise. When your body feels some minute pain, such as the prick of a thorn, the reason you dislike it is that you believe in the notion of an individual self. You therefore think, "Me . . . my body . . . my happiness . . . my suffering." The fact that when other people experience exactly the same pain it hardly bothers you at all is proof of the extent to which you believe in an "I."

This skandha, feeling, is the bond that ties you to the three worlds of existence. Feeling is the basic reaction of like and dislike that occurs when you encounter anything in the phenomenal world. It comes about through the functioning of the sense organs and their corresponding consciousness. If you examine it, you will recognize it to be devoid of any real entity; feeling then becomes the wisdom of sameness, and its nature is none other than the aspect of Chenrezi known as Bountiful Lasso, Amoghapāsha in Sanskrit.

Amoghapāsha belongs to the jewel family, and he is imbued with so much power that merely to hear his name and mantra will broaden your meditation experience, deepen your wisdom, lengthen your life span, and greatly amplify your merit and wealth. Yet this astonishingly powerful aspect of Chenrezi is in truth nothing other than your own mind. When, through the realization of voidness, you perceive saṃsāric phenomena as infinite purity, you unlock the enlightened counterpart of the skandha of feeling, the treasury of ever-enriching qualities; this is the Jewel-Born Buddha, Ratnasambhava.

Amoghapāsha, Bountiful Lasso, is a synonym for the wish-granting gem. Like a lasso, the wish-granting gem can bring even the most powerful gods and men under its control and pull all sentient beings up to enlightenment. When you feel yourself about to fall into the abyss of obscuring emotions, pray to Chenrezi; at the last moment, when the lasso of his compassion catches you, you will be filled with confidence in his enlightened omniscience. Therefore, with conviction and one-pointed devotion, recite the six-syllable mantra.

Appraisal

57. Appraisal, if you keep taking it as valid, is delusion;
When you turn to all beings with compassion, it is Chenrezi—
It is none other than the Sublime One Who Dredges the Depths of Saṃsāra.
In compassion without bias, recite the six-syllable mantra.

Your mind ceaselessly appraises whatever you encounter, thinking, "This might please me, this might harm me." It is as a result of this process that you keep craving what might be pleasurable and fearing what might be unpleasant. The assessments that your mind makes arise from its ego-centered way of perceiving everything. But now, instead of appraising things in terms of how much happiness and suffering they will bring you, you should focus on the happiness and suffering of the whole infinity of sentient beings. This will give birth to a vast compassion without any bias, and you will then recognize this third skandha, appraisal, as the aspect of Chenrezi known as He Who Dredges the Depths of Saṃsāra.

When you dredge the depths of the sea, whatever is at the bottom will be lifted up to the surface. Likewise, Chenrezi's compassionate activity lifts up to the higher realms all those beings who have sunk to the depths of existence, the lower realms of saṃsāra.

If, even for the sake of a single being, Chenrezi had to toil until the end of time, his great compassion would never diminish. He Who Dredges the Depths of Saṃsāra is constantly ready to come to the help of beings. This is illustrated by the following parable.

Long ago, a company of merchants put to sea in search of the fabled island of jewels. Shipwrecked by a storm, they sought refuge on an island inhabited by man-eating ogres. The ogres, to overpower the merchants, magically transformed themselves into comely princesses, and appearing to the merchants in this guise, they were soon able to charm them and win their confidence. Before long, the ogre princesses had taken all of the merchants as their husbands; thenceforth, the merchants were kept under close watch and never allowed to stray far from their homes.

One day, however, the captain of the merchants happened to go further than usual without being noticed. He came upon a huge building made of iron. From within a voice cried out, "Listen, you out there! We too are merchants who were shipwrecked on this island and imprisoned here. Be careful! You are being fooled; the princesses you have married are actually ogres, and they plan to murder and devour all of you." At this, the captain at last realized that he and his men had been tricked and were the prisoners of the ogre princesses. "We are in a terrible trap," he said. "But is there no way to escape?"

The voice said: "For us there is none, but for you there is one chance. To the east of the city there is a lake, and upon the shore of the lake is a grove called the Grove of Golden Grass. On the night of each new and full moon, Chenrezi, in the form of the royal stallion Valāha, or Mighty Cloud, comes to the grove from the Celestial Realm of the Thirty-Three to graze, drink, and roll on the golden sand. He calls whoever wishes to leave this isle of ogres for the continent of Jambudvīpa to come and ride on his back. I have heard the ogre princesses say that anyone who holds on to Valāha's mane and refuses to listen to their false pleas cannot be prevented from escaping safe and sound to India."

> The captain hurried back to tell his companions what he had learned, and all of them, appalled at their plight and realizing that this was their only hope to regain their freedom, prayed to Chenrezi from the depth of their hearts.
>
> As foretold, at the time of the full moon the celestial stallion appeared, grazing peacefully in the Grove of Golden Grass. Just as he was about to take flight, he called out to the merchants to mount quickly on his back. The ogre princesses, seeing that their captives were on the point of escape, began to wail and lament. They brought out the children they had borne with the merchants and implored their husbands to stay behind to look after their poor sons and daughters, who, they cried, would otherwise surely all starve. A few of the merchants, unable to sever their attachments and resist the pleas of their ogre wives, fell back to earth; but all the others, deaf to these tearful entreaties, prayed to Chenrezi with great faith and were able to escape safely to the continent of Jambudvīpa.

Chenrezi's compassion, free from the skandha of appraisal, falls equally on all beings. He will tirelessly dredge the depths of saṃsāra until not even a single being is left behind.

The first skandha is your first apprehension of an object. The second skandha is your feeling that the object is pleasant, unpleasant, or neutral to you. The third skandha is your appraisal of the intensity of that feeling as strong, medium, or weak; your mind then holds on to this appraisal as something real and valid, which forms the basis for the subsequent two stages. It is through this sequence of processes, the five aggregates, that all suffering comes about. However, by reciting the six-syllable mantra with total devotion, you can be free from the shackles of appraisal and thus escape the trap of saṃsāra.

Impulse

58. Impulse, as saṃsāric actions, keeps you circling in the six realms;
If you realize saṃsāra and nirvāṇa are the very same, it is Chenrezi—
It is none other than the Greatly Compassionate Transformer of Beings.
Acting for others in one single taste, recite the six-syllable mantra.

Impulse is the compulsion to take action on the basis of your feelings of desire and aversion, thus accumulating karma; impulse is therefore the architect of saṃsāra and nirvāṇa. Completely enslaved by impulse, you have been wandering from one life to the next since beginningless time. Yet if you realize that the nature of impulse is void, and that your endless impulses are in truth the myriad facets of wisdom, you will no longer be subject to their dominion.

According to the Vajrayāna, Chenrezi pervades all maṇḍalas as the Mighty Lord of the Lotus Dance. Although in essence a fully enlightened Buddha displaying inexhaustible resources of compassion, he assumes the form of a Bodhisattva in order to help sentient beings directly according to their needs. Everything a Bodhisattva does is to benefit beings; he has no selfish aims, whatever the circumstances. This exalted level of compassion brings with it countless enlightened qualities, in particular the realization that saṃsāra and nirvāṇa are of one single taste.

At present, you might find it difficult to identify with such inconceivably vast attributes as Chenrezi's realization, compassion, and ability to help others. But if you recite his mantra with single-minded devotion, you too will one day be able to benefit beings on the same immense scale. Aspire from your heart to help all beings, and dedicate to them all your merit, with the conviction that Chenrezi acknowledges your aspirations and gives you his blessing to bring them to fulfillment.

Consciousness

> 59. Consciousness, the expression of ordinary mind,
> has eight functions;
> If you realize ultimate mind to be Dharmakāya,
> it is Chenrezi—
> It is none other than the Sublime Ocean of
> Conquerors.
> Knowing that your own mind is the Buddha,
> recite the six-syllable mantra.

If a seed in the ground comes from a poisonous plant, the roots and leaves that develop from it are sure to be poisonous, or even lethal. In the same way, whenever the five aggregates are present, suffering is bound to ensue. The king-pin of the aggregates is consciousness, for it is consciousness that clings to the aggregates as truly existent, to pleasure as pleasure, and to suffering as suffering. Consciousness is, in fact, the deluded mind and its deluded thoughts. Now, once you recognize that consciousness has never come into true existence and can therefore neither continue to exist nor come to an end, you will be free from its grip. But until you reach that point, consciousness, constantly perpetuating delusion, will continue to generate more and more karma. It is therefore crucial that you focus all your efforts on recognizing the void nature of consciousness. When that recognition arises clearly, it is like the light of day breaking into the darkness of night.

The pure nature of consciousness is the aspect of Chenrezi known as the Ocean of Conquerors. "Conquerors" refers to the Buddhas, who have won the victory of complete enlightenment, and "Ocean" refers to the vastness of the infinity of Buddhas united in Chenrezi. Pray that the day will come when you, too, achieve such perfection that just by hearing your name beings will be purified of their defilements and liberated from the lower realms.

Knowing that Chenrezi dwells within yourself as the continuity of unchanging oneness, recite the six-syllable mantra.

The Four Essential Points Related to Body, Speech, Mind, and Dharmakāya

BODY

60. Believing the body to be solid is what causes
    servitude;
    If you recognize it as the deity, appearing yet void,
    it is Chenrezi—
    It is none other than the Sublime Khasarpaṇi.
    In the recognition of the deity's body, appearing
    yet void, recite the six-syllable mantra.

It is our ordinary perception of the body as a solid structure of bones and flesh that causes it to attract suffering like a magnet. But by training yourself in the practices of visualization and mantra recitation, you can learn to break away from your fixation on the body's solidity; by training in perceiving your body as Chenrezi's unlimited, unborn wisdom-body, you can attain the state beyond suffering. The body of Chenrezi, all-pervading like the sky, is neither flesh and blood nor something concrete like a statue. Rather, it is transparent like a rainbow, appearing clearly yet void and without any substance. What is more, Chenrezi is not just a visual image—he is alive, radiant with wisdom, love, and power, responsive to anyone who so much as makes a simple gesture of prayer or recites a single maṇi.

SPEECH

61. Conceptualizing speech and sound is what causes
 delusion;
 If you recognize it as mantra, resounding yet void,
 it is Chenrezi—
 It is none other than the Sublime Lion's Roar.
 In the recognition of sound as mantra, recite the
 six-syllable mantra.

When your visualization of the deity's body is clear and stable, mantra recitation, as described in the section on the vajra speech, will further enhance your practice. The first syllable of Chenrezi's mantra, OṂ, symbolizes the five wisdoms; as the syllable of auspiciousness, it begins most mantras. MAṆI means "jewel," PADME means "lotus," and HŪṂ is the syllable proclaiming and invoking Chenrezi's omniscience. The whole mantra can be rendered: "You, the Lotus Jewel, grant your omniscience." By repeating his name in the six-syllable mantra, you remember and invoke his boundless qualities, as if you were calling to him from afar. In answer, his compassion manifests effortlessly, fulfilling all your wishes.

In order to bless beings, Chenrezi empowered his mantra to be exactly the same as himself. It is the resounding of the unborn void. Written, the mantra liberates by sight; as sound, it liberates by hearing; arising in the mind, it liberates by recollection; worn on the body, it liberates by contact. If you accustom yourself to perceiving all sound as mantra, you will feel no fear when you hear the terrifying sounds of the bardo. Through his mantra, Chenrezi performs his vast and compassionate activity on an infinite scale. So with fervent devotion, hearing all the many sounds of the universe as the reverberation of the mantra, recite the six syllables.

MIND

62. Clinging to mind's perceptions as true is the
 delusion that causes saṃsāra;
 If you leave mind in its natural state, free from
 thoughts, it is Chenrezi—
 It is none other than the Sublime Unwinding in
 Ultimate Mind.
 In ultimate mind, the Dharmakāya, recite the
 six-syllable mantra.

People always say, "Meditate! Meditate!" but unless you have established a firm and unmistaken understanding of the view of voidness, what is the point of meditating? Failure to recognize the void nature of mind is the very source of saṃsāra. This void nature, with its inherent compassion, is recognized when the mind, free of the influence of thoughts, awakens to the simple awareness of the present.

Given free rein, thoughts create the whole of saṃsāra. Unexamined, they retain their apparent reality and hence their power to perpetuate saṃsāra. Yet no thought, virtuous or harmful, has even the slightest tangible existence. Without exception, thoughts are completely void, like a rainbow which, though appearing in the sky brilliant and vivid in its five colors, can never be caught, worn as clothing, or used in any way at all. The void nature remains absolutely unchanged by anything, even when it is veiled from view by superficial obscurations. Indeed, those obscurations are not really things in the way that need to be removed, since the moment we recognize their void nature they vanish into thin air. When the delusion of obscuring thoughts fades away, the mind remains free and serene, effortlessly at rest in its own nature. This is the meaning of Chenrezi's name Unwinding in Ultimate Mind.

The sky is never disturbed or changed by the occurrence of clouds. The sky neither entertains the hope that rainbows will arise nor suffers disappointment if they don't. Chenrezi's vajra mind never moves from the absolute nature, no matter how extensive or pervasive his compassionate activity for beings. Appearing to beings in innumerable ways, in reality he never moves from the sphere of voidness.

Chenrezi is one with the primordial nature of your own mind; do not look for him elsewhere. In order to realize this nature within yourself, request and receive the teachings with unfabricated, heartfelt devotion; then contemplate and assimilate them into your being. Finally, you will achieve ultimate realization. All karmic tendencies and obscuring emotions will dissolve, and you will know directly the voidness of all phenomena. At that point you will unwind into a state of rest, far from the torments of saṃsāra. Like a serene old man watching children at play, you will view with unshakable equanimity the ever-changing display of unreal phenomena.

If you find it difficult to visualize the deities with their ornaments, the emanation of light, and all the other details, simply maintain the recognition of the natural state; this is the heart-yoga of the Dharmakāya. Watching everything arise in the single flavor of absolute reality, recite the six-syllable mantra.

DHARMAKĀYA

> 63. Everything that exists is the primordially pure continuum of the Dharmakāya;
> If you meet the Dharmakāya face to face, it is Chenrezi—
> It is none other than the Sublime Sovereign of the Universe.
> In the continuum of all-pervading purity, recite the six-syllable mantra.

Chenrezi and all the Buddhas in all their aspects, whether on the Sambhogakāya or Nirmāṇakāya level, arise from the ground of Dharmakāya. The Dharmakāya is the absolute expanse beyond any intellectual fabrication. It includes within its nature all the enlightened qualities of Buddhahood.[66] It is the primordial wisdom which has been with us from beginningless time. This inherent wisdom can be recognized through the meditation practices of tranquility and insight. Tranquility is the pacification of the mind's usual state of turmoil, and insight is the development of vaster vision and profound realization that follows. When tranquility and insight are inseparably merged, the Dharmakāya is realized.

As you progress along the Bodhisattva path, continually maintaining the practice in both meditation and postmeditation, you eventually reach the first bhūmi[67] and enter the path of vision, so called because for the first time you actually glimpse ultimate reality, the void nature of everything. This experience of voidness, however, has still not reached its full extent and must be progressively enlarged through each successive level until finally, at the tenth bhūmi, the fabric of the two obscurations vanishes forever, and primordial, adamantine wisdom is fully revealed. You reach what is called the path of no more learning, the level of Buddhahood, where the mind is one with the wisdom mind of Dharmakāya. Whoever achieves this nondual level of enlightenment truly embodies the highest ideals of all in the three worlds of existence.

Chenrezi himself is the Tathāgata, the very essence of Buddhahood, and all the qualities of the Dharmakāya will develop effortlessly through the recitation of his six-syllable mantra.

Conclusion of the Second Discourse

64. One deity, Chenrezi, embodies all Buddhas;
One mantra, the six syllables, embodies all mantras;
One Dharma, bodhichitta, embodies all practices
of the development and completion stages.
Knowing the one which liberates all, recite the
six-syllable mantra.

The Buddha Shākyamuni himself is an emanation of Chenrezi; the Dharma, which shows us what to avoid and what to cultivate, is perfectly contained in the six-syllable mantra; the Saṅgha, the Bodhisattvas who help us along the path, are emanations of Chenrezi as well. Chenrezi is thus the union of the Three Jewels. Just as one reservoir collects countless drops of rain, Chenrezi's compassion includes all the wisdom of Mañjushrī and all the power of Vajrapāṇi. With this one deity, one mantra, and one practice, you can accomplish everything.

The many deities are infinitely diverse: peaceful or wrathful, with one, three, or many heads, and with two, four, six, or many more arms, each one symbolizing a different quality. Yet you can be confident that all of them are included in Chenrezi. In the same way, since all the beneficial power of the immense variety of other mantras is contained in the six-syllable mantra by itself, you can put all your heart into reciting just the one mantra. Your body, speech, and mind are essentially one with the enlightened body, speech, and mind of Chenrezi; this you should recognize as the quintessence of the practice.

At the same time, to follow the path of enlightenment all the way to its ultimate goal it is vital to constantly sustain and strengthen the vast attitude of bodhichitta. According to the pith-instructions of the precious Kadampa teachers, you are first introduced to the nature of the mind, absolute bodhichitta, and you then cultivate compassion for all beings, relative bodhichitta.

It would be difficult to bring the wild mind under control without first recognizing that wandering thoughts are in reality never born and can therefore neither remain nor come to an end. With this recognition, not pursuing thoughts as they arise but remaining in the unbroken simplicity of the natural state of the mind is called absolute bodhichitta.

Once you have glimpsed the nature of mind in this way, your realization of absolute bodhichitta is deepened through the cultivation of relative bodhichitta in its two aspects: aspiring to achieve enlightenment for the sake of all beings and actually putting this aspiration into practice. As we have seen before, it is not enough simply to wish to help people. You have to undertake to truly benefit all beings, just like Chenrezi, and it is in order to achieve this goal that you visualize Chenrezi, recite his mantra, and meditate on the nature of his wisdom. As you continue to practice in this way, deluded thoughts become fewer and fewer, while wisdom blooms in your being, enabling you to fulfill the immediate and ultimate needs of yourself and others.

Part Three

Determination to Be Free from Saṃsāra

Leaving Saṃsāric Activity Behind

The primary point of renunciation is to leave all saṃsāric activities behind in order to practice the Dharma single-mindedly.

Actions

65. What use is all you've done? Being so busy just
    causes saṃsāra—
Look how meaningless all you've done has been.
Now you'd better just stop trying to do anything;
Dropping all activities, recite the six-syllable mantra.

Only a Buddha can count how many times you have taken birth in beginningless saṃsāra, and only a Buddha can say when saṃsāra began. It is said in the *Sublime Dharma of Clear Recollection* that if you could pile up all the bodies you have had in your past lives as an insect, the heap would be higher than Mount Meru; and if you could collect all the tears of grief you have shed, they would form an ocean bigger than any on earth. During all these innumerable lives, everything you have done has only perpetuated your suffering without bringing you even an inch closer to liberation. Why? Because, until now, all your actions have been harmful, or at best futile.

Living creatures are constantly busy. We humans are always busy competing with one another, buying, selling, making, destroying. Birds are always busy building nests, hatching eggs, feeding nestlings. Bees are always busy collecting nectar, making honey. Other animals are always busy feeding, hunting, watching for danger, rearing their young. The more you do, the more you have to do and the more your hardships multiply—but the final outcome of all your toil and trouble will last no longer than a drawing made on water with your finger. When you acknowledge the frustration and futility of so much meaningless activity it becomes clear that the only truly worthwhile undertaking is to practice the Dharma.

Speaking

> 66. What use is all you've said? It was all just pointless prattle—
> Look how much irrelevant distraction it has brought.
> Now you'd better just keep silent;
> Ceasing completely to speak, recite the six-syllable mantra.

When people get together and talk, most of what they say is entirely inconsequential. Their conversation, inspired principally by attachments and antipathies, only serves to heighten their poisonous emotions. All this pointless talking agitates the mind, making thoughts flutter like so many paper flags in the wind.

"The mouth is the doorway of sin," goes the saying. Superfluous speech, lies, harsh words, and gossip all cause endless distractions and inner disquiet; and even the gift of articulate and compelling eloquence more often than not just leads to wasted time and trouble. This is why it is said in the Mantrayāna that to spend a single month reciting mantra while otherwise keeping silent is more beneficial than to spend a whole year reciting mantra but intermixing it with ordinary talking. Done properly without the intrusion of any other form of speech, as in the first case, the recitation of mantra retains its full power and ultimately leads to a clear vision of the truth beyond words, for the maṇi is the natural resonance of this inexpressible truth.

Your practice will therefore progress quickly if you eliminate the endless chatter of everyday life by taking a vow of silence, and utter nothing but the six-syllable mantra.

Moving Around

67. What use is rushing around? Coming and going
just tires you out—
Look how far your wandering has taken you from
the Dharma.
Now you'd better just settle down and relax your
mind;
Staying put, carefree and at ease, recite the six-
syllable mantra.

Racing around, hither and thither, only tires us out for no reason. We are always rushing off to see what is happening somewhere else and getting involved in all sorts of events in the world outside. But all this time there is actually more than enough to look at inwardly, in the movement of our thoughts, and plenty to be done to master them.

Until now you have been wandering around, lost in the different realms of saṃsāra where there is little else but suffering. Gathering karma and experiencing the pain of its fruition, you have strayed further and further away from the Dharma. Would it not now be better to stay by yourself in a quiet place conducive to meditation? To meditate on the sublime teacher and the sublime teachings until the true meaning of Dharma completely suffuses your mind is the only way to render this rare and precious human life truly worthwhile. If you are able to do that, even for a short while, it is a great blessing.

Eating

68. What use is all you've eaten? It all just turned
into excrement—

Look how insatiable your appetite has been.
Now you'd better nourish yourself with the food
of samādhi;
Quit all that eating and drinking, and recite the
six-syllable mantra.

Whatever we eat, however delicious or tasteless it might be, is only going to end up as excrement, so why crave for it so much? It would be better to consider the food we eat as an offering, thereby accumulating merit instead of intensifying our attachment.

When you eat, visualize your food and drink as pure nectar and first offer it to the Three Jewels. Then, imagining that the Buddhas return to you the food you have offered them, eat it as a blessing. At the end of the meal, visualize that you are Chenrezi and that the food you have just eaten is transformed into nectar, which flows out from your hands and from your whole body to relieve the hunger and thirst of all the beings in the realm of starving spirits; the ordinary act of eating thus becomes a way to accumulate merit. By integrating the Dharma into all your actions, every aspect of your daily life can be made into a practice which enriches your understanding.

Why long for lavish meals? Trying to satisfy your craving is like drinking salt water: the more you drink the thirstier you feel. Look how much time, effort, and money people spend just for the sake of a delicious meal! Instead of all that, content yourself with simple food and take delight in the nectar of samādhi,[68] the meditation of tranquility and insight, which will bring deep satisfaction and rid you of all your obscurations. Recognizing the source of true nourishment, recite the six-syllable mantra.

Thinking

69. What use are all your thoughts? They've just
brought more delusion—

Look how few of all your aims you've managed
to achieve.
Now for this life's concerns you'd better not think
too far ahead;
Dropping all your plans, recite the six-syllable
mantra.

Without extending past thoughts or welcoming future ones, maintain a clear awareness of the present moment. Otherwise there can be no end to the succession of deluded thoughts. As the wise and holy Gyalse Thogme said, "All these so-called joys and sorrows are like drawings on water; why chase after them? If you really must have something to think about, then contemplate how everything that has been collected will be lost and everything that has been built will fall apart."

The futility of planning for the unpredictable future is illustrated by the story of Famous Moon's father.

> One night a farmer, before going to sleep, tied up the big bag of barley he had just harvested and hung it from a beam above his bed. He stretched out on his mattress and lay there on his back, with his hands behind his head, looking up at the bag. "I shall certainly be able to sell this barley for a good sum of money," he thought. "With that amount I shall be in a position to make a good marriage to a fine and beautiful woman. . . . Once married, it won't be long before I have a handsome son. . . . Let me think, what shall I call him?" Glimpsing the full moon shining brilliantly through the window, he suddenly had an idea. "I know! I shall call him *Famous Moon*. . . ." But at that very moment a mouse that had been gnawing away at the rope that held up the bag finished its work. The heavy bag fell on the farmer, putting an end to both him and his plans.

Don't let your mind get lost in speculation. Drop completely all plans for the ordinary concerns of this life, and remembering what a precious opportunity to practice the Dharma each passing instant affords, direct your every thought toward Chenrezi. Instead of succumbing to the power of delusion, fill your mind with love and compassion for all beings; and instead of exhausting yourself in vain trying to fulfill all your ordinary aims, remain in the equanimity that comes from deep meditation.

To practice like this, even for as little as one hour, is an effective antidote to the obscuring emotions and is sure to foster your progress on the path. So cutting through all hopes, plans, and expectations, which serve only to stir up the mind, recite the six-syllable mantra.

Possessions

70. What use is all you own? Property is just clinging—
Look how soon you'll leave whatever you've got behind.
Now you'd better put an end to your possessive grasping;
Ceasing to acquire and hoard things, recite the six-syllable mantra.

Possessions, like everything material, are bound to disintegrate sooner or later. Wealth causes endless anxiety and all kinds of negative behavior. "As your affluence grows, so does your misery," the saying goes. You might spend your whole life piling up possessions and money until you are as rich as the God of Wealth himself—and then suddenly death will rob you of it all. Consider the fate of so many powerful rulers and wealthy dynasties, struck down by intrigues, tragedies, upheavals, wars, and all the other sufferings they seem to attract.

Would it not be agonizing to watch someone toy briefly with a precious jewel as if it were just an ordinary stone, and then throw it away? Well, it is even more distressing to watch those who have the precious opportunity of practicing the Dharma waste their lives in the mistaken pursuit of meaningless goals. To use this human life for other than its true purpose is like filling a golden vessel with excrement.

Do not waste or misuse this precious opportunity. Do not spend your time accumulating things that are totally unnecessary. It would be so much better spent building up the merit of spiritual practice.

Even reciting a few maṇis or doing an instant of practice will make you rich in the heart-treasure of the enlightened ones. Realizing that no amount of worldly wealth will bring true benefit either in this life or the next, recite the six-syllable mantra with diligence, devotion, and joy.

Sleeping

71. What use is all the time you've slept? It was all
    just spent in a stupor—
  Look how easily your life is running out in
    indolence.
  Now you'd better start to exert yourself whole-
    heartedly;
  Day and night, spurning all distraction, recite
    the six-syllable mantra.

At the age of seventy, you will have spent 70 times 365 nights, or more than twenty years, just sleeping like a corpse. Ordinary sleep is not only of no use for your Dharma practice; it also reinforces your karmic propensity for ignorance, to the point that excessive indolence can be enough to cause rebirth in the lower realms of saṃsāra. It is therefore most important that you abandon laziness and focus all your efforts single-mindedly on the practice of Dharma.

It is also important to make use of the methods of transforming ordinary sleep into a practice which will further your progress on the path. Before you go to sleep at night, reflect on what you have done during the day. Confess any actions that were negative, and resolve firmly to avoid repeating them. Remembering whatever you did that was positive, dedicate all the merit you might have accumulated through the course of the day to the swift liberation of all beings. Then assume the "lion posture," lying down on your right side with your right hand beneath your right cheek and your left arm resting upon your left side; this is the position Lord Buddha took when he entered parinirvāṇa. Next, visualize Chenrezi, about the size of your thumb, sitting on a four-petaled red lotus in the center of your heart. Light rays stream out from him, filling your body, your room, and gradually the whole universe, melting everything into a mass of radiant light. Fall asleep while maintaining this visualization.

If you can use sleep in this way for practice, the practice of day will blend continuously with the practice of night. Similarly, when you can make use of the methods for transforming all your daily activities into practice, postmeditation will blend continuously into meditation; each will enhance the other and your progress will be rapid. Persevering both day and night, recite the six-syllable mantra.

The Urgent Need to Practice

72. There's no time, no time! There's no time to rest!
When suddenly death is upon you, what will you do?
Now you'd better start practicing the sublime Dharma
right away;
Now, quick, hurry—recite the six-syllable mantra.

You can be sure that death will come, but you can never be sure when, where, or how—it could even be today. Death is unimpressed before even all the power and military might in the world, unmoved by even the most eloquent of entreaties, impervious to even the most dazzling beauty, untempted by even the most fabulous bribe. Nothing at all can put off death, even for an instant. When your time has come, there is only one thing that will be of any use to you: whatever Dharma practice you have done. Always remember death. As the Kadampa masters said, "It is contemplating death that will first turn your mind to Dharma, then spur on your efforts to practice, and finally allow you to recognize death as the Dharmakāya."

The moment of death, however, is not the time to begin meditating. Now is the time, while your mind is free from worry and your body free from illness. Begin to practice now, and even if death strikes unexpectedly you will already be prepared, without regret or fear.

Never forget how swiftly this life will be over, like a flash of summer lightning or the wave of a hand. Now that you have the opportunity to practice Dharma, do not waste a single moment on anything else, but with all your energy and effort recite the six-syllable mantra.

73. What can you say about years, months, or days—
Look how things change every moment, right now!
Each moment that passes brings you closer to death;
Now, this very moment, recite the six-syllable mantra.

Nothing ever stands still; from moment to moment everything is changing. In spring seeds send out shoots; in summer the shoots grow into leaves, stems, and flowers; in autumn the grain ripens and is harvested; and in winter the earth is again prepared to receive next year's crop. As the moon waxes and wanes over the course of a month, as the sun rises and sets over the course of a day, everything undergoes incessant change. Noon might see a thousand people singing and dancing in a fairground, yet dusk finds the whole place silent and empty. In the meantime, each one of those revelers will have slipped a few hours closer to death.

Just as every single thing is always moving inexorably closer to its ultimate dissolution, so also your own life, like a burning butterlamp, will soon be consumed. It would be foolish to think that you can first finish all your work and then retire to spend the later stages of your life practicing the Dharma. Can you be certain that you will live that long? Does death not strike the young as well as the old? No matter what you are doing, therefore, remember death and keep your mind focused on the Dharma. In this way recite the six-syllable mantra.

74. As your life runs out like the setting sun sinking away,
Death closes in like the lengthening shadows of evening.
Now what's left of your life will vanish as fast as the last fading shadows;
There's no time to waste—recite the six-syllable mantra.

From the very moment of your birth, you are doomed to die. No doctor, however skilled, can prevent it. Death is advancing relentlessly upon you like the shadow of the western mountains at sunset, engulfing in darkness everything in its path. Lord Buddha described, as the paragon of speed, a man who could catch in flight all four arrows shot simultaneously in the four directions by four strong bowmen. Yet swifter still, he said, is the coming of death.

Once Lord Buddha came across four powerfully built men trying to move an enormous boulder. With a single effortless movement of his foot, the Buddha flicked the massive rock into the air, where it shattered into pieces. Astonished, the men asked how he had acquired such miraculous strength, and the Buddha replied that it was through accumulation of merit. They asked him if there could be anybody stronger than he. "Yes," said the Buddha, "Death—and because of Death I shall have to leave even this body endowed with all its perfect marks and signs." The Buddha always taught that reflection on death and impermanence is the strongest incentive to practice Dharma.

Mastering the Mind

> 75. The six-syllable mantra, although perfect as Dharma,
> Is fruitless recited while chatting and looking around;
> And to cling to the number recited is to miss the point outright.
> Undistractedly watching the mind, recite the six-syllable mantra.

The six-syllable mantra has the power to counteract all your negative emotions and to bring you unimaginable benefit, but it cannot be fully effective if you do not recite it with the proper concentration. If you are always being distracted as you recite it by bodily sensations, different things to look at, idle talk with others, or your own wandering thoughts, the mantra's power, like the luster of a piece of gold encrusted with dirt, will never make itself felt. Even if the beads of your rosary whirl through your fingers at breakneck speed, what use could such an empty façade of practice possibly be? The point is not to accumulate a huge number of recitations at any cost, but to gain a deeper understanding of the practice and its goal.

To harvest the full fruit of the mani recitation, it is important to maintain your body in the correct posture without any restless movements; to restrict your speech to the recitation of the mantra alone, without any other talking; and to keep your mind concentrated on the visualization, without letting it be distracted by memories of the past or plans for the future.

Aspire to emulate Jetsun Milarepa, who left behind all the

busy activities and useless distractions of ordinary life, banished laziness and negative emotions from his mind, and gave himself entirely to the practice of Dharma. If you practice in this way, your mind-stream will without any doubt be blessed by all the Buddhas and Bodhisattvas.

> 76. If you check your mind over and over again,
> Whatever you do becomes the perfect path.
> Of all the hundreds of vital instructions, this is the very quintessence;
> Fuse everything into this one single point, and recite the six-syllable mantra.

The whole thrust of the Buddha's teaching is to master the mind. If you master the mind, you will have mastery over body and speech, and your own and others' suffering can only come to an end. But if you leave the mind full of negative emotions, then however perfect the actions of your body and the words you speak might seem, you are far from the path.

Mastery of the mind is achieved through constant awareness of all your thoughts and actions. Check your mind over and over again, and as soon as negative thoughts arise, remedy them with the appropriate antidotes. When positive thoughts arise, reinforce them by dedicating the merit they bring, wishing that all sentient beings be established in ultimate enlightenment. Maintaining this constant mindfulness in the practices of tranquility and insight, you will eventually be able to sustain the recognition of wisdom even in the midst of ordinary activities and distractions. Mindfulness is thus the very basis, the cure for all saṃsāric afflictions.

The practice of Dharma should bring you to the point where you can maintain the same constant awareness whether in or out of practice sessions. This is the quintessential point of all spiritual instructions; without it, however many mantras and prayers you recite, however many thousands of prostrations and circumambulations you do, as long as your mind remains distracted none of it will help to get rid of your obscuring emotions. Never forgetting this most crucial point, recite the six-syllable mantra.

Concluding Verses

77. The first part, my sorrowful tirade at this decadent age's ways,
Was a reproof I had intended for myself.
This sad lament has affected me deeply;
Now I offer it to you, thinking you might feel the same.

The first part of this teaching points out the extent to which people in this decadent age fall under the sway of their actions and emotions, shows up the pointlessness of ordinary life, and depicts the destructive effect of people's behavior on the happiness they seek. If you clearly recognize, in accordance with the Buddha's first teaching, that saṃsāra is pervaded by suffering, then the determination to be free from it will be firmly set in your mind as the very cornerstone of your Dharma practice. It is to bring about this change of attitude that Patrul Rinpoche expresses the sadness and weariness he feels at the ways of saṃsāra.

78. If that is not the case, and you have total confidence in the loftiness of your view and meditation,
Wise ideas about how to combine the worldly and the spiritual,
And the diplomatic skill to settle problems to the satisfaction of all—
If you have all that, then I offer you my apologies.

Patrul Rinpoche has condemned the confused and deceitful behavior of people in this dark age, not in a spirit of animosity, but rather to reveal and correct his own shortcomings. He also hoped that by speaking out he might encourage others, too, to wake up to the delusions of this age and to recognize that the Dharma is the only way to liberation.

The intention behind the first section, therefore, was to turn the confused mind toward the Dharma. But Patrul Rinpoche then adds that should the reader have already transcended the crooked ways of our time and gained perfect confidence and accomplishment in the view, meditation, and action of the sūtras and tantras, should his mind be always set on the sublime thought of benefiting others, and should he have successfully integrated the essence of Dharma with involvement in the affairs of the world, in that case he, Patrul Rinpoche, apologizes for presumptuously offering this irrelevant advice.

79. The second part, my dissertation establishing view and meditation—
Since of course I have no experience of realization at all—
Just sets out what I've understood by the grace of the teachings
From the precious lineage of the all-knowing father and son.

The underlying framework of all teachings of the Hīnayāna, Mahāyāna, and Vajrayāna is the explanation of view, meditation, and action. Patrul Rinpoche humbly denies having any inner experience of these three. In reality, of course, he had thoroughly studied and assimilated the teachings of Longchen Rabjam and Jigme Lingpa, "father and son" of the lineage of the Great Perfection. He had then attained total realization and brought inconceivable benefit to beings. In this discourse he flawlessly sets out the vital points of the Buddhist path: how to identify delusion, demolish its dominion, and finally transform it into wisdom.

80. The third part, my exhortation to relinquish everything and practice,
Though you may well miss the point, just slipped out by itself.
Yet, since it in no way contradicts the words of the Buddhas and Bodhisattvas,
It would be truly kind of you to put it into practice.

Contemplating the unending miseries of saṃsāra will make you feel sad and sickened at so much suffering, and this feeling will develop into a strong desire to be free from it all. That determination to relinquish saṃsāra should then lead you to the conclusion that the best thing you can do for yourself and others is to practice the Dharma. You might have already set yourself various aims in life, but now for your own good you must make up your mind which of them is the most important and urgent. If you take the Dharma at all seriously, you will see that Dharma practice is not something that can be postponed till later. How many people in the world will die within the next hour? Can you be certain that you won't be one of them? In any case, there is surely never anything to be gained from wasting the time you have, however long your life might turn out to be.

81. This discourse, virtuous in the beginning, middle, and end,
Was written in the siddha's cave of White Rock Victory Peak,
For an old friend whose pleas could no longer be resisted,
By that ragged old fellow Apu Hralpo, ablaze with the five poisons.

At the persistent request of one of his students, this text was composed by Patrul Rinpoche, Orgyen Jigme Chökyi Wangpo, at Trakar Tsegyal, the cave of White Rock Victory Peak, in

Kham, Eastern Tibet, not far from Datsedo, on the ancient border between Tibet and China.[69] In this beautiful place of high white cliffs full of natural caves, Patrul Rinpoche lived in retreat with five of his disciples. There he gave many teachings, like this one, in the light of his own experience of meditation.

Apu Hralpo is the name by which Patrul Rinpoche was familiarly known. Apu in the language of Eastern Tibet is a respectful term of address. According to literary tradition, Apu can also be interpreted as the combination of the syllables *A*, symbol of the unborn void nature, and *Pu*, meaning "son," referring to Patrul Rinpoche's love for all beings as if they were his own children. Because of his great tenderness and compassion for all, he was also often called Kind Apu.

Patrul Rinpoche mocks the honorific Apu given to him, by calling himself Apu Hralpo, *hralpo* meaning someone clad in torn old rags—as indeed he was for most of the time. In fact, it can be said that Patrul Rinpoche was someone who had completely torn into shreds the fabric of delusion, the taking of subject and object as having true existence. As Khenpo Shenga,[70] an accomplished master himself and a disciple of Patrul Rinpoche, said of him, commenting on this line, "He completely burned up the five poisons in the fire of wisdom."

Dedication of Merit

82. I have just been prattling on and on, but so what?
My theme is of great worth and its meaning
unerring; so the merit it brings
I offer to you, and to all of us throughout the
three worlds—
May all the wishes we make, inspired by the
teachings, come true!

Patrul Rinpoche apologizes that his unpolished discourse has been going on and on like the monotonously twanging strings of a broken old lute. Nevertheless, he maintains, the meaning of his words, being faithful to the teaching of Lord Buddha, is free from error, and this makes what he says worth hearing, worth studying, and worth putting into practice. Should any merit have accrued, therefore, from having expounded the three parts of his discourse, he goes on to dedicate it to all beings, so that following the path of the Bodhisattvas they may reach the supreme level of Chenrezi.

Epilogue

In Tibet, the Land of Snow, Buddhism has flourished for more than a thousand years. Over three successive centuries, three great Tibetan kings—Songtsen Gampo, Trisong Detsen, and Tri Ralpachen—each developed great faith in the teachings of the Buddha and the practice of meditation, and they established in Tibet the necessary conditions for the spread of the teachings. Through the succeeding centuries, Tibetans have sustained their great faith in the Three Jewels and have been able to incorporate the meaning of the Buddhist Dharma into their daily lives.

It is mentioned a number of times in the *Maṇi Kabum* of King Songtsen Gampo that Lord Buddha himself entrusted the care of the people of Tibet to the sublime Chenrezi, who blessed the whole country as the Paradise of the Potala Mountain, all the men as himself, and all the women as Jetsun Drölma.

In recent decades, adverse conditions and terrible conflict have befallen Tibet. Fortunately, through the compassionate activity of all the Buddhas and particularly of Chenrezi, in 1959, while Tibet was being invaded, His Holiness the Dalai Lama was able to escape to safety in India. A living emanation of Chenrezi, His Holiness works tirelessly to preserve and disseminate the sacred teachings. Through his blessings, not only has the Buddhadharma now returned to its birthplace, India, but also our prayers that the Dharma may flourish once again in Tibet may actually be realized.

The teachings given here focus on Chenrezi, the lord of all maṇḍalas. Because he is the Buddha of Compassion, and because compassion is the heart of the Buddhist teachings, Chenrezi is the supreme meditation deity; and the recitation of his mantra is particularly powerful, imbued with great blessing and effective in relieving the suffering of beings. To meditate constantly on Chenrezi with unwavering devotion is therefore a particularly effective way to make progress on the path of the great vehicle and to burnish the jewel of bodhichitta.

In his outer, or relative, aspect Chenrezi dwells in the Buddha-field of the Potala Mountain, personifying the compassion of all the Buddhas. In his inner, or absolute, aspect he is our own innate wisdom and compassion. To understand how both absolute and relative coexist is called the view.

Mere knowledge by itself, however, is not enough and, if not applied, is of little use. As with any skill, this knowledge must be put to work and integrated into our being through a process of familiarization, usually referred to as meditation, and consisting in this case of the actual practice focused on Chenrezi.

Once you have recognized the view, as you practice it through meditation, all your actions, words, and thoughts will become naturally more and more wholesome. Eventually, whether resting, working, eating, or sleeping, whether happy or sad, you will constantly have the thought of Chenrezi present in your mind; this is called action.

After receiving these teachings, it is now up to you to sew them into the fabric of your life so that they become integrated into all your thoughts, words, and actions. This is not easy to do, but through the blessing of Chenrezi and the efficacy of his mantra, you will gradually make progress, overcome obstacles, and gain liberation as the fruit of your efforts.

In Tibet after 1959, under conditions of intense persecution, tens of thousands of people continued to practice the Dharma secretly, and they have emerged from their ordeal with even greater faith. But in your case nobody is forbidding you to pray or to practice. So recite the *maṇi,* reflect on the teachings, and fuse them into your being by meditating on them every day, even if it is for no more than a few moments. The Dharma is something that you yourself have to practice; no one else can do it for you.

Whether practicing formally in a session or carrying the practice into the activities of your daily life, you should remember three supreme points applied to the preparation, the substance, and the conclusion of whatever you are doing. The preparation is to wish that what you are about to do may benefit all beings, bringing them happiness and ultimately leading them to enlightenment. The substance is to be fully attentive to what you are doing, without ever taking subject, object, or action as having any true existence. The conclusion is to dedicate to all beings the merit you may have accumulated through your practice or activity. By sealing everything you do with this dedication, you ensure that the merit will ripen into the fruit of Buddhahood both for yourself and for others.

In this age troubled by war, famine, disease, disasters, and physical and mental suffering of all kinds, to think even for an instant of the welfare of others is of inconceivable merit. Please take these teachings to heart and put them into practice. That will render everything I have said here truly worthwhile.

THE HEART TREASURE OF THE ENLIGHTENED ONES

The Practice of View, Meditation, and Action

A Discourse Virtuous in the Beginning, Middle, and End

THE ROOT TEXT IN TIBETAN AND ENGLISH

༄། །ཐོག་མཐའ་བར་གསུམ་དུ་དགེ་བའི་གཏམ་ལྟ་སྒོམ་སྤྱོད་གསུམ་
ཉམས་ལེན་དམ་པའི་སྙིང་ནོར་ཞེས་བྱ་བ་
བཞུགས་སོ། །

༄༅། །ན་མོ་ལོ་ཀེ་ཤྭ་རཱ་ཡ།
།གང་མཚན་བདུད་རྩིའི་ཟེགས་མ་གཅིག་ལྷུང་བས།
།ཚེ་རབས་དུ་མར་རྒྱ་བར་ཆོས་ཀྱི་སྒྲས།
།འགེངས་པའི་ངོ་མཚར་རིན་ཆེན་རྣམ་གསུམ་ཞེས།
།གྲགས་པའི་དཔལ་དེས་ཀུན་ཏུ་ཤིས་གྱུར་ཅིག

།གང་ཞིག་སྔོན་གྱི་དུས་ན་ཨ་མྲའི་འབྲས།
།ཁ་ཅིག་ནང་མ་སྨིན་ཀྱང་ཕྱི་སྨིན་འདྲ།
།སྣང་བ་དེ་ལྟར་ཆོས་པའི་གཟུགས་བརྙན་བདག
།སེམས་དང་ཆོས་མ་འདྲེས་ཕྱིར་ཆོས་གཏམ་དཀོན།

།དེ་ལྟན་ཡང་དམ་པ་ཁྲིད་ཀྱི་བཀས།
།བསྐུལ་བའི་ནན་མ་ལྡོག་ཕྱིར་དྲང་པོའི་ངག
།སྙིགས་སྤྱོད་ཐལ་བའི་ཚུལ་དང་མི་མཐུན་པར།
།ག་ཡོ་སྒྱུ་མེད་པའི་སེམས་ཀྱིས་གསོལ་འདེར་དགོངས།

།དྲང་སྲོང་ཆེན་པོ་ཐུབ་དབང་ལྷའི་ཡང་ལྷས།
།དྲང་པོའི་ལམ་ནས་དྲང་པོའི་གོ་འཕང་བརྙེས།
།དྲང་པོའི་ལམ་བཟང་འགྲོ་ལ་དྲང་པོར་སྟོན།
།དེ་སླད་དྲང་སྲོང་ཆེ་ཞེས་གྲགས་མིན་ནམ།

The Root Text

NAMO LOKESHVARĀYA

1. If but a single drop of the nectar of your name were to fall upon my ears,
They would be filled with the sound of Dharma for countless lives.
Wondrous Three Jewels, may the brilliance of your renown
Bring perfect happiness everywhere!

2. Like some persimmons in the autumn
Which, though inside still unripe, look ripe outside,
I myself am just the semblance of a Dharma practitioner,
And since my mind and the Dharma haven't mixed, my Dharma teaching won't be up to much.

3. But since you, worthy friend, entreat me insistently,
I cannot refuse—I will speak out frankly.
Unusual though it is in this decadent age,
I offer you these words without treachery, so listen well.

4. The True Ṛiṣhi, the Munīndra, god of gods,
Attained the true level through the true path,
And truly showed this true and excellent path to others.
Isn't that why he's known as the True Ṛiṣhi?

།ཀྱེ་མ་སྙིགས་མའི་དུས་འདི་ར་འགྲོ་བའི་རྒྱུད།
།དྲང་པོའི་གཞུང་བཟང་ཉམས་ནས་གཡོ་སྒྱུ་སྤྱོད།
།དེ་སླད་འཁྱོག་པོའི་བློ་དང་འཁྱོག་པོའི་ངག
།གྲུ་གྲུས་གཞན་སེམས་བསླུ་ལ་སླུ་ཡིད་གཏོད།

།ཀྱེ་ཧུད་སྙིགས་འགྲོ་མཐོང་ནས་བློ་འདི་སྐྱོངས།
།ཀྱེ་མ་སུ་ཡི་ངག་ལ་སུ་ཡིད་རྟོན།
།མི་ལྷུན་སྲིན་པོའི་གླིང་ན་གནས་འདྲ་འདི།
།དགོངས་ནས་རང་དྲིན་རང་ལ་ཆེ་བར་མཛོད།

།སྔོན་ཡང་རང་སེམས་རྣམ་ཤེས་གཅིག་པུ་ཞིག
།འཁྲུམས་ཤིང་ལས་ཀྱིས་བདས་ནས་འདིར་སྐྱེས་ཟིན།
།ད་ཡང་མར་གྱི་དཀྱིལ་ནས་སྐྲ་བཏོན་ལྟར།
།ཐམས་ཅད་བཞག་ནས་རང་ཉིད་གཅིག་པུར་འགྲོ།

།རང་སེམས་རང་ལ་མི་དཀར་ཐབས་མེད་ཀྱིས།
།རང་བློ་རང་ལ་མི་དྲང་མི་སྲིད་ཀྱིས།
།རང་དོན་སྙིང་པོའི་ལྷ་ཆོས་མ་འགྲུབ་ན།
།རང་སྲིད་རང་གིས་བརླག་པ་མ་ཡིན་ནམ།

5. Alas for people in this age of residues!
The mind's wholesome core of truth has withered, and people live deceitfully,
So their thoughts are warped, their speech is twisted,
They cunningly mislead others—who can trust them?

6. Alas! How depressing to see the beings of this degenerate age!
Alas! Can anyone trust what anyone says?
It's like living in a land of vicious man-eating demons—
Think about it, and do yourself a big favor.

7. Not long ago, your consciousness was wandering alone.
Swept along by karma, it took this present birth.
Soon, like a hair pulled out of butter,
Leaving everything behind, you'll go on again alone.

8. Of course what we want is our own good,
So we have to be honest with our own selves:
If we don't accomplish the essence of the Dharma for our own sake,
Won't we be ruining our own life?

།སྙིགས་མའི་སྐྱེ་བོ་བསམ་སྤྱོད་དམན་ཆེས་བས།
།སུས་ཀྱང་རང་ལ་མི་ཕན་གཡོ་སྒྱུས་བསླུ།
།སུ་ལའང་རང་གིས་ཕན་པ་འགྲུབ་དཀའ་བས།
།འདུ་འཛིའི་འབྲེལ་ཐག་བཅད་ན་མི་ལེགས་སམ།

།བཀུར་ཀྱང་གོང་མ་མཉེས་དུས་མི་འོང་གིས།
།སྐྱོང་ཡང་འོག་མ་མགུ་དུས་མི་འོང་གིས།
།བརྩེ་ཡང་ཕར་བསམ་རྒྱུར་ལ་མི་སེམས་པའི།
།རྒྱུ་པ་འདི་དགོངས་ལ་བློ་ཐག་ཆོད་པར་མཛོད།

།མཁས་ཀྱང་བསྟན་དོན་མི་འགྲུབ་རྩོད་པ་འཕེལ།
།གྲུབ་ཀྱང་གཞན་དོན་མི་འབྱུང་སྒྲོ་སྐུར་མང་།
།མཐོ་ཡང་སྡེ་རྒྱུས་མི་འོང་ཞེངས་ལོག་ཆེ།
།ད་ལྟའི་དུས་འདི་དགོངས་ལ་སྐྱོ་བར་མཛོད།

།བཤད་ཀྱང་བདེན་དུ་མི་འཛིན་གཞན་དུ་གོ།
།ཕན་སེམས་གཉིང་ནས་དཀར་ཀྱང་ལོག་པར་འཛིན།
།འཁྱོག་པོས་དྲང་པོ་འཁྱོག་པོར་མཐོང་དུས་འདིར།
།སུ་ལའང་ཕན་པ་མི་འགྲུབ་རེ་ཐག་ཆོད།

9. In this dark age, what people think and do is vile.
None of them will help you, they'll deceive and trick you;
And for you to be of any help to them will be hard;
Wouldn't it be best to quit the whole rat race?

10. Though you serve your superiors, they will never be pleased;
Though you look after your inferiors, they will never be satisfied;
Though you care about others, they won't care about you.
Think about it, and make a firm decision.

11. Being learned these days doesn't help the teachings—it just leads to more debate;
Being realized these days doesn't help others—it just leads to more criticism;
Being in a responsible position these days doesn't help govern the country well—it only spreads revolt.
Think about these times with sorrow and disgust.

12. Though you explain, people miss the point or don't believe you;
Though your motivation is truly altruistic, people think it's not.
These days, when the crooked see the straight as crooked,
You can't help anyone—give up any hope of that.

།ཆོས་ཀུན་སྒྱུ་མ་ལྟ་བུར་རྒྱལ་བས་གསུངས།
།དེ་ནི་སྒྱུ་མ་ལས་ཀྱང་སྒྱུ་ཆེན་ཏེ།
།གཡོ་སྒྱུའི་སྒྱུ་མ་ཞེམ་པའི་མིག་འཕྲུལ་མཁན།
།སྙིགས་སྤྱོད་སྒྱུ་མ་འདི་ལ་འཇིགས་པར་མཛོད།

།གཏམ་རྣམས་བྲག་ཅ་ལྟ་བུར་རྒྱལ་བས་གསུངས།
།དེ་ནི་བྲག་ཅ་ལས་ཀྱང་ཡང་ཅ་སྟེ།
།ཁ་དང་དོན་དུ་མི་མཚུངས་བྲག་ཅའི་གཏམ།
།སྙུ་ཚིག་བྲག་ཅ་འདི་ལ་སྐྱུན་པ་སྐྱེད།

།སྣུ་མཐོང་མི་མ་ལགས་ཏེ་སྣུ་བྱེད་མཁན།
།ཀྱུས་པ་ཞེད་གཏམ་མ་ལགས་ཏེ་བསླུ་བྲིད་ཚིག
།དེ་ནི་སུ་ལ་འང་བློ་གཏད་མི་འདུག་གིས།
།རང་ཉིད་གཅིག་པུ་རང་དགར་གནས་པར་མཛོད།

།ལུས་སྤྱོད་ཆོས་བཞིན་སྤྱོད་ན་ཀུན་དང་འགལ།
།ངག་གཏམ་དྲང་པོར་བཤད་ན་ཕལ་ཆེར་ཁྲོ།
།སེམས་བཟང་གཏིང་ནས་དཀར་ཀྱང་སྐྱོན་དུ་སྟེ།
།དེ་ནི་རང་རྒྱུ་ལ་སྦེད་པའི་དུས་ལ་བབ།

13. "All phenomena are like magical illusions," said the Buddhas;
But these days the illusions are more illusory than ever,
Trickeries conjured up by devious illusionists—
Beware of the illusions of this degenerate age's ways.

14. "All talk is like an echo," said the Buddhas,
But these days it's more like the re-echo of an echo.
What the echoes say and what they mean are not the same,
So don't take any notice of these insidious echo-words.

15. Whoever you see isn't human, but a fraud;
Whatever people say isn't right, but just lies.
So since these days there's no one you can trust,
You'd better live alone and stay free.

16. If your actions conform with Dharma, you'll antagonize everyone;
If your words are truthful, most people will get angry;
If your mind is truly good and pure, they will judge it a defect.
Now is the time to keep your own way hidden.

།ལུས་སྣང་དབེན་པའི་རི་ལ་གཅིག་པུར་སྡོད།
།ངག་སྣང་སླབ་མ་མང་འབྲེལ་ཐག་ཆོད།
།སེམས་སྣང་རང་སྐྱོན་བོན་རྩེར་རེ་ལྟོས།
།སྣང་བའི་རྒྱལ་འཛིན་ཟེར་ན་དེ་ལ་ཟེར།

།སྐྱུ་ལ་ར་རང་བློ་ག་ཏ་དྲན་མི་འདུག་ཞེ་ཁོག་གོ།
།གང་ལ་ར་རང་སྙིང་པོ་མི་འདུག་སྐྱོ་ཆད་དེ།
།གང་བསམ་འགྲུབ་དུས་མི་འདུག་རྒྱང་ཐག་ཆོད།
།འདི་ག་སུམ་ག་ཏན་དུ་འགྲོགས་ནས་ཡན་པར་མཆིས།

།སྐྱིད་དུས་མི་འདུག་སྐྱིད་པོ་དེ་ནི་ཟད།
།སྡུག་པོ་མི་འདོད་སྡུག་མཐར་ཆོས་ཀྱིས་ཆོད།
།སྐྱིད་སྡུག་ཅི་འོང་སྔོན་ལས་བཙན་པོས་ཤེས།
།དེ་ནི་སྐྱུ་ལ་ར་རང་མི་རེ་མི་དགོས་སོ།

།མི་ལ་རེ་ཆེ་རེ་བ་འཛུམ་སྐྱུ་ལ་སྐྱུ་ལ།
།རང་ལ་དགོས་མང་དགོས་དགོས་སྐྱུབ་པའི་ཤེམས།
།འདི་བྱ་འདི་བྱེད་ཕྱི་ཆོས་རེ་དོགས་བློ།
།དེ་ནི་ཅི་ལ་བབ་ཀྱང་མི་བྱེད་དོ།

17. Hide your body by staying alone in a mountain wilderness;
Hide your speech by cutting off contact and saying very little;
Hide your mind by being continuously aware of your own faults alone.
This is what it means to be a hidden yogī.

18. Disgust, because there's no one to be trusted,
Sadness, because there's no meaning in anything,
Determination, because there'll never be time to get everything you want;
If you always keep these three things in mind, some good will come of it.

19. There's no time to be happy; happiness is over just like that;
You don't want to suffer, so eradicate suffering with Dharma.
Whatever happiness or suffering comes, recognize it as the power of your past actions,
And from now on have no hopes or doubts regarding anyone at all.

20. Expecting a lot from people, you do a lot of smiling;
Needing many things for yourself, you have many needs to meet;
Making plans to do first this, then that, your mind's full of hopes and fears—
From now on, come what may, don't be like that.

།དེ་རིང་ཤི་ཡང་མི་འགྱོད་འཁོར་བའི་ཆོས།
།ལོ་བརྒྱར་བསྟུད་ཀྱང་མི་དགའ་ལང་ཚོ་སོང་།
།ད་ནི་ཤི་ཡང་གསོན་ཡང་ཚེ་འདིས་ཅི།
།ཕྱི་མའི་ཆོས་ཙམ་འགྲུབ་ན་དེ་ག་རང་།

།ཀྱེ་མ་བདག་གི་མགོན་གཅིག་ཐུགས་རྗེའི་གཏེར།
།རྩ་བའི་བླ་མ་མགོན་པོ་སྤྱན་རས་གཟིགས།
།གསུང་གི་སྙིང་པོ་དམ་ཆོས་ཡི་གེ་དྲུག
།ད་ནི་རེ་ས་ཁྱེད་ལས་མི་འདུག་གོ།

།ཤེས་ཚོད་གོ་བར་ལུས་ནས་དམ་ཕན།
།བྱས་ཚོད་ཚེ་འདིར་ཤོར་ནས་དམ་ཕན།
།བསམ་ཚོད་འཁྲུལ་པར་སོང་ནས་དམ་ཕན།
།ཕན་རེས་ཡི་གེ་དྲུག་བགྲང་བའི་དུས་ལ་བབ།

།མི་བསླུ་གཏན་གྱི་སྐྱབས་གཅིག་དཀོན་མཆོག་གསུམ།
།དཀོན་མཆོག་ཀུན་འདུས་ངོ་བོ་སྤྱན་རས་གཟིགས།
།ཁྱེད་ཤེས་བློ་གཏད་གཅིག་ལས་མི་འགྱུར་བའི།
།ངེས་ཤེས་བློ་ཐག་ཆོད་ལ་ཡི་གེ་དྲུག་སྒྲོངས།

21. Even if you die today, why be sad? It's the way of saṃsāra.
Even if you live to be a hundred, why be glad? Youth will have long since gone.
Whether you live or die right now, what does this life matter?
Just practice Dharma for the next life—that's the point.

22. Ah! Fount of compassion, my root teacher, Lord Chenrezi,
You are my only protector!
The six-syllable mantra, essence of your speech, is the sublime Dharma;
From now on I have no hope but you!

23. Whatever I know I've left it as theory; it's no use to me now.
Whatever I've done I've spent on this life; it's no use to me now.
Whatever I've thought was all just delusion; it's no use to me now.
Now the time has come to do what's truly useful—recite the six-syllable mantra.

24. The only never-failing, constant refuge is the Three Jewels;
The Three Jewels' single essence is Chenrezi.
With total, unshakable trust in his wisdom,
Convinced and decisive, recite the six-syllable mantra.

།ཐེག་ཆེན་ལམ་གྱི་རྩ་བ་བྱང་ཆུབ་སེམས།
།སེམས་མཆོག་རྒྱལ་བ་ཀུན་གྱི་བགྲོད་གཅིག་ལམ།
།ལམ་བཟང་བྱང་ཆུབ་སེམས་དང་མི་འབྲལ་ཞིང་།
།འགྲོ་ལ་སྙིང་རྗེའི་ངང་ནས་ཡིག་དྲུག་སྒྲོངས།

།ཐོག་མེད་འཁོར་བར་འཁྱམས་ནས་ད་ཕན་ཆད།
།ཅི་བྱེད་སྡིག་ཏུ་སོང་ནས་སྲིད་པར་འཁྱམས།
།སྡིག་ལྟུང་སྙིང་ནས་མཐོལ་ཞིང་བཤགས་སེམས་ཀྱིས།
།སྟོབས་བཞི་ཚང་བའི་ངང་ནས་ཡིག་དྲུག་སྒྲོངས།

།བདག་འཛིན་ཞེན་པའི་བློ་འདི་སྲིད་པའི་རྒྱུ།
།དེ་སྤང་ལུས་དང་ལོངས་སྤྱོད་དགེ་བའི་ཚོགས།
།ཡར་མཆོད་མར་སྦྱིན་འཁོར་འདས་ཀུན་ལ་བསྔོ།
།གཅེས་འཛིན་རྒྱངས་ཀྱིས་སྐྱུར་ལ་ཡིག་དྲུག་སྒྲོངས།

།སངས་རྒྱས་ཀུན་གྱི་ངོ་བོ་བླ་མ་རྗེ།
།སྐུ་དྲིན་སངས་རྒྱས་ཀུན་ལས་ལྷག་པའི་མགོན།
།བླ་མ་སྤྱན་རས་གཟིགས་དང་དབྱེར་མེད་དུ།
།དད་པའི་གདུང་ཤུགས་སྐྱེད་ལ་ཡིག་དྲུག་སྒྲོངས།

25. The basis of the Mahāyāna path is the thought of
enlightenment;
This sublime thought is the one path trodden by all the
Buddhas.
Never leaving this noble path of the thought of
enlightenment,
With compassion for all beings, recite the six-syllable
mantra.

26. Wandering in saṃsāra from beginningless time until
now,
Whatever you've done was wrong and will lead to
further wandering.
From your heart acknowledge all wrongdoing and
downfalls, and, confessing them,
With the four powers complete, recite the six-syllable
mantra.

27. The mind, holding on to an "I," clings to
everything—this is the cause of saṃsāra;
So, as offerings to the exalted in nirvāṇa and charity to
the lowly in saṃsāra,
Give everything—body, possessions, and virtue—and
dedicate the merit to all;
Casting all attachments far away, recite the six-syllable
mantra.

28. The noble teacher has the nature of all Buddhas,
And of all Buddhas, it is he who is the kindest.
Seeing the teacher as inseparable from Chenrezi,
With fervent devotion, recite the six-syllable mantra.

།སྒྲིབ་བྱང་ལམ་སྒོམ་སྐུ་བཞི་མངོན་དུ་བྱེད།
།དབང་བཞིའི་བདག་ཉིད་བླ་མ་སྤྱན་རས་གཟིགས།
།རང་སེམས་བླ་མར་ཤེས་ན་དབང་བཞི་རྫོགས།
།རང་དབང་རང་ཐོབ་ངང་ནས་ཡིག་དྲུག་སྒྲོངས།

།འཁོར་བ་རང་སྣང་ཙམ་སྟེ་ལོགས་ན་མེད།
།སྣང་སྲིད་ལྷ་རུ་ཤེས་ན་གཞན་དོན་རྫོགས།
།དག་སྣང་དབང་བཞི་འགྲོ་ལ་དུས་གཅིག་བསྐུར།
།འཁོར་བ་དོང་སྤྲུགས་ངང་ནས་ཡིག་དྲུག་སྒྲོངས།

།བསྐྱེད་རིམ་རྣམ་གྲངས་མང་མང་དགོས་མི་འབྲུད།
།བདེ་གཤེགས་གཅིག་བསྒོམ་རྒྱལ་བ་ཀུན་གྱི་ངང་།
།གང་སྣང་སྣང་བ་ཐུགས་རྗེ་ཆེན་པོའི་སྐུ།
།སྣང་སྟོང་ལྷ་སྐུའི་ངང་ནས་ཡིག་དྲུག་སྒྲོངས།

།བཟླས་བརྗོད་བསྙེན་སྒྲུབ་ལས་སྔགས་སྤྲོས་པ་ཙམ།
།ཚིག་ཚོད་ཡི་གེ་དྲུག་པ་ཆོས་ཀྱི་སྒྲ།
།སྒྲ་གྲགས་འཕགས་པའི་གསུང་དང་འདུ་འབྲལ་མེད།
།གྲགས་སྟོང་སྔགས་སུ་ཤེས་པས་ཡིག་དྲུག་སྒྲོངས།

29. Purifying the obscurations, initiating the practice of the path and actualizing the four kāyas,
The essence of the four empowerments is the teacher Chenrezi;
If you recognize your own mind as the teacher, all four empowerments are complete;
Receiving innate empowerment by yourself, recite the six-syllable mantra.

30. Saṃsāra is nothing other than how things appear to you;
If you recognize everything as the deity, the good of others is consummated.
Seeing the purity of everything confers the four empowerments on all beings at once;
Dredging the depths of saṃsāra, recite the six-syllable mantra.

31. The mind cannot cope with all the many visualization practices;
To meditate on one Sugata is to meditate on them all.
Whatever appears, appearances are the form of the Great Compassionate One;
In the realm of the deity's body, apparent yet void, recite the six-syllable mantra.

32. Recitations, sādhanas, and powerful spells are just complications;
The all-inclusive six-syllable mantra is the very sound of the Dharma.
All sounds have never been other than the speech of Sublime Chenrezi;
Recognizing them as mantra, resounding yet void, recite the six-syllable mantra.

།སྒྲིབ་གཉིས་རྣམ་རྟོག་ཞི་ན་ཉམས་རྟོགས་རྒྱས།
།རང་སྣང་དབང་དུ་འདུས་ན་དགྲ་བགེགས་ཐུལ།
།མཆོག་ཐུན་ཆེ་འདིར་སྐྱོལ་མཛད་སྤྱན་རས་གཟིགས།
།ལས་བཞི་ལྷུན་གྲུབ་ངང་ནས་ཡིག་དྲུག་སྒྲོངས།

།གང་ཤར་གཏོར་མ་ཤར་གྲོལ་མགྲོན་ལ་བསྔོས།
།སྣང་སྟོང་སྣ་ཚྪོ་གང་སྣང་ས་ལ་འདེབས།
།གཉིས་མེད་ལྷ་ཕྱག་སེམས་ཉིད་མགོན་ལ་འཚལ།
།ཆོས་སྐྱོང་ཡོངས་རྫོགས་ངང་ནས་ཡིག་དྲུག་སྒྲོངས།

།ཞེ་སྡང་དགྲ་བོ་བྱམས་པའི་མཚོན་གྱིས་ཐུལ།
།རིགས་དྲུག་གཉེན་འཁོར་སྙིང་རྗེའི་ཐབས་ཀྱིས་སྐྱོངས།
།དད་པའི་ཞིང་ལ་ཉམས་རྟོགས་ལོ་ཏོག་རྨོས།
།ཚེ་འདིས་ལས་རྫོགས་ངང་ནས་ཡིག་དྲུག་སྒྲོངས།

།བདེན་ཞེན་རོ་རྒྱན་ཞེན་མེད་མེ་ལ་སྲེགས།
།འདིར་སྣང་བདུན་ཚོགས་སྙིང་པོའི་ཆོས་ཀྱིས་དེད།
།ཚོགས་བསགས་ས་རོ་བརྒྱགས་ཚེ་རབས་གསུར་དུ་བསྔོས།
།གཤིན་པོའི་དགེ་རྫོགས་ངང་ནས་ཡིག་དྲུག་སྒྲོངས།

33. As thoughts and the two obscurations are pacified, experience and realization increase;
As your perceptions come under control, enemies and obstructing influences are subjugated.
It is Chenrezi who bestows in this very life the supreme and common siddhis;
As the four activities are accomplished by themselves, recite the six-syllable mantra.

34. Offer the torma of whatever arises to the guests of immediate liberation;
Mold the clay of whatever appears into the tsa-tsa of void appearance;
Offer the prostration of nonduality to the Lord of Mind Nature.
Consummating these Dharma activities, recite the six-syllable mantra.

35. Overcome your enemy, hatred, with the weapon of love;
Protect your family, the beings of the six realms, with the skillful means of compassion;
Harvest from the field of devotion the crop of experience and realization.
Consummating your life's work, recite the six-syllable mantra.

36. Cremate that old corpse of clinging to things as real in the fire of nonattachment;
Conduct the weekly funeral ceremonies of ordinary life by practicing the essence of Dharma;
As the smoke-offering to provide for the departed, dedicate your accumulated merit for all their future lives.
Consummating all positive actions done for the sake of the dead, recite the six-syllable mantra.

།དད་པའི་བུ་ཚ་ཙམ་ལས་ལེན་ཆོས་སྐོར་རྒྱུད།
།འདིར་སྣང་ཁྱིམ་དུ་ཞེན་ལོག་བུ་ཐང་ཞོག
།སྙིང་རྗེའི་བུ་མོ་ཁམས་གསུམ་མག་པར་བྱིན།
།གསོན་པོའི་རྒྱུས་རྫོགས་ངང་ནས་ཡིག་དྲུག་སྒྲོགས།

།སྣང་ཚོད་འཁྲུལ་པ་ལགས་ཏེ་བདེན་པར་མེད།
།འཁོར་འདས་རྣམ་རྟོག་ཙམ་སྟེ་ལོགས་ན་མེད།
།རྣམ་རྟོག་ཤར་གྲོལ་ཤེས་ནས་ལམ་རྫོགས།
།གྲོལ་ལུགས་གནད་ཀྱི་ངང་ནས་ཡིག་དྲུག་སྒྲོགས།

།རང་སེམས་རིག་སྟོང་གཉིས་མེད་ཆོས་སྐུའི་ངང་།
།མ་བཅོས་གཉུག་མར་བཞག་ན་རང་གསལ་འཆར།
།ཁྱུར་མེད་ཆིག་ཆོད་ངང་དུ་བྱུས་ཆོས་ཟིན།
།རིག་སྟོང་རྗེན་པར་ཞོག་ལ་ཡིག་དྲུག་སྒྲོགས།

།གནས་པའི་སྟེང་ནས་འགྱུ་བའི་རྗེས་མཐུད་ཆོད།
།འགྱུ་བའི་ངང་ནས་གནས་པའི་རང་ངོ་ལྟོས།
།གནས་འགྱུ་གཉིས་མེད་ཐ་མལ་ཤེས་པ་སྐྱོངས།
།རྩེ་གཅིག་ཉམས་ཀྱི་ངང་ནས་ཡིག་དྲུག་སྒྲོགས།

37. Put your child, devotion, at the doorway of your practice;
Give your son, renunciation, mastery over the household of ordinary life;
Wed your daughter, compassion, to the bridegroom of the three worlds.
Consummating your duty to the living, recite the six-syllable mantra.

38. Whatever appears is delusion and has no true existence;
Saṃsāra and nirvāṇa are just thoughts and nothing more.
If you can liberate thoughts as they arise, that includes all stages of the path;
Applying the essential instruction for liberating thoughts, recite the six-syllable mantra.

39. Your own mind, aware and void inseparably, is Dharmakāya.
Leave everything as it is in fundamental simplicity, and clarity will arise by itself.
Only by doing nothing will you do all there is to be done;
Leaving everything in naked void-awareness, recite the six-syllable mantra.

40. Let stillness cut the momentum of moving thoughts;
Within movement see the very nature of stillness.
Where stillness and movement are one, maintain the natural mind;
In the experience of one-pointedness, recite the six-syllable mantra.

།ཀུན་རྫོབ་བརྟགས་ནས་དོན་དམ་གཏན་ལ་ཕབ།
།དོན་དམ་ངང་ནས་ཀུན་རྫོབ་འཆར་ཚུལ་ལྟོས།
།བདེན་གཉིས་དབྱེར་མེད་བློ་བྲལ་གཉུག་མའི་གཤིས།
།སྤྲོས་བྲལ་ལྟ་བའི་ངང་ནས་ཡིག་དྲུག་བསྒྲོངས།

།སྣང་བའི་སྟེང་དུ་སེམས་ཀྱི་ཞེན་པ་ཆོད།
།སེམས་ཀྱི་སྟེང་དུ་སྣང་བའི་རྫུན་ཕུག་རྡིབ།
།སྣང་སེམས་གཉིས་མེད་རྒྱ་གྲོལ་ལྷུག་པ་ཆེ།
།རོ་གཅིག་རྟོགས་པའི་ངང་ནས་ཡིག་དྲུག་བསྒྲོངས།

།སེམས་ཀྱི་རང་བཞིན་རིག་སྟོང་གཉུག་མར་གྲོལ།
།རིག་པའི་རང་རྩལ་སེམས་རྟོག་རང་སར་དག
།སེམས་རིག་གཉིས་མེད་ཐིག་ལེ་གཅིག་གི་ངང་།
།བསྒོམ་མེད་ཆོས་སྐུའི་ངང་ནས་ཡིག་དྲུག་བསྒྲོངས།

།གཟུགས་སྣང་ལྷ་རུ་ཤེས་ན་བསྐྱེད་རིམ་གནད།
།མཛེས་དང་མི་མཛེས་སྣང་ཞེན་རང་སར་གྲོལ།
།ཞེན་མེད་སེམས་ཀྱི་སྣང་ཆ་འཕགས་པའི་སྐུ།
།མཐོང་སྣང་རང་གྲོལ་ངང་ནས་ཡིག་དྲུག་བསྒྲོངས།

41. By examining relative truth, establish absolute truth;
Within absolute truth, see how relative truth arises.
Where the two truths are inseparable, beyond intellect, is the state of simplicity;
In the view free of all elaboration, recite the six-syllable mantra.

42. From appearances, cut away the clinging of mind;
From mind, demolish the lair of fictitious appearances;
Where mind and appearances are one is infinite openness;
In the realization of one taste, recite the six-syllable mantra.

43. In the nature of mind, the simplicity of void awareness, everything is freed;
Thoughts, the spontaneous creativity of awareness, are purified in their own sphere.
Mind and awareness are one in the single essence.
In the nonmeditation of Dharmakāya, recite the six-syllable mantra.

44. To recognize as the deity whatever forms appear is the crucial point of the development stage;
Clinging to appearance as beautiful or ugly is liberated into its own nature.
Free of clinging, mind as it appears is the body of Supreme Chenrezi.
In the self-liberation of visual experiences, recite the six-syllable mantra.

།སྒྲ་སྣང་སྔགས་སུ་ཤེས་ན་བཟླས་བརྗོད་གནད།
།སྙན་དང་མི་སྙན་སྣང་ཞེན་རང་སར་གྲོལ།
།ཞེན་མེད་འཁོར་འདས་རང་སྒྲ་ཡིག་དྲུག་གསུང་།
།ཐོས་སྣང་རང་གྲོལ་ངང་ནས་ཡིག་དྲུག་སྒྲོགས།

།དྲི་སྣང་སྐྱེ་མེད་ཤེས་ན་རྫོགས་རིམ་གནད།
།ཞིམ་དང་མི་ཞིམ་ཞེན་སྣང་རང་སར་གྲོལ།
།ཞེན་མེད་དྲི་སྣང་འཕགས་པའི་ཚུལ་ཁྲིམས་དང་།
།དྲི་སྣང་རང་གྲོལ་ངང་ནས་ཡིག་དྲུག་སྒྲོགས།

།རོ་སྣང་ཚོགས་སུ་ཤེས་ན་མཆོད་པའི་གནད།
།བཅུད་དང་མི་བཅུད་ཞེན་སྣང་རང་སར་གྲོལ།
།ཞེན་མེད་བཟའ་བཏུང་འཕགས་པ་དགྱེས་པའི་རྫས།
།རོ་སྣང་རང་གྲོལ་ངང་ནས་ཡིག་དྲུག་སྒྲོགས།

།རེག་སྣང་མཉམ་ཉིད་ཤེས་ན་རོ་སྙོམས་གནད།
།འགྲང་ལྟོགས་ཚ་གྲང་སྣང་བ་རང་སར་གྲོལ།
།ཞེན་མེད་ཕྱི་ནང་རེག་བྱ་ལྷའི་ཕྲིན་ལས།
།རེག་སྣང་རང་གྲོལ་ངང་ནས་ཡིག་དྲུག་སྒྲོགས།

45. To recognize sounds as mantra is the crucial point of recitation practice;
Clinging to sound as pleasant or unpleasant is liberated into its own nature.
Free of grasping, the spontaneous sound of saṃsāra and nirvāṇa is the voice of the six syllables.
In the self-liberation of hearing, recite the six-syllable mantra.

46. To recognize smells as unborn is the crucial point of the completion stage;
Clinging to odor as fragrant or foul is liberated into its own nature.
Free of grasping, all smells are the fragrant discipline of Supreme Chenrezi;
In the self-liberation of smelling, recite the six-syllable mantra.

47. To recognize flavors as a sacramental feast is the crucial point of offering.
Attachment to taste as delicious or disgusting is liberated into its own nature;
Free of grasping, food and drink are substances to delight Supreme Chenrezi;
In the self-liberation of taste, recite the six-syllable mantra.

48. To recognize sensations as essential sameness is the crucial point of equal taste;
Feelings of repletion and hunger, hot and cold, are liberated into their own nature.
Free of grasping, all sensations and feelings are the deity's activity;
In the self-liberation of sensation, recite the six-syllable mantra.

།ཆོས་ཀུན་སྟོང་པར་ཤེས་ན་ལྟ་བའི་གནད།
།བདེན་རྫུན་བློ་ཡི་འཛིན་སྟངས་རང་སར་གྲོལ།
།ཞེན་མེད་སྣང་སྲིད་འཁོར་འདས་ཆོས་སྐུའི་ངང་།
།རྟོག་ཚོགས་རང་གྲོལ་ངང་ནས་ཡིག་དྲུག་སྒྲོངས།

།ཞེ་སྡང་ཡུལ་རྗེས་མ་འབྲེང་ཁྲོ་བློ་ལྟོས།
།ཁྲོ་སྣང་རང་ཤར་རང་གྲོལ་གསལ་སྟོང་དང་།
།གསལ་སྟོང་མེ་ལོང་ཡེ་ཤེས་གཞན་ན་མེད།
།ཞེ་སྡང་རང་གྲོལ་ངང་ནས་ཡིག་དྲུག་སྒྲོངས།

།ང་རྒྱལ་ཡུལ་རྗེས་མ་འཛིན་འཛིན་བློ་ལྟོས།
།མཆོག་འཛིན་རང་ཤར་རང་གྲོལ་ཡེ་སྟོང་དང་།
།ཡེ་སྟོང་མཉམ་ཉིད་ཡེ་ཤེས་གཞན་ན་མེད།
།ང་རྒྱལ་རང་གྲོལ་ངང་ནས་ཡིག་དྲུག་སྒྲོངས།

།འདོད་ཆགས་ཡུལ་རྗེས་མ་ཞེན་ཞེན་བློ་ལྟོས།
།ཞེན་སྣང་རང་ཤར་རང་གྲོལ་བདེ་སྟོང་དང་།
།བདེ་སྟོང་སོར་རྟོག་ཡེ་ཤེས་གཞན་ན་མེད།
།འདོད་ཆགས་རང་གྲོལ་ངང་ནས་ཡིག་དྲུག་སྒྲོངས།

49. To recognize all phenomena as void is the crucial point of the view;
Belief in true and false is liberated into its own nature.
Free of grasping, everything there is, all of saṃsāra and nirvāṇa, is the continuum of the Dharmakāya;
In the self-liberation of thoughts, recite the six-syllable mantra.

50. Don't follow after the object of hatred; look at the angry mind.
Anger, liberated by itself as it arises, is the clear void;
The clear void is none other than mirrorlike wisdom.
In the self-liberation of hatred, recite the six-syllable mantra.

51. Don't chase after the object of pride; look at the grasping mind.
Self-importance, liberated by itself as it arises, is primordial voidness;
This primordial voidness is none other than the wisdom of essential sameness.
In the self-liberation of pride, recite the six-syllable mantra.

52. Don't hanker after the object of desire; look at the craving mind.
Desire, liberated by itself as it arises, is bliss-void;
This bliss-void is none other than all-discriminating wisdom.
In the self-liberation of desire, recite the six-syllable mantra.

།ཕྲག་དོག་ཡུལ་རྗེས་མ་འབྲང་དཔྱོད་བློ་ལྟོས།
།རྟོག་དཔྱོད་རང་ཤར་རང་གྲོལ་བློ་སྟོང་དང་།
།བློ་སྟོང་བྱ་གྲུབ་ཡེ་ཤེས་ལོགས་ན་མེད།
།ཕྲག་དོག་རང་གྲོལ་ངང་ནས་ཡིག་དྲུག་སྒྲོངས།

།གཏི་མུག་ཡུལ་ལ་མ་རློམ་རང་ངོ་ལྟོས།
།རྟོག་ཚོགས་རང་ཤར་རང་གྲོལ་རིག་སྟོང་དང་།
།རིག་སྟོང་ཆོས་དབྱིངས་ཡེ་ཤེས་ལོགས་ན་མེད།
།གཏི་མུག་རང་གྲོལ་ངང་ནས་ཡིག་དྲུག་སྒྲོངས།

།གཟུགས་ཕུང་ཡེ་སྟོང་སྐྱེ་མེད་ནམ་མཁའི་ངང་།
།སྟོང་ཉིད་རིག་པའི་ཐིག་ལེ་སྤྱན་རས་གཟིགས།
།འཕགས་པ་ནམ་མཁའི་རྒྱལ་པོ་ལོགས་ན་མེད།
།སྟོང་ཉིད་ལྟ་བའི་ངང་ནས་ཡིག་དྲུག་སྒྲོངས།

།ཚོར་བ་ཡུལ་སེམས་གཉིས་སྦྲེལ་འཆིང་བའི་ཞགས།
།མཉམ་ཉིད་གཉིས་མེད་རྟོགས་ན་སྤྱན་རས་གཟིགས།
།འཕགས་པ་དོན་ཡོད་ཞགས་པ་ལོགས་ན་མེད།
།རོ་མཉམ་རྟོགས་པའི་ངང་ནས་ཡིག་དྲུག་སྒྲོངས།

53. Don't follow after the object of jealousy; look at the critical mind.
Jealousy, liberated by itself as it arises, is void intellect;
This void intellect is none other than all-accomplishing wisdom.
In the self-liberation of jealousy, recite the six-syllable mantra.

54. Don't just take for granted ideas forged by ignorance; look at the nature of ignorance itself.
The hosts of thoughts, liberated by themselves as they arise, are awareness-void;
This awareness-void is none other than the wisdom of the absolute expanse.
In the self-liberation of ignorance, recite the six-syllable mantra.

55. Form is unborn, primordially void, like the sky;
The quintessence of this awareness-void is Chenrezi—
It is none other than the Sublime King of the Sky.
In the view of voidness, recite the six-syllable mantra.

56. Feeling is the lasso that binds mind and object together;
When you know it as nondual sameness, it is Chenrezi—
It is none other than the Sublime Bountiful Lasso.
In the realization of same taste, recite the six-syllable mantra.

།འདུ་ཤེས་མཚན་མར་འཛིན་པ་འཁྲུལ་པའི་བློ།
།འགྲོ་ཀུན་སྙིང་རྗེས་འཛིན་ན་སྤྱན་རས་གཟིགས།
།འཕགས་མཆོག་འཁོར་བ་དོང་སྤྲུགས་ལོགས་ན་མེད།
།དམིགས་མེད་སྙིང་རྗེའི་ངང་ནས་ཡིག་དྲུག་སྒྲོངས།

།འདུ་བྱེད་འཁོར་བའི་ལས་ཀྱིས་རིགས་དྲུག་འཁོར།
།སྲིད་ཞི་མཉམ་ཉིད་རྟོགས་ན་སྤྱན་རས་གཟིགས།
།འགྲོ་འདུལ་ཐུགས་རྗེ་ཆེན་པོ་ལོགས་ན་མེད།
།གཞན་ཕན་རོ་གཅིག་ངང་ནས་ཡིག་དྲུག་སྒྲོངས།

།རྣམ་ཤེས་སེམས་ཀྱི་རང་བཞིན་ཚོགས་བརྒྱད་ཀ།
།སེམས་ཉིད་ཆོས་སྐུར་རྟོགས་ན་སྤྱན་རས་གཟིགས།
།འཕགས་མཆོག་རྒྱལ་བ་རྒྱ་མཚོ་ལོགས་ན་མེད།
།རང་སེམས་སངས་རྒྱས་ཤེས་པས་ཡིག་དྲུག་སྒྲོངས།

།ལུས་སྣང་གདོས་བཅས་འཛིན་པ་འཆིང་བའི་རྒྱུ།
།སྣང་སྟོང་ལྷ་རུ་ཤེས་ན་སྤྱན་རས་གཟིགས།
།འཕགས་མཆོག་ཁ་སརྤ་ཎི་ལོགས་ན་མེད།
།སྣང་སྟོང་ལྷ་སྐུའི་ངང་ནས་ཡིག་དྲུག་སྒྲོངས།

57. Appraisal, if you keep taking it as valid, is delusion;
When you turn to all beings with compassion, it is Chenrezi—
It is none other than the Sublime One Who Dredges the Depths of Saṃsāra.
In compassion without bias, recite the six-syllable mantra.

58. Impulse, as saṃsāric actions, keeps you circling in the six realms;
If you realize saṃsāra and nirvāṇa are the very same, it is Chenrezi—
It is none other than the Greatly Compassionate Transformer of Beings.
Acting for others in one single taste, recite the six-syllable mantra.

59. Consciousness, the expression of ordinary mind, has eight functions;
If you realize ultimate mind to be Dharmakāya, it is Chenrezi—
It is none other than the Sublime Ocean of Conquerors.
Knowing that your own mind is the Buddha, recite the six-syllable mantra.

60. Believing the body to be solid is what causes servitude;
If you recognize it as the deity, appearing yet void, it is Chenrezi—
It is none other than the Sublime Khasarpaṇi.
In the recognition of the deity's body, appearing yet void, recite the six-syllable mantra.

།ངག་སྣང་བརྗོད་པའི་སྒྲ་རྟོགས་འཁྲུལ་པའི་རྒྱུ།
།གྲགས་སྟོང་སྔགས་སུ་ཤེས་ན་སྤྱན་རས་གཟིགས།
།འཕགས་མཆོག་སེངྒེ་སྒྲ་ཞེས་ལོགས་ན་མེད།
།སྒྲ་གྲགས་སྔགས་སུ་ཤེས་པས་ཡིག་དྲུག་སྒྲོངས།

།སེམས་སྣང་བདེན་ཞེན་འཁྲུལ་པ་འཁོར་བའི་རྒྱུ།
།རྟོག་བྲལ་ག་ཤེས་ལ་བཞག་ན་སྤྱན་རས་གཟིགས།
།འཕགས་མཆོག་སེམས་ཉིད་ངལ་བསོ་ལོགས་ན་མེད།
།སེམས་ཉིད་ཆོས་སྐུའི་ངང་ནས་ཡིག་དྲུག་སྒྲོངས།

།སྣང་སྲིད་ཡེ་ནས་དག་པ་ཆོས་སྐུའི་ངང་།
།ཆོས་སྐུའི་རང་ཞལ་མཇལ་ན་སྤྱན་རས་གཟིགས།
།འཕགས་མཆོག་འཇིག་རྟེན་དབང་ཕྱུག་ལོགས་ན་མེད།
།དག་པ་རབ་འབྱམས་ངང་ནས་ཡིག་དྲུག་སྒྲོངས།

།ལྷ་གཅིག་རྒྱལ་བ་ཀུན་འདུས་སྤྱན་རས་གཟིགས།
།སྔགས་གཅིག་སྙིང་པོ་ཀུན་འདུས་ཡི་གེ་དྲུག
།ཆོས་གཅིག་བསྐྱེད་རྫོགས་ཀུན་འདུས་བྱང་ཆུབ་སེམས།
།གཅིག་ཤེས་ཀུན་གྲོལ་ངང་ནས་ཡིག་དྲུག་སྒྲོངས།

61. Conceptualizing speech and sound is what causes delusion;
If you recognize it as mantra, resounding yet void, it is Chenrezi—
It is none other than the Sublime Lion's Roar.
In the recognition of sound as mantra, recite the six-syllable mantra.

62. Clinging to mind's perceptions as true is the delusion that causes saṃsāra;
If you leave mind in its natural state, free from thoughts, it is Chenrezi—
It is none other than the Sublime Unwinding in Ultimate Mind.
In ultimate mind, the Dharmakāya, recite the six-syllable mantra.

63. Everything that exists is the primordially pure continuum of the Dharmakāya;
If you meet the Dharmakāya face to face, it is Chenrezi—
It is none other than the Sublime Sovereign of the Universe.
In the continuum of all-pervading purity, recite the six-syllable mantra.

64. One deity, Chenrezi, embodies all Buddhas;
One mantra, the six syllables, embodies all mantras;
One Dharma, bodhichitta, embodies all practices of the development and completion stages.
Knowing the one which liberates all, recite the six-syllable mantra.

།བྱས་པས་ཅི་བྱ་བྱ་བྱེད་འབོར་བའི་རྒྱུ།
།བྱས་ཚད་སྙིང་པོ་མེད་པའི་ཚུལ་ལ་ལྟོས།
།དེ་ནི་བྱར་མེད་ངང་ལ་བཞག་ན་དགའ།
།བྱ་བྱེད་ཙམས་སེ་ཞོག་ལ་ཡིག་རྡུག་སྒྲོངས།

།སྨྲས་པས་ཅི་བྱ་སྨྲས་ཚད་ཁྲེ་མོའི་གཏམ།
།འབྲེལ་མེད་རྣམ་གཡེང་སྐྱེད་པའི་ཚུལ་ལ་ལྟོས།
།དེ་ནི་བརྗོད་མེད་ངང་ལ་གནས་ན་དགའ།
།སྨྲ་བརྗོད་ཐད་ཀྱིས་ཆོད་ལ་ཡིག་རྡུག་སྒྲོངས།

།སོང་བས་ཅི་བྱ་འགྲོ་འདུག་ངལ་བའི་རྒྱུ།
།འཁྱམས་ཤིང་ཆོས་ལས་རིང་བའི་ཚུལ་ལ་ལྟོས།
།དེ་ནི་གཅིག་ཏུ་སེམས་བག་ཕབ་ན་དགའ།
།བག་ཕེབ་ལྷོད་ཀྱིས་སྡོད་ལ་ཡིག་རྡུག་སྒྲོངས།

།ཟོས་པས་ཅི་བྱ་ཟོས་ཚད་མི་གཙང་རྒྱུ།
།ཟ་འདོད་ཚིམ་པ་མེད་པའི་ཚུལ་ལ་ལྟོས།
།དེ་ནི་ཏིང་འཛིན་ཟས་སུ་ཟོས་ན་དགའ།
།བཟའ་བཏུང་བྱེད་འཕྲོ་བོར་ལ་ཡིག་རྡུག་སྒྲོངས།

65. What use is all you've done? Being so busy just causes saṃsāra—
Look how meaningless all you've done has been.
Now you'd better just stop trying to do anything;
Dropping all activities, recite the six-syllable mantra.

66. What use is all you've said? It was all just pointless prattle—
Look how much irrelevant distraction it has brought.
Now you'd better just keep silent;
Ceasing completely to speak, recite the six-syllable mantra.

67. What use is rushing around? Coming and going just tires you out—
Look how far your wandering has taken you from the Dharma.
Now you'd better just settle down and relax your mind;
Staying put, carefree and at ease, recite the six-syllable mantra.

68. What use is all you've eaten? It all just turned into excrement—
Look how insatiable your appetite has been.
Now you'd better nourish yourself with the food of samādhi;
Quit all that eating and drinking, and recite the six-syllable mantra.

།བསམ་པས་ཅི་བྱ་བསམ་ཚོད་འཁྲུལ་པའི་རྒྱུ།
།བསམ་དོན་ཐོག་ཏུ་མི་ཐེལ་རྒྱལ་པ་ལ་ལྟོས།
།དེ་ནི་ཚེ་འདིའི་བློ་སྣ་བསྐྱུངས་ན་དགའ།
།བློ་ཐག་ཐད་ཀྱིས་ཚེད་ལ་ཡིག་དྲུག་སྒྲོངས།

།འབྱོར་པས་ཅི་བྱ་ལོངས་སྤྱོད་ཞེན་པའི་བློ།
།བསགས་མཛོད་ཤུལ་དུ་ལུས་པའི་རྒྱལ་ལ་ལྟོས།
།དེ་ནི་བདག་འཛིན་ཞེན་པ་བཅད་ན་དགའ།
།གསོག་འཇོག་རྩོལ་སྒྲུབ་བོར་ལ་ཡིག་དྲུག་སྒྲོངས།

།ཉལ་བས་ཅི་བྱ་གཉིད་ཚོད་གཏི་མུག་དང་།
།སོས་དལ་མི་ཚེ་འཛད་པའི་རྒྱལ་ལ་ལྟོས།
།དེ་ནི་སྙིང་ནས་བརྩོན་འགྲུས་བསྐྱེད་ན་དགའ།
།ཉིན་མཚན་རྣམ་གཡེང་སྤངས་ནས་ཡིག་དྲུག་སྒྲོངས།

།ལོང་མེད་ལོང་མེད་སྙོད་པའི་ལོང་མི་འདུག
།འཆི་བདག་གློ་བུར་སླེབ་ན་ཅི་ཞིག་བྱ།
།དེ་ནི་འཕྲལ་ལ་ལྷ་ཆོས་འགྲུབ་ན་དགའ།
།ད་ལྟ་ལ་ཐུར་ཉིད་དུ་ཡིག་དྲུག་སྒྲོངས།

69. What use are all your thoughts? They've just brought more delusion—
Look how few of all your aims you've managed to achieve.
Now for this life's concerns you'd better not think too far ahead;
Dropping all your plans, recite the six-syllable mantra.

70. What use is all you own? Property is just clinging—
Look how soon you'll leave whatever you've got behind.
Now you'd better put an end to your possessive grasping;
Ceasing to acquire and hoard things, recite the six-syllable mantra.

71. What use is all the time you've slept? It was all just spent in a stupor—
Look how easily your life is running out in indolence.
Now you'd better start to exert yourself wholeheartedly;
Day and night, spurning all distraction, recite the six-syllable mantra.

72. There's no time, no time! There's no time to rest!
When suddenly death is upon you, what will you do?
Now you'd better start practicing the sublime Dharma right away;
Now, quick, hurry—recite the six-syllable mantra.

།ལོ་དང་ཟླ་གྲངས་ཞག་གི་རྩིས་ཀྱིས་ཅི།
།ད་ལྟ་སྐད་ཅིག་འགྱུར་བའི་རྒྱུ་ལ་ལྟོས།
།སྐད་ཅིག་རེ་རེར་སོང་བཞིན་འཆི་ལ་ཉེ།
།ད་ལྟ་ད་ལྟ་ཉིད་ནས་ཡིག་དྲུག་སྒྲོངས།

།ཚེ་ནི་ཉི་མ་བཞིན་དུ་ཕར་ཕར་འགྲོ།
།འཆི་བདག་གྲིབ་སོ་བཞིན་དུ་ཚུར་ཚུར་འོང་།
།ད་ནི་ཚེ་ལྷག་ཉི་རྨུས་གྲིབ་སོ་ཙམ།
།སྡོད་པའི་ལོང་ཡོམ་མི་འདུག་ཡིག་དྲུག་སྒྲོངས།

།ཆོས་སུ་ཡི་གེ་དྲུག་པ་བཟང་མོད་དེ།
།ཁ་ཡེངས་མིག་ཡེངས་བཟླས་པས་འབྲས་མི་འབྱིན།
།ངག་བཟླས་གྲངས་ལ་ཞེན་པ་ཨ་འཐས་སློ།
།རྩེ་གཅིག་སེམས་ལ་ལྟོས་ལ་ཡིག་དྲུག་སྒྲོངས།

།ཡང་དང་ཡང་དུ་རང་གི་སེམས་བརྟགས་ན།
།ཅི་ལྟར་བྱས་ཀྱང་ཡང་དག་ལམ་ལ་འགྲོ།
།གདམས་པའི་གནད་བརྒྱ་འདུས་པ་འདི་བོན།
།གནད་དོན་གཅིག་ལ་སྒྲིལ་ལ་ཡིག་དྲུག་སྒྲོངས།

73. What can you say about years, months, or days—
Look how things change every moment, right now!
Each moment that passes brings you closer to death;
Now, this very moment, recite the six-syllable mantra.

74. As your life runs out like the setting sun sinking away,
Death closes in like the lengthening shadows of evening.
Now what's left of your life will vanish as fast as the last fading shadows;
There's no time to waste—recite the six-syllable mantra.

75. The six-syllable mantra, although perfect as Dharma,
Is fruitless recited while chatting and looking around;
And to cling to the number recited is to miss the point outright.
Undistractedly watching the mind, recite the six-syllable mantra.

76. If you check your mind over and over again,
Whatever you do becomes the perfect path.
Of all the hundreds of vital instructions, this is the very quintessence;
Fuse everything into this one single point, and recite the six-syllable mantra.

།ངང་པོར་སྙིགས་མའི་སྤྱོད་ལ་སྐྱོ་བའི་གཏམ།
།གཏམ་འདི་རང་གིས་རང་ལ་གདམས་པ་སྟེ།
།རང་བློ་གཏིང་ནས་འབྱུང་བའི་སྐྱོ་ཤུགས་ཅིག
།ཁྱེད་ལའང་འདྲའམ་སྙམ་ནས་ཕུལ་བ་ལགས།

།མི་འདྲ་ལྷ་སྒོམ་མཐུན་པོའི་གདེངས་ཚོད་དང་།
།ལུགས་གཉིས་བྱ་བཞག་འགྲུབ་པའི་རྣམ་དཔྱོད་བློ།
།རང་གཞན་སྒྲོག་ཏད་ཕེར་བའི་འདུན་གྲོས་ཤོམས།
།ཁྱེད་ལ་ཡོད་པར་གྱུར་ན་མཐོལ་ལོ་བཤགས།

།བར་དུ་ལྷ་སྒོམ་གཏན་ལ་འབེབས་པའི་གཏམ།
།རྟོགས་པའི་ཉམས་སྐྱོང་བདག་ལ་མེད་མོད་ཀྱང་།
།ཀུན་མཁྱེན་ཡབ་སྲས་བརྒྱུད་པ་རིན་པོ་ཆེའི།
།གསུང་གིས་བསྐུངས་པའི་གོ་ཡུལ་བཤད་པ་ལགས།

།ཐམ་ངེས་འབྱུང་ཆོས་ལ་སྐུལ་བའི་གཏམ།
།གཏམ་འདི་བརྗོད་དོན་མེད་ཀྱང་ཤུགས་ཀྱིས་ཐལ།
།འོན་ཀྱང་སྲས་བཅས་རྒྱལ་བའི་བཞེད་གཞུང་དང་།
།མི་འགལ་ཉམས་སུ་བླངས་ན་སྐུ་དྲིན་ཆེ།

77. The first part, my sorrowful tirade at this decadent age's ways,
Was a reproof I had intended for myself.
This sad lament has affected me deeply;
Now I offer it to you, thinking you might feel the same.

78. If that is not the case, and you have total confidence in the loftiness of your view and meditation,
Wise ideas about how to combine the worldly and the spiritual,
And the diplomatic skill to settle problems to the satisfaction of all—
If you have all that, then I offer you my apologies.

79. The second part, my dissertation establishing view and meditation—
Since of course I have no experience of realization at all—
Just sets out what I've understood by the grace of the teachings
From the precious lineage of the all-knowing father and son.

80. The third part, my exhortation to relinquish everything and practice,
Though you may well miss the point, just slipped out by itself.
Yet, since it in no way contradicts the words of the Buddhas and Bodhisattvas,
It would be truly kind of you to put it into practice.

།དེ་ལྟར་གྲོགས་མཐའ་བར་དུ་དགེ་བའི་གཏམ།
།ཐུག་དཀར་རྗེ་རྒྱལ་སྒྲུབ་པའི་ཐུག་ཕྱུག་ཅུ།
།སྨྲར་འདྲིས་གྲོགས་ཀྱིས་བསྐུལ་བམ་བཟོད་ནས།
།དུག་ལྔ་མི་འབར་ཨ་བུ་ཧྲལ་པོས་བྲིས།

།ཁ་བཤད་རྒྱུད་པར་སོང་ཡང་ཅི་ཆ་སྟེ།
།དོན་བཟང་འབྲེལ་པ་མེད་པའི་དགེ་ཚོགས་རྒྱུན།
།བྱེད་དང་བདག་བཅས་ཁམས་གསུམ་འགྲོ་བ་ཀུན།
།ཆོས་མཐུན་བསམ་པ་འགྲུབ་པའི་རྒྱུར་བསྔོ། །དགེའོ།། །།

81. This discourse, virtuous in the beginning, middle, and end,
Was written in the siddha's cave of White Rock Victory Peak,
For an old friend whose pleas could no longer be resisted,
By that ragged old fellow Apu Hralpo, ablaze with the five poisons.

82. I have just been prattling on and on, but so what?
My theme is of great worth and its meaning unerring; so the merit it brings
I offer to you, and to all of us throughout the three worlds—
May all the wishes we make, inspired by the teachings, come true!

Notes

1. Saṃsāra (Tib. *'khor-ba*): the endless round of birth, death, and rebirth, pervaded by suffering, of which this present life is but a single instance.
2. Sentient being (Tib. *sems-can*): literally, "one who has a mind."
3. Dharma (Tib. *chos*): Dharma has several meanings; here it refers to the various teachings given by Buddha Shākyamuni and other enlightened beings. The Dharma was taught in order to show beings what to do and what to avoid, so that they might free themselves from saṃsāra and ultimately reach perfect Buddhahood.
4. Buddha-field: an emanation of a Buddha's wisdom. There are various levels corresponding to the three kāyas. Some can only be seen by a Buddha, some can also be seen by a Bodhisattva, and some, such as the Blissful Paradise of Sukhāvatī, can be seen by the ordinary beings reborn there. One may secure rebirth in such a Buddha-field through constantly keeping in mind four things: the qualities of the Buddha-field itself, the fervent wish to be reborn there, the desire to establish all sentient beings in perfect bliss, and the accumulation of merit and wisdom.
5. Chenrezi (Tib.), (Skt. Avalokiteshvara): the Buddha of Compassion, the principal deity of the practice described in this text.
6. Three defects of the vessel:
    - *i.* Not to pay attention to the teachings is to be like a pot turned upside down; whatever is poured onto it will be wasted.
    - *ii.* To forget the teachings is to be like a pot with a hole in the bottom; whatever is poured into it will just leak out again.
    - *iii.* To listen with a mind full of negative thoughts is to be like a pot containing poison; whatever wholesome substance is poured into it will just be contaminated.

Six stains:

i. To listen with pride, thinking that you are just as good as the teacher

ii. To listen without faith, finding fault with the teacher and his teachings

iii. To be indifferent toward the teachings, thinking that whether you receive the teachings or not is of no great importance

iv. To be either distracted by your surroundings or withdrawn inside to the point of becoming drowsy

v. To be annoyed, thinking that the teachings are too long or that the external conditions are inhospitable

vi. To be discouraged, thinking that you are incapable of practicing these teachings or of attaining realization

Five wrong ways of retaining the teachings:

i. To remember the words but not the meaning

ii. To remember the meaning but not the words

iii. To remember the words and what they mean, but to fail to recognize their ultimate intention

iv. To remember the words and the meaning but confuse the order

v. To remember the wrong meaning

7. Six pāramitās: the transcendent actions, or perfections, that lead out of saṃsāra: generosity, discipline, patience, diligence, concentration, and wisdom. They are transcendent because they are beyond the attachment associated with ordinary generosity, discipline, etc.

8. Shāntideva: One of the eighty-four siddhas, he was the great paṇḍita who wrote the *Bodhicharyāvatāra* (Tib. byang-chub sems-dpa'i spyod-pa la 'jug-pa), *Engaging in the Activity of the Bodhisattvas,* widely considered the most fundamental and essential Mahāyāna text on the Bodhisattva's path of compassion.

9. Tripiṭaka (Tib. *sde-snod gsum*): literally, "the Three Baskets." The Vinaya (*'dul-ba*) is the collection of precepts given by Lord Buddha establishing lay and monastic discipline. The Sūtras (*mdo-sde*) are the sermons of Lord Buddha. The Abhidharma (*mngon-chos*) details the formation, structure, and processes of the universe and the beings it contains, as well as classifying the various levels on the path to enlightenment.

10. Shāstra (Tib. *bstan-bcos*): Of the nine kinds of shāstra (*bstan-bcos dgu*) listed below, only the first, sixth, and ninth are valid; the other six are to be discarded.

    i. Shāstras on appropriate subjects (*don dang ldan-pa'i* bstan-bcos)
    ii. Shāstras on inappropriate subjects (*don log-pa'i . . .*)
    iii. Shāstras on meaningless subjects (*don med-pa'i . . .*)
    iv. Shāstras written to gain fame for the author (*thos-pa lhur len-pa'i . . .*)
    v. Shāstras written to incite controversy (*rtsos-pa lhur len-pa'i . . .*)
    vi. Shāstras written to inspire spiritual practice (*sgrub-pa lhur len-pa'i . . .*)
    vii. Deceitful shāstras (*ngan gyo'i . . .*)
    viii. Shāstras not inspired by loving-kindness (*brtse-ba dang bral-ba'i . . .*)
    ix. Shāstras that free one from the sufferings of the lower realms of saṃsāra (*ngan-song dang ngan-'gro'i sdug-bsngal 'bying-par byed-pa'i . . .*)

11. The Hīnayāna, or lesser vehicle, is for those who seek liberation from saṃsāra chiefly for their own sake. The Mahāyāna, or great vehicle, is for those who seek complete enlightenment for the sake of all sentient beings.

12. Sūtrayāna: the corpus of teachings found in the sūtras, the words spoken by Buddha Shākyamuni. There are both Hīnayāna and Mahāyāna sūtras. Mantrayāna: The corpus of teachings found in the tantras, which were expounded by Buddha Shākyamuni as well as by other Buddhas not only on the manifested level of the Nirmāṇakāya, but on the subtle and ultimate levels of the Sambhogakāya and Dharmakāya, respectively. The Mantrayāna, or vehicle of mantras, is also referred to as Vajrayāna, the adamantine vehicle.

13. Four Noble Truths:

    i. The truth of suffering, which is to be understood
    ii. The truth of the cause of suffering, which is to be discarded
    iii. The truth of the path, which is to be traveled
    iv. The truth of cessation of suffering, which is to be achieved

14. Degenerate age (Tib. *snyigs-dus*), equivalent to the Skt. kaliyuga: the "age of debris," or dark age, in which all that remains of the perfections of the golden age of the distant past are degenerated traces. In particular, this age is characterized by five degenerations (*snyigs-ma lnga*): shortening of life span, degeneration of the environment, degeneration of the views of beings, decline of their faculties, and increase of negative emotions. Further explanations are given in the commentary on verse 5.

15. Chandrakīrti (Tib. *zla-ba'grags-pa*): Born in South India to a Brahmin family, Chandrakīrti became one of the chief disciples of Nāgārjuna. An outstanding scholar, he also attained supreme realization and was famous for his ability to work miracles, such as feeding the Saṅgha by milking a drawing of a cow or repelling an invasion by magically inducing a stone lion to roar ferociously. He was a teacher at Nālandā University, where for seven years he debated with Chandragomin, the latter assisted by Avalokiteshvara in person.

    This famous quote of Chandrakīrti comes from the verses in praise of compassion which open the *Madhyamakāvatāra* (Tib. *dbu-ma la 'jug-pa*), *Supplement to the Middle Way.*

16. Shrāvaka: literally, "listener"; one who listens to the Buddha's teachings and practices accordingly. Pratyekabuddha: literally, "Buddha by himself"; one who progresses on the path without, in that life, the aid of a teacher. These two, together with the Arhats, "foe destroyers"—those who have vanquished the enemy of conflicting emotions—are the Saṅgha of the lesser vehicle, the Hīnayāna. Their goal is limited to securing liberation for themselves alone, whereas Bodhisattvas aspire to liberate all sentient beings from saṃsāra. It is because of this altruistic and courageous attitude that Bodhisattvas can progress through the ten supreme levels (bhūmi) of the Mahāyāna to attain perfect and complete Buddhahood, the ultimate level.

17. Three worlds of saṃsāra: the worlds of desire, of form, and of no-form. These are the three main states of existence within saṃsāra, in which are included the six realms:

    i. The world of desire, comprising hell beings, pretas (tortured spirits), animals, humans, asuras (demigods), and devas (gods), all of whom have strong negative emotions *ii.* The world of form, comprising higher celestial beings, or gods, whose mode of existence is the fruit of meritorious deeds or meditation practice performed in a previous life

iii. The formless world, comprising the celestial beings, who, unlike those of the form world, do not possess bodies of "form" as such; there are four levels, which correspond to levels of samādhi, or meditative concentration. Although the beings of the two higher worlds are characterized by a life span that is extremely long by human standards, as well as by the absence of the negative emotions found in the world of desire, they are still pervaded by ignorance, since they have not eliminated the false belief in the existence of an "I." Even though the gross emotions have been temporarily suppressed, the propensities to such emotions have not been uprooted by the insight of selflessness. For this reason the beings of the form and formless worlds will again fall into the intense suffering of the lower realms. Only when the negative emotions have been thoroughly dispelled by the realization of emptiness can one recognize the true nature of mind and attain liberation from saṃsāra.

18. Vajrāsana: the "Diamond Throne" of India, the present Bodh-Gayā, in Bihar.
19. Parinirvāṇa: the passing away of a Buddha in order to further train sentient beings, especially with regard to impermanence. According to the Mantrayāna, although a Buddha or an enlightened master dissolves his physical body, his mind merges with the all-pervading Dharmakāya, and therefore his blessings remain stronger than ever.
20. Jamyang Khyentse Wangpo (*'Jam-dbyangs mkhyen-brtse'i dbang-po;* 1820–92): Incarnation of the speech aspect of Rigdzin Jigme Lingpa, and a contemporary of Patrul Rinpoche, he was one of the greatest masters of his time. For thirteen years he roamed throughout Tibet in order to receive transmissions of many precious teachings whose hitherto unbroken lineages were on the verge of extinction. He also revived many already extinct lineages after receiving the transmissions

in visions from various great masters of the past. Jamgön Khyentse Wangpo assembled all these transmissions, together with many other important teachings, in his collection *The Five Great Treasures.* He had five principal emanations, including Jamyang Khyentse Chökyi Lodrö (1893–1959) and H. H. Dilgo Khyentse Rinpoche, whose activity for the sake of beings and for the teachings has been ceaseless and all-encompassing.

21. Orgyen Jigme Chökyi Wangpo (*O-rgyan 'jigs-med chos-kyi dbang-po;* 1808–87): Patrul Rinpoche's name. Shāntideva: The great Bodhisattva mentioned above (note 8). Shavaripa: a great siddha of India who manifested himself in the form of a hunter. Spontaneous Liberation of Suffering (Tib. *sdug-bsngal rang-grol*): one of the names of Chenrezi.
22. *Kun-bzang bla-ma'i shal-lung* (Tib.): the famous work in which Patrul Rinpoche, with his characteristically vigorous style and a wealth of colorful anecdotes, sets out the practice of Dharma in general and the preliminary practices of the Longchen Nyingthig in particular. Translated in English as *The Words of My Perfect Teacher,* this text will soon be published.
23. Kalpa: a vast period of time corresponding to the life-cycle of a universe, including its formation, duration, destruction, and the interim period that follows.
24. Thought of enlightenment (Skt. *bodhichitta*): relatively, the inspiration and determination to gain perfect Buddhahood in order to liberate all beings from the sufferings of saṃsāra; absolutely, emptiness indivisible from compassion and beyond all concepts.
25. Age of the five degenerations: see note 14.
26. Ten negative actions: three concerning the body (killing, taking what is not given, and sexual misconduct); four for speech (lies, idle talk, slander, and harsh words); and three for the mind (malice, envy, and wrong views). The ten positive actions are the opposite of these.
27. Spontaneous harvest and the bountiful cow: inexhaustible sources of nourishment for the beings of the golden age at an early stage of degeneration, during which they need solid food but are not yet obliged to toil to produce it. In the symbolic world-system of the maṇḍala offering, the spontaneous harvest is associated with the northern continent and the bountiful cow with the western continent.

28. Prātimokṣha vows: the eight degrees of lay and monastic vows according to the Vinaya, which lead to liberation from the lower realms and set one on the path toward enlightenment.
29. Kusha grass: a delicate fine-stranded grass; the Buddha was sitting upon a seat made of kusha grass at the moment of his enlightenment, and for this reason it has a particular symbolic significance and is commonly used in many Buddhist rituals.
30. Five branches of knowledge, or sciences (Tib. *rigs-pa'i gnas lnga*): languages (*sgra*), logic (*tshad-ma*), crafts (*bzo-ba*), medicine (*gso-ba*), and philosophy (*nang-gi rig-pa*).
31. Samaya (Tib. *dam-tshig*): the commitments and precepts of the Mantrayāna, which formalize the all-important bond between disciple and guru, fellow disciples and practice.
32. Guru Rinpoche: the great master Padmasambhava. He and the paṇḍita Vimalamitra were the two great Indian teachers and adepts of the Mantrayāna invited to Tibet in the eighth century by King Trisong Detsen to establish the Buddhist teachings there. Their extraordinary resourcefulness and power, derived from mastery of the tantras, proved indispensable in overcoming resistance and obstacles to the spread of Buddhism, which even the finest teachers of the Mahāyāna sūtras had hitherto been unable to eliminate.
33. Five kinds of supernatural knowledge (Tib. *mngon-shes-lnga*):
    i. The ability to perform miracles (*rdzu-'phrul gyi mngon-par shes-pa*)
    ii. Divine sight (*lha'i mig-gi mngon-par shes-pa*)
    iii. Divine hearing (*lha'i rna-ba'i mngon-par shes-pa*)
    iv. Knowledge of others' minds (*gzhan-gyi sems shes-pa*)
    v. Recollection of former lives (*sngon-gyi gnas rjes-su-dran-pa*)
34. Chain of interdependent events (Skt. pratītya-samutpāda; Tib. *rten-'brel*): the cascade of mutually dependent causes and effects through which, starting from ignorance, relative phenomena arise.
35. Eight ordinary concerns: As defined by Nāgārjuna, they are gain and loss, pleasure and pain, praise and defamation, fame and obscurity.
36. Mantra: literally, "that which protects the mind." There are various kinds of mantras. The principal categories are awareness mantras, dhāraṇīs, and secret mantras, which correspond respectively to method, wisdom, and their nondual nature.

37. Twelve branches of the Buddha's teachings (Tib. *bstan-pa'i-yan lag bcu-gnyis*) In Tibetan (phonetic and transliterated spellings) these are:

i. Do-de (*mdo-sde*): the corpus of the sūtras, in which the condensed (*mdor-bsdus*) meaning is arranged in sections (*sde*)

ii. Yang Nye (*dbyangs-bsnyad*): texts in which teachings formerly expounded in very detailed prose are now told (*bsnyad*) in versified songs (*dbyangs*)

iii. Lungten (*lung-bstan*): texts in which predictions (*lung-bstan*) for future ages are given

iv. Tsikche (*tshigs-bcad*): texts originally written in verse (*tshigs-bcad*)

v. Chetu Jöpa (*ched-du bjod-pa*): teachings which were expounded (*bjod-pa*) purposely (*ched-du*) for the sake of preserving the doctrine, without anyone in particular having requested them

vi. Lengshi (*gleng-gzhi*): texts in which elaborate teachings are given on the basis (*gzhi*) of a discourse (*gleng*) which had been given as a precept following someone's improper actions

vii. Tokjö (*rtogs-bjod*): texts in which anecdotes (*rtogs-bjod*) about others' contemporary deeds are retold by the Buddha

viii. Detabu Jungwa (*de lta-bu byung-ba*): "So it happened . . ." (*de lta-bu byung-ba*), texts which relate stories of the past

ix. Kyerab (*skye-rabs*): texts which relate the series (*rabs*) of past births (*skyes*) of Lord Buddha as various Bodhisattvas

x. Shintu Gyepa (*shin-tu rgyas-pa*): texts in which the vast and profound teachings are expounded in extreme detail (*shin-tu rgyas-pa*)

xi. Mejung (*rmad-byung*): texts which expound wondrous (*rmad-byung*) and extraordinary teachings never disclosed before

xii. Tenla Pabpa (*gtan-la dpab-pa*): texts in which the meaning of the vinaya and the sūtras is established (*gtan la dpab pa*) with precision through classifications (*rab-dbye*) of the aggregates, the elements, the subjects and objects of perception, and other dharmas of saṃsāra; descriptions (*rnam-bshag*) of the stages, path, samādhis, and other dharmas of the path; and enumeration (*rnam-grangs*) of the kāyas, wisdoms, and other dharmas of the fruit.

38. *Kāraṇḍavyūha-sūtra* (Tib. *mdo-sde za-ma-tog bkod-pa*): a scripture on Chenrezi; one of the first Buddhist sūtras to reach Tibet, appearing miraculously on the palace roof of King Lha-Thothori Nyentsen, twenty-eighth king of the Chögyal Dynasty, in 433 C.E.

39. Four kāyas (Tib. *sku bzhi*): the Nirmānakāya, or "emanation body"; the Sambhogakāya, or "enjoyment body"; the Dharmakāya, or "truth body"; and the Svabhāvikakāya, or "essence body," which is the union of these three.

    Five wisdoms (Tib. *ye-shes lnga*): Descriptions of how the five poisons are transformed into the five wisdoms are found in verses 50–54 of the root text.

40. Yama, Yamarāja: the Lord of Death, a personification of the law of cause and effect, which determines what will become of beings in accordance with the actions they have done.

41. Five sins of immediate effect (Tib. *mtshams-med lnga*): to kill one's father, one's mother, or an Arhat; to cause a schism within the Saṅgha; or to shed the blood of a Tathāgata. The "immediate effect" is that as a result of these sins one will be drawn to the hell realms immediately after death without even going through the experiences of the bardo, the intermediate state.

    Ten nonvirtuous actions: see note 26.

    Vows of the three vehicles (Tib. *sdom gsum*): for the Hīnayāna, the prātimokṣha vows (see note 28) or the refuge vows; for the Mahāyāna, the Bodhisattva vow; and for the Vajrayāna the samaya vows (see note 31).

42. *Sublime Dharma of Clear Recollection* (Skt. *Saddharmānusmṛityupashṭhāna*; Tib. *dam-pa'i chos dran-pa nye-bar gzhag-pa*): a sūtra which explains the laws of karma in great detail. In the sūtra itself, its title is explained as "to distinguish those [actions, words, and thoughts] which are suitable from those which are unsuitable, and to keep one's sustained attention focused upon this distinction."

43. Bodhisattva Taktu-ngu (Tib.), Skt. Sadāprarudita.

44. Four obscurations (Tib. *sgrib-pa bzhi*): the obscurations of body, speech, and mind, and the subtle defilements of all three together.

45. Maṇḍala (Tib. *skyil-'khor*): usually to be understood as the deity, retinue, and environment, visualized as an array of figures and structural elements of symbolic significance distributed geometrically in a broadly circular pattern. The Tibetan term literally means "center and periphery," referring outwardly to the main deity at the center of the maṇḍala and the retinue around him or her, and inwardly to the unchanging nature which encompasses all phenomena.

46. Five aggregates, or skandhas (Tib. *phung-po nga*): the five psychophysical aggregates, or processes, that characterize sentient beings.

    i. Form: the way an object first appears to the mind
    ii. Feeling: the qualitative perception of the object as good, bad, or neutral
    iii. Appraisal: the quantitative evaluation of that perception
    iv. Impulse: the impulse to seize the pleasant and reject the unpleasant, thus compounding karma
    v. Consciousness: that which is conscious of the other skandhas and experiences suffering

    See also verses 55–59.

47. Ten directions: the four cardinal points of the compass, the four intermediate directions, and the zenith and nadir.

48. Karma Chagme Rāga Asya (*Ka-rma chags-med rā-ga a-sya;* 1613–78): a great saint and *tertön,* who belongs both to the Nyingma and Kagyu traditions. His writings, particularly his instructions for retreat practice (Tib. *ri-chos*), have been and remain a source of inspiration to many practitioners.

49. Ordinary and supreme accomplishments (Tib. *thun-mong dang mchog-gi dngos-grub*): The ordinary accomplishments, or siddhis, are long life, health, prosperity, etc., as well as the ability to perform miraculous deeds. The supreme accomplishment is enlightenment, the full realization of one's innate Buddha-nature.

50. This quote from the *Prajñāpāramitā* is a concise summary of Lord Buddha's three turnings of the wheel of Dharma.

    i. "Mind" (Skt. chitta; Tib. *sems*) is the deluded aspect of awareness. In the first turning of the wheel, Lord Buddha taught the four truths: there is suffering; the cause of suffering is the ego with its negative emotions; the antidote is the Buddhist path; the result is the cessation of suffering.

ii. "Mind does not exist" refers to the void nature. In the second turning of the wheel, Lord Buddha taught that all phenomena, including the mind, are void of intrinsic existence.

iii. "Its expression is clarity" refers to the luminous or aware aspect of mind. In the third turning of the wheel, Lord Buddha taught that the void nature is not a mere blank but is pervaded by the wisdom qualities of the Buddha-nature.

The first turning of the wheel pertains to the relative truth of causality, or the interdependent origination of phenomena, both mental and physical; the second in some aspects pertains to the absolute truth and in some aspects to the relative truth; and the third pertains to the absolute truth.

51. Ten powers (Tib. *dbang bcu*):

i. Power over life (*tshe la dbang-ba*)
ii. Power over mind (*sems la dbang-ba*)
iii. Power over matter (*yo-byad la dbang-ba*)
iv. Power over karma (*las la dbang-ba*)
v. Power over rebirth (*skye-ba la dbang-ba*)
vi. Power of aspiration (*mos-pa la dbang-ba*)
vii. Power of prayer (*smon-lam la dbang-ba*)
viii. Power of miracles (*rdzu-'phrul la dbang-ba*)
ix. Power of wisdom (*ye-shes la dbang-ba*)
x. Power of Dharma (*chos la dbang-ba*)

These ten powers should not be confused with the ten strengths (*stobs bcu*).

52. Mastering the sky treasure (Tib. *nam-mkha' mdzod*) refers to the ability to materialize objects, as if from the sky, according to the needs of beings; this is one of the abilities referred to in the category of power over matter (see note 51). Such mastery over the elements accompanies the realization of a great yogī.

53. Once, a terrible famine struck the country of Magadha, lasting for twelve years. Saraha asked Nāgārjuna to provide for the monks of

Nālandā, who lacked all necessities. Nāgārjuna decided to find out how to make gold. He took two sandalwood leaves and, with the appropriate mantras, gave them the power to transport him instantly to wherever he wished. Holding one of the leaves in his hand and concealing the other in the sole of his sandal, he traveled across the ocean to an island where lived a famous alchemist. Nāgārjuna requested the alchemist to teach him how to make gold. Now, the alchemist had realized that Nāgārjuna must have crossed over the sea by some secret magical technique, and, hoping to acquire his secret, he said, "We should agree to exchange either our craft or our wealth." "We should exchange crafts," answered Nāgārjuna, and he gave him the leaf he held in his hand. The alchemist, thinking that Nāgārjuna would now no longer be able to leave the island, taught him how to make gold. But once Nāgārjuna had learned the alchemist's secret, he left, using the other sandalwood leaf he had hidden in his shoe, and returned to India. Arriving back in Nālandā, he was able to transform a large quantity of iron into gold, thus providing the whole saṅgha with all their needs.

54. Torma (Tib. *gtor-ma*): a symbolic three-dimensional form that can be made of flour, clay, or precious substances. According to context, it can be seen as an offering, as a maṇḍala of deities, as a weapon for destroying obstacles, or as a power-object from which one can receive blessings.

55. Stūpa (Tib. *mchod-rten*): a geometrical structure symbolizing a Buddha's mind, in other words the Dharmakāya, and constructed according to the proportions of a Buddha's body. It is filled with relics of saints, maṇḍalas, written mantras and prayers, and tsa-tsas.

56. Four yogas of Mahāmudrā (Tib. *phyag-chen gyi rnal 'byor bzhi*):
    - One-pointedness (Tib. *rtse-gcig;* Skt. ekāgra)
    - Simplicity (Tib. *spros-bral;* Skt. niṣhprapañcha)
    - One taste (Tib. *ro snyom;* Skt. rasāsama)
    - Nonmeditation (Tib. *sgom-med;* Skt. abhavanam)

    The four yogas are also described in detail in the final chapter of Takpo Tashi Namgyal's *Mahāmudrā: The Quintessence of Mind and Meditation* (Boston and London: Shambhala Publications, 1986).

57. Tranquility (Tib. *zhi-gnas;* Skt. shamatha). Insight (Tib. *lhag-mthong;* Skt. vipashyanā), sometimes translated as "vast perspective" or "wider seeing."

58. Five paths (Tib. *lam lnga*): On the path of accumulation (*tshogs-lam*) and the path of union (*sbyor-lam*) one can only have an idea of the absolute nature. Only when reaching the first bhūmi, thus entering the path of seeing (*mthong-lam*), does one see the absolute, void nature of phenomena as it is. This vision then deepens and becomes more vast as one progresses through the path of meditation (*sgom-lam*) up to the eleventh bhūmi, the path of no more learning (*mi-slob-pa'i-lam*), which is full enlightenment, the level of the Buddha.

59. Primordial continuous mind (Tib. *gnyug-ma*).

60. See note 50.

61. Feast-offering (Tib. *tshogs;* Skt. gaṇachakra): an essential and regularly performed ritual and experiential element found in almost all Mantrayāna sādhanas, whether practiced in a group or individually. During the visualization of the maṇḍala of deities, offerings of food and drink are perceptually transformed and consecrated as pure samaya-substances, then offered to the deities of the maṇḍala, embodying the teacher, before being consumed by the participants both as a purification of broken precepts and as a celebration in the context of pure vision.

62. Eighth level: the eighth of the ten levels (Tib. *sa bcu;* Skt. dashabhūmi) corresponding to the point at which a Bodhisattva enters the final phase of the path of meditation (see note 59).

63. Jetsun Trakpa Gyaltsen (*rje-btsun grags-pa rgyal-mtshan;* 1147–1216): son of Jetsun Kunga Nyingpo, he became one of the main patriarchs of the Sakya order.

64. Five realms: In this context, the more usual classification of the experiences of saṃsāra into six realms is modified to a fivefold division, by counting the realms of the gods and the demigods as one.

65. Five aspects of Chenrezi: King of the Sky (*nam-mkha'i rgyal-po*), Bountiful Lasso (*don-yod zhags-pa*), He Who Dredges the Depths of Saṃsāra (*'khor-ba dong-sprugs*), Great Compassionate Transformer of Beings (*'gro-'dul thugs-rje chen-po*), and Ocean of Conquerors (*rgyal-ba rgya-mtsho*), who are the pure nature of, respectively, the skandhas of form, feeling, appraisal, impulse, and consciousness.

66. Enlightened qualities of Buddhahood: The innumerable specific qualities and abilities realized by a fully enlightened Buddha are classified by Maitreya-Asaṅga in the *Abhisamayālaṃkāra* (*mngon-rtogs rgyan*) into twenty-one different categories:

   i. The 37 dharmas leading to enlightenment
   ii. The 4 boundless attitudes
   iii. The 8 liberations
   iv. The 9 gradual meditations
   v. The 10 all-pervading perceptions
   vi. The 8 overwhelming perceptions
   vii. Absence of the negative emotions
   viii. Knowledge through prayers
   ix. The 5 kinds of clairvoyance
   x. The 4 kinds of perfectly discriminating awareness
   xi. The 4 complete purities
   xii. The 4 powers
   xiii. The 10 strengths
   xiv. The 4 kinds of fearlessness
   xv. The 3 absences of pretence
   xvi. The 3 kinds of maintained mindfulness
   xvii. Infallible memory
   xviii. Complete destruction of habitual tendencies
   xix. Great compassion toward living beings
   xx. The 18 distinctive qualities
   xxi. The 3 kinds of omniscience

   and in the *Uttaratantra* (*rgyud bla-ma*) into sixty-four principal attributes, comprising:

   - The 10 strengths
   - The 4 kinds of fearlessness
   - The 18 distinctive qualities of Buddhahood
   - The 32 major marks of Buddhahood

67. Bhūmi: "level." See also notes 58 and 62.

68. Samādhi (Tib. *ting-nge-'dzin*): meditative concentration, literally, "to remain with what is profound and absolute"; includes the practices of tranquility and insight (see note 57).

69. Trakar Tsegyal (*brag-dkar rtse-rgyal*): The cave of White Rock Victory Peak is located at the upper end of a valley between Minyak and Tao,

near Gyaphak Gön, a monastery founded by the great siddha Gyaphak Kili Kunzang (*rgya-'phag ki-li kun-bzang*).

Datsedo (Tib.): nowadays usually spelled *Tatsiendo* or *Tarstedo* and known in Chinese as *Kangding*.

70. Khenpo Shenga (*mkhan-po gzhan-phan chos-kyi snang-ba*): 1871–1927.

Bibliography

Commentary on the Root Text

The Excellent Path of the Bodhisattvas: A Word-by-Word Commentary on the Discourse Virtuous in the Beginning, Middle, and End (thog mtha' bar gsum dge ba'i gtam gyi 'bru 'grel rgyal sras lam bzang), written by Dzogchen Khenpo Shenphen Nangwa (gzhan phan snang ba), also known as Khenpo Shenga (gzhan dga'), at the behest of Khenpo Yeshe Gyatso (ye shes rgya mtsho). 31 folios, from a unique woodblock made in Dzogchen Monastery.

Works of Patrul Rinpoche

The Collected Works of dPal-sprul O-rgyan 'Jigs-med Chos-kyi dBang-po. Reproduced from H. H. Dudjom Rinpoche's xylographic collection by Sonam Kazi, 6 vols. Gangtok, Sikkim, 1971.

The Collected Works of dPal-sprul O-rgyan 'Jigs-med Chos-kyi dBang-po. Reproduced from a newly calligraphed set of manuscripts edited by Alla Zenkar, Thubten Nyima. Chengdu, China: Office for the Kangyur and Tangyur, 1988.

The Heart Treasure of the Enlightened Ones: The Practice of View, Meditation, and Action: A Discourse Virtuous in the Beginning, Middle, and End (thog mtha' bar gsum dge-ba'i gtam lta sgom spyod gsum mnyams-len dam-pa'i snying nor). Vol. 6 of *Collected Works,* pp. 195–209.

The Words of My Perfect Teacher (kun-bzang bla-ma'i shal-lung). Vol. 5 of *Collected Works.* Translated into French as *Le Chemin de la Grande Perfection.* France: Editions Padmakara, 1987. English translation by the Padmakara Translation Group forthcoming.

Biographies of Patrul Rinpoche

Jamyang Khyentse Wangpo ('Jams-dbyangs mKhyen-brtse'i dBang-po). "Praise to Patrul Rinpoche" *(rgyal-ba'i myu-gu chos-kyi dbang-po rjes-su dran-pa'i ngag-gi 'phreng-ba bkra-shis bil-ba'i ljong bzang kun tu dga'-ba'i tshal*). Appended to vol. 6 of *Collected Works*, pp. 245–50.

Khenpo Kunpal (mKhan-chen Kun-bzang dPal-ldan). *The Elixir of Faith* (*o-rgyan 'jigs-med chos kyi dbang-po'i rnam-thar dad-pa'i gsos sman bdud rtsi'i bum bcud*). Vol. 2 of *Collected Writings* (*gsung-'bum*) of mKhan-chen Kun-bzang dPal-ldan, pp. 353–484. Published by H. H. Dilgo Khyentse Rinpoche, Bhutan, 1986. Forthcoming in French and English translations by the Padmakara Translation Group under the title *The Life and Teachings of Patrul Rinpoche.*

The Third Dodrup Chen, Tenpai Nyima (mDo-grub bsTan-pa'i Nyima). *The Dew Drop of Amṛita* (*mtshungs bral rgyal-ba'i myu-gu o-rgyan jigs-med chos-kyi dbang-po'i rtogs-brjod tsam gleng-ba bdud rtsi'i zil thig*). Vol. 4 of *Collected Writings*, pp. 101–136. Gangtok, Sikkim: Dodrup Sangye, 1972.

Scriptures Quoted in This Volume

Engaging in the Activity of the Bodhisattvas (Skt. *Bodhicharyāvatāra;* Tib. *byang-chub sems-dpa'i spyod-pa la 'jug-pa*). Shāntideva.

Heart Essence of the Vast Expanse (*longchen nyingthig; klong-chen-snying gi thig-le*). Jigme Lingpa. ('Jigs-med gLing-pa). 4 vols. Published by Lama Ngödrup for H. H. Dilgo Khyentse Rinpoche, Paro, Bhutan, 1972.

King of Samādhis Sūtra (Skt. *Samādhirāja-sūtra;* Tib. *ting-nge-'dzin gyi rgyal-po'i mdo*).

Sublime Dharma of Clear Recollection (Skt. *Saddharmānusmṛityupasḥtḥāna;* Tib. *dam-pa'i chos dran-pa nye-bar gzhag-pa*).

Sūtra Designed as a Jewel Chest (Skt. *Kāraṇḍavyūha-sūtra;* Tib. *za-ma-tog bkod-pa'i-mdo*).

About Patrul Rinpoche
(1808–1887)

Patrul Rinpoche was an enlightened master who, though he lived the life of a vagabond, was one of the most illustrious spiritual teachers of the last century. His memory is still very much alive today and offers a constant source of inspiration to all practitioners of Tibetan Buddhism.

Patrul Rinpoche was born in 1808 in Dzachuka, a nomad area of Kham to the north of Shechen and Dzogchen. The child's sharp intelligence, natural kindness, and exceptional abilities soon became evident. He was recognized as the *tülku* of a master who had lived in that region, named Palge Samten Phuntshok, famous for having erected a wall of a hundred thousand stones engraved with the mantra OṂ MAṆI PADME HŪṂ. Later, several great lamas recognized him as being an emanation of Shāntideva, and he was also said to be the speech incarnation of Jigme Lingpa. The young Palge Tülku—Patrul for short—was duly installed as head of his predecessor's monastic seat.

Soon afterward, he met his principal teacher, Jigme Gyalwai Nyugu. This great master had lived many years in central Tibet as one of the foremost disciples of Jigme Lingpa and, since returning to Kham, had spent several years meditating alone near the snowline in the remote valley of Dzama Lung. On the windswept mountainside where he lived, there was not even the shelter of a cave. His only home was a depression in the ground, and he survived by eating wild plants and roots. As the years passed, the renown of this remarkable ascetic spread far and wide. Hundreds of disciples came to visit him, living in tents nearby. He was the exemplar of the Dharma practitioner who keeps his life very simple, who just makes up his mind to stay where he is until he accomplishes realization. From Jigme Gyalwai Nyugu, Patrul Rinpoche received no less than twenty-five times the teachings on the foundation practices of the Longchen Nyingthig, as well as many other important transmissions, all of which he studied and practiced with great energy. In his teens, Patrul Rinpoche spent long periods traveling to meet his teachers or accompanying them on their own journeys—for many of them had no permanent residence. In addition to Jigme Gyalwai Nyugu, Patrul met and studied with most of the great lamas of the time, including the first Dodrup Chen, Jigme Trinle Öser; Jigme Ngotsar; Dola Jigme; Gyelse Shenpen Thaye of Dzogchen; and the great *siddha* Do Khyentse Yeshe Dorje.

Do Khyentse Yeshe Dorje was the mind incarnation of Rigdzin Jigme Lingpa. He had been naturally clairvoyant from an early age and worked countless miracles. Patrul Rinpoche felt strong devotion toward this unconventional master, whom he perceived as the Buddha in person. One day, when Do Khyentse was in Dzachu, he saw Patrul passing nearby and hailed him: "Hey! Palge! Come over here! Or don't you dare?" As soon as Patrul drew near, Do Khyentse caught him by the hair, knocked him down onto the ground, and dragged him around in the dust. Patrul could tell that Do Khyentse had been drinking heavily; his breath reeked of beer. He thought to himself: "Even a great realized master like him can get drunk and behave in such an incoherent manner!" And Lord Buddha's description of the defects of alcohol came to his mind.

At that very moment, Do Khyentse abruptly relaxed his grip, let go of Patrul, and stared fiercely into his eyes. "Paah!" he said. "What iniquitous, pedantic ideas you have! You old dog!" He spat in Patrul's face, showed him his little finger (a gesture of utter contempt), and left. Suddenly, Patrul realized: "I am completely deluded. This is a profound instruction, pointing out the ultimate nature of mind." He sat in meditation posture, and the experience of unobstructed awareness came spontaneously to him, clear as a cloudless sky. When Jigme Gyalwai Nyugu had earlier given him the introduction to primordial awareness, it had been like the dawn; this experience with Do Khyentse was for him like full sunrise. Patrul Rinpoche would later joke about it, saying: "Old Dog is the secret initiation name Do Khyentse gave me." Some of Patrul's writings are signed "Old Dog."

On the death of his predecessor's nephew, Patrul Rinpoche decided to spend the rest of his life without home or possessions. Setting everything at his monastery in order, he departed for a life of wandering.

The steeply wooded hills and valleys around Dzogchen Monastery are dotted with shelters and overhangs where Patrul Rinpoche often stayed during this first period of his homeless life and to which he was to return often. At Dzogchen he received many teachings from Gyelse Shenpen Thaye and the *siddha* Mingyur Namkhai Dorje, the fourth Dzogchen Rinpoche. Here also, in the Yamantaka Meditation Cave, he composed his famous text, "The Words of My Perfect Teacher," the *Kunzang Lame Shelung*.

Wandering in the mountains, living in caves, forests, and hermitages lost in the wilderness, he constantly meditated on love, compassion, and *bodhichitta*—the wish to bring all sentient beings to freedom and enlightenment. These he held as the very root of spiritual practice. To everyone, high and low, he would say, "Have a good heart, and act with kindness; nothing is more important." As his bodhichitta became more and more vast, so also did his realization of the ever-present Great Perfection.

At the age of forty-three, Patrul Rinpoche set out for the province of Amdo to meet the great master Shabkar Tsokdruk Rangdrol. On the way, however, he heard that Shabkar had died. So he went instead to Golok, where again he was often with Gyelse Shenpen Thaye. He inspired the whole region with his teaching, even persuading bandits to give up robbery and hunters to abandon killing.

In his youth, he had studied with the greatest teachers of his time and, with his extraordinary memory, committed most of the teachings to heart. Later in life, he could teach the most complex subjects of Buddhist philosophy for months at a time without relying on a single page of text. When he taught, people's minds were completely changed. Everyone listening would feel serene and able to rest effortlessly in contemplation. Spoken by him, even a few simple words could open the door to a whole succession of new insights into spiritual life. He taught in a direct language which people could immediately apply to their own inner experience. His immense knowledge, the warmth of his blessings, and the depth of his inner realization gave his teachings a quality quite different from those of any other teacher.

From his outward appearance, his clothes, and the way he behaved with people who did not know who he was, nothing distinguished Patrul Rinpoche from a completely ordinary person. People who met him by chance would never have guessed that he was a great lama. It even happened that other lamas, not recognizing him, gave him teaching on his own writings. He kept no possessions at all. Utterly detached from the affairs of this world, he would never accept offerings. If people insisted on presenting him with valuables—silver, gold, or whatever they were—he would just abandon them wherever he happened to be and go off, carefree and alone. When he stayed somewhere, it was without fixed plans, and when he left somewhere, he had no particular destination. He would just take off with his walking stick, the clothes he was wearing, a small cloth bag containing the clay pot in which he boiled tea, and a copy of the *Bodhicharyāvatāra.* He would stop anywhere he liked, in forests, caves, or the middle of nowhere, for an undetermined time.

Everyone who spent time with him said that he only spoke about the Dharma. He might teach, or he might tell stories from the lives of the great lamas of old; but no one ever heard him just chat about ordinary worldly goings-on. He rarely spoke anyway, and when he did it was in a blunt and very direct way, uncomfortable for anyone hoping for flattery. His presence inspired awe and respect, even fear at first, and only people who genuinely needed his spiritual guidance would approach him. But all those who persisted ended up finding it very difficult to part from him.

Patrul Rinpoche is remembered today by all the most illustrious contemporary teachers as an outstanding contemplative master who indubitably attained the realization of absolute reality. His Holiness the Dalai Lama often praises in public Patrul Rinpoche's bodhichitta teachings, which he himself upholds and transmits. Dilgo Khyentse Rinpoche referred to Patrul Rinpoche as a perfect example of a practitioner of the view, meditation, and action of *Dzogchen,* Atiyoga.

Patrul Rinpoche knew practically by heart the famed *Seven Treasures* and other works of the fourteenth-century master Gyalwa Longchenpa, whom he considered the ultimate authority on the various levels of the Buddhist path. From time to time, secluded in a cave or a rough hermitage, he would write a text of his own, and most of these profound and original treatises were later collected into the six volumes of his writings. His most popular work, *The Words of My Perfect Teacher* (*Kunzang Lame Shelung;* see bibliography), describes in a trenchant vernacular style with a wealth of anecdotes the fundamental practices of the Nyingmapa tradition as taught by Jigme Gyelwai Nyugu, and is revered by masters and disciples of all schools of Tibetan Buddhism.

Patrul Rinpoche instructed followers of all schools without partiality and—together with Jamgon Kongtrul Lodrö Thaye, Jamyang Khyentse Wangpo, and Lama Mipham—played a major role in the development of the nonsectarian movement which flourished in the nineteenth century, reviving the entirety of Tibetan Buddhism at a time when many rare lineages and practices were on the verge of extinction. A strong exponent of the joys of solitude and monastic simplicity, he always stressed the futility of worldly striving and pursuits.

In 1885, Patrul Rinpoche, then seventy-seven, came back to his birthplace in Dzachuka, and he remained there until his death in 1887. His last hours were described by his attendant Sonam Tsering:

> On the 17th, he took a little food and recited the Confession Tantra. He then did a few prostrations, the fivefold yogic exercise, and an exercise to untie the heart channels. Early the next morning he took some curd and drank some tea. When the sun begun to shine, he took off his clothes, sat upright, crossed his legs in the *vajra* posture, and rested his two hands upon his knees. When I put some of his clothes back on him, he said nothing. There were three of us in his presence—Kungyam, the physician, and myself. Sometime later he gazed straight into space, snapped the fingers of both hands, rested them under his clothes in the *mudrā* of evenness, and entered the great, luminous, inner space of primordial purity, the perfect sublimation of death.

Among Patrul Rinpoche's many important disciples were the third Dodrupchen Rinpoche, Nyoshul Lungthok Tenpai Nyima, Adzom Drukpa, Mipham Rinpoche, Tertön Sogyal, the fifth Dzogchen Rinpoche, the second Katok Situ Rinpoche, Khenpo Kunzang Pelden, Khenpo Yonga, and Khenpo Shenga. Many of today's great lamas hold the direct lineage of Patrul Rinpoche's teachings, separated only by one or two generations. Dilgo Khyentse Rinpoche himself was blessed as a young child by Mipham Rinpoche and received teachings from several of these direct disciples of Patrul Rinpoche. Patrul Rinpoche's teachings, his blessings, and his power to inspire are therefore still very much with us today.

About H.H. Dilgo Khyentse Rinpoche (1910–1991)

His Holiness Dilgo Khyentse Rinpoche was one of the last of the generation of great lamas who completed their education and training in Tibet. He was one of the principal lamas of the ancient Nyingmapa tradition, an outstanding upholder of the Practice Lineage who spent twenty-two years of his life meditating in retreat, accomplishing the fruits of the many teachings he had received.

He composed numerous poems, meditation texts, and commentaries and was a *tertön*, a discoverer of "treasures" containing the profound instructions hidden by Padmasambhava. Not only was he one of the leading masters of the pith instructions of Dzogchen, the Great Perfection; he was also the holder of hundreds of lineages, which he sought, received, and taught throughout his life. In his generation he was the exemplary exponent of the *Rime* (nonsectarian) movement, renowned for his ability to transmit the teachings of each Buddhist lineage according to its own tradition. Indeed, there are few contemporary lamas who have not received teachings from him, and a great many, including His Holiness the Dalai Lama himself, who venerate him as one of their principal teachers.

Scholar, sage, and poet, teacher of teachers, Rinpoche never ceased to inspire all who encountered him through his monumental presence, his simplicity, dignity, and humor. Khyentse

Rinpoche was born in 1910 in Denkhok Valley, in eastern Tibet, to a family descended from the royal lineage of the ninth-century king Trisong Detsen. His father was a minister to the king of Derge. When still in his mother's womb, he was recognized as an extraordinary incarnation by the illustrious Mipham Rinpoche, who later named the infant Tashi Paljor and bestowed a special blessing and Mañjushrī empowerment upon him.

Even as a little boy, Rinpoche manifested a strong desire to devote himself entirely to the religious life. But his father had other ideas. His two elder sons had already left home to pursue monastic careers; one had been recognized as an incarnate lama and the other wanted to become a doctor. Rinpoche's father hoped that his youngest son would follow in his own footsteps, and he could not accept that he might also be a *tülku,* or incarnate lama, as had been indicated by several learned masters.

At the age of ten, the boy was taken ill with severe burns; he was bedridden for nearly a year. Knowledgeable lamas advised that unless he was allowed to embrace the spiritual life he would not live long. Yielding to everyone's entreaties, his father agreed that the child could follow his own wishes and aspirations in order to fulfil his destiny.

At the age of eleven, Rinpoche entered Shechen Monastery in Kham, East Tibet, one of the six principal monasteries of the Nyingmapa school. There, his root guru, Shechen Gyaltsap, Mipham Rinpoche's Dharma heir, formally recognized and enthroned him as an incarnation of the wisdom-mind of the first Khyentse Rinpoche, Jamyang Khyentse Wangpo (1820–1892), the peerless lama who—along with the first Jamgon Kongtrul—set in motion a Buddhist renaissance throughout Tibet. All contemporary Tibetan masters draw inspiration and blessings from this movement.

Khyen-tse means wisdom and love. The Khyentse tülkus are incarnations of several key figures in the development of Tibetan Buddhism. These include King Trisong Detsen and Vimalamitra, who, along with Guru Rinpoche, brought tantric Buddhism to Tibet in the ninth century; the great Gampopa, disciple of Milarepa and founder of the Kagyü tradition; and Jigme Lingpa, who, in the eighteenth century, discovered the Longchen Nyingthig, the Heart Essence of the Vast Expanse.

At Shechen, Rinpoche spent much of his time studying and meditating with his root guru in a hermitage above the monastery. It was during this time that Shechen Gyaltsap gave him all the essential empowerments and instructions of the Nyingma tradition. Rinpoche also studied with many other great masters, including the renowned disciple of Patrul Rinpoche, Dzogchen Khenpo Shenga, who imparted to him his own major work, the *Thirteen Great Commentaries.* In all, he received extensive teachings and transmissions from more than fifty teachers.

Before Shechen Gyaltsap died, Khyentse Rinpoche promised his beloved master that he would unstintingly teach whoever asked him for Dharma. Then, from the ages of fifteen to twenty-eight, he spent most of his time meditating in silent retreat, living in isolated hermitages and caves, or sometimes simply under the shelter of overhanging rocks, in the mountainous countryside near his birthplace in Denkhok Valley.

Dilgo Khyentse Rinpoche later spent many years with Dzongsar Khyentse, Chökyi Lodrö (1896–1959), who was also an incarnation of the first Khyentse. After receiving from Chökyi Lodrö the many empowerments of the Rinchen Terdzö, the collection of Revealed Treasures *(termas)*, Rinpoche told him he wished to spend the rest of his life in solitary meditation. But Khyentse Chökyi Lodrö's answer was: "The time has come for you to teach and transmit to others the countless precious teachings you have received." Since then Rinpoche has worked constantly for the benefit of beings with the tireless energy that is the hallmark of the Khyentse lineage.

After leaving Tibet, Khyentse Rinpoche spent much of his

time traveling all over the Himalayas, India, Southeast Asia, and the West, transmitting and explaining the teachings to his many disciples. He was often accompanied by his wife, Sangyum Lhamo, and his grandson and spiritual heir, Rabjam Rinpoche.

Wherever he was, he would rise well before dawn to pray and meditate for several hours before embarking on a ceaseless series of activities until late into the night. He accomplished a tremendous daily workload with total serenity and apparent effortlessness. Whatever he was doing—and he was often giving his attention to several different tasks at the same time—seemed to make no difference to the flow of his view, meditation, and action. Both his teaching and his lifestyle combined into a harmonious whole all the different levels of the path. He made extensive offerings and during his life offered a total of a million butter lamps. Wherever he went, he also supported many practitioners and people in need, in such a discreet way that very few people were aware of the extent of his charity.

Rinpoche held that building stūpas and monasteries in sacred places helps to avert conflict, disease, and famine, promotes world peace, and furthers Buddhist values and practice. He was an indefatigable builder and restorer of stūpas, monasteries, and temples in Bhutan, Tibet, India, and Nepal. In Bhutan, following predictions he had received for the peace of the country, he built several temples dedicated to Guru Padmasambhava and a number of large stūpas, gradually becoming one of the most respected teachers of all the Bhutanese people from the royal family down. Rinpoche made three extended visits to Tibet in recent years, where he inaugurated the rebuilding of the original Shechen Monastery, destroyed during the Cultural Revolution; and he contributed in one way or another to the restoration of over two hundred temples and monasteries in Tibet, especially the monasteries of Samye, Mindroling, and Shechen. In India, too, he built a new stūpa at Bodh-Gayā, the site of Shākyamuni Buddha's enlightenment beneath the Bodhi tree, and initiated plans to construct stūpas in each of the seven other great pilgrimage places sacred to Lord Buddha in northern India.

In Nepal, he transplanted the rich Shechen tradition to a new home—a magnificent monastery in front of the great stūpa of Bodhnath. This became his principal seat, and it houses a large community of monks, led by their abbot Rabjam Rinpoche. It was Khyentse Rinpoche's particular wish that this should be a place where the Buddhist teachings are continued in all their original purity, just as they were previously studied and practiced in Tibet, and he invested enormous care in the education of the promising young lamas capable of continuing the tradition.

After the systematic destruction of books and libraries in Tibet, many works existed in only one or two copies. Rinpoche was involved for many years in publishing as much of Tibet's extraordinary heritage of Buddhist teaching as possible, a total of three hundred volumes, including the five treasures of Jamyang Kongtrul. Till the end of his life, Rinpoche was still seeking lineages he had not received and transmitting to others those that he had. During his life, among countless other teachings, he twice transmitted the hundred and eight volumes of the Kangyur and five times the sixty three volumes of the Rinchen Terdzö.

He first visited the West in 1975 and thereafter made a number of visits, including three North American tours, and taught in many different countries, particularly at his European seat, Shechen Tennyi Dargyeling in Dordogne, France, where people from all over the world were able to receive extensive teaching from him and where several groups of students undertook the traditional three-year retreat program under his guidance.

Through his extensive enlightened activity, Khyentse Rinpoche unsparingly devoted his entire life to the preservation and dissemination of the Buddha's teaching. What brought him the greatest satisfaction was to see people actually putting the teachings into practice and their lives being transformed by the blossoming of bodhichitta and compassion.

Even in the last years of his life, Khyentse Rinpoche's extraordinary energy and vigor were little affected by his advancing age. However, he began to show the first signs of ill health in early 1991, while teaching in Bodh-Gayā. Completing his program there nevertheless, he traveled to Dharamsala, where, without apparent difficulty, he spent a month transmitting a set of important Nyingmapa empowerments and transmissions to His Holiness the Dalai Lama, which the latter had been requesting for many years.

Back in Nepal, as spring advanced, it became obvious that his health was steadily deteriorating. He passed much of the time in silent prayer and meditation, setting aside only a few hours of the day to meet those who needed to see him. He decided to travel to Bhutan, to spend three and a half months in retreat opposite the "Tiger's Nest," Paro Taktsang, one of the most sacred places blessed by Padmasambhava.

Completing his own retreat, Rinpoche visited several of his disciples who were also in retreat and spoke to them of the ultimate Guru, beyond birth and death, beyond any physical manifestation. Shortly afterward he was again showing signs of illness. On 27 September 1991, at nightfall, he asked his attendants to help him sit in an upright position. In the early hours of the morning, his breathing ceased and his mind dissolved in the absolute expanse.

Index

Index

Index

preoccupation with one's own, 29
temporary, 4
Hardships, 34
Harsh words, 44
Hatred, 97, 125
and anger, analysis of, 125
as one's worst enemy, 96
Hawk, story of, 74
Hells, 8, 66, 113, 126, 216
He Who Dredges the Depths of Saṃsāra (Chenrezi), 135, 232
Hidden defects, 8
Hidden yogī, 47, 48
Higher realms, 28
Hīnayāna, 54, 216, 221
definition, 215
Homelessness, 23
Hopes, 154
Human life, as a tool, 3, 155
Humility, 128
Hungry ghosts, 8

Ignorance, 131, 132, 217
root of 84,000 negative emotions, 131
Illusion(s), 41–42, 96, 112
phenomenal world as, 103
Impermanence, 43, 72, 104, 129, 153, 157, 159
Impulse, skandha of, 138, 222
analysis of, 138
Impure perceptions, 80, 113
India
Buddhadharma returned to, 167
Diamond Throne of. *See* Vajrasana
Indivisible
instants of consciousness, 110
particles, 110
Indra, 49, 61
Infatuation, 37
Infinite purity, 88, 118, 134
Initiation. *See* Empowerment(s)
Inner realization, need for, 60
Insight (vipashyanā), 110, 144, 225
Intention to benefit others, 66
Interdependent events, 219
Intermediate state. *See* Bardo

Jambudvīpa, 40
Jamyang Khyentse Wangpo, 15, 217
Jealousy, 37, 130
Jewel
family, 134
symbolism of, 86
Jewels. *See* Three Jewels
Jigme Chökyi Wangpo, 15. *See also* Patrul Rinpoche
Jigme Lingpa, 163, 223, 236
Joy, 39

Kadampa, 8, 24, 34, 36, 39, 68, 116, 145, 157
Kagyu, 116
Kalpa, 13, 21, 40
definition, 224
Karma, 73, 95, 111
Karma Chagme, 89, 222
Kāyas, 227
two, 71
three, 64, 213
four, 61, 76, 79–81
Khasarpaṇi, 140
Khenpo Shenphen Nangwa (Shenga), 165, 227
Kindheartedness, 98
King
story of the King, the dove, and the hawk, 74

Index

Index

Merit, true, 71. *See also* Dedication of merit
  dreamlike, 72
  as source of Buddha's strength, 158
Mighty Lord of the Lotus Dance (Chenrezi), 138
Milarepa, Jetsun, 39, 51, 54, 114, 116, 159
Mind, 142
  and body, 105
  capriciousness of, 104
  constantly changing, 104
  deluded, 92, 105
  dualistic, 104
  gaining control over, 105
  as main focus of Buddhist practice, 4
  mastering as essence of Buddhism, 160
  movement of, 107, 115
  natural serenity of, 107
  nature of, 88, 103, 106, 114–15
  primordial continuous, 115
  sixth sense, 123
  and speech, 105
  stillness of, 107, 115
  void nature of, 105
  voidness and clarity, 115
  work on one's, 40
Mindfulness, 24, 160
Mind-stream, 108
Mind-training, 39
Miserliness, 72
  story of man who got rid of, 100
Monastic vows, 46
Money, 154
Motivation
  channels force of actions, 3
  checking one's, 4
  right, 2
Mountain of jewels, 73
Mount Meru, 28, 69, 72
Movement, 107, 115
Moving around, as useless activity, 151

Nāgārjuna, 31, 225
  transmuting iron into gold, 93
Nature
  of mind, 103, 106
  unchanging, 119
Negative actions, 1, 32, 69
  result of, 50
Negative forces, 78, 91, 94
News, good and bad, 120
Nirmānakāya, 12, 215
Nirvāṇa, 103
  definition, 5
  nonattachment to, 124
  as recognition of mind's nature, 115
Niṣhprapañcha, 224. *See also* Simplicity
Noble Truths, Four, 7, 13, 54–55, 215
Nonaction, 106
Nonexistence of a self, 84
  as essence of the Dharma, 99
Nonmeditation, 106, 114, 115, 224. See also Abhavanam
Notions of "I" and "mine", 123

Obscurations, 94, 142
  four, 81, 228
  two, 91, 144
Obscuring emotions, 10, 21, 49
Obstacles, 94
Ocean of Conquerors (Chenrezi), 139, 225

Index

Index

Index

Sovereign of the Universe (Chenrezi), 143
Speech, 150
  as mantra, 141
Spiritual guide, 32, 33
Spiritual master, 46
  as Buddha, 75
Spontaneous harvest, 24, 218
Spontaneous Liberation of Suffering (Chenrezi), 15, 218
Stillness, 107, 115
Story
  of famous moon, 153
  of Buddha and rock, 158
  of four bowmen, 158
  of merchants and ogres, 136
Stūpa, 96
  definition, 224
Subject and object, dividing notions of, 123
Sublime Dharma of Clear Recollection (Saddharmānusmṛitbyupashṭhāna). *See* Sūtra
Suffering, 26, 149, 215
  causes of, 65
  as reminder, 49
  taking others', 50
  using it and happiness as the path, 104
Sukhāvatī (Buddha-field), 59, 87, 90, 213
Sūtra, 13, 214
  Designed as a Jewel Chest (Kāraṇḍavyūha), 59, 221
  Prajñapāramitā, 13, 83, 92, 115, 222
  Samādhirāja, 103
  Sublime Dharma of Clear Recollection (Saddharmānusmṛitbyupashṭhāna), 69, 149, 222
Sūtrayāna, 56, 79
  definition, 215
Symbolic empowerment, 80, 81

Takpo Tashi Namgyal, 224
Taktu-ngu (Sadaprarudita), Bodhisattva, 77
Talking, meaninglessness of, 150
Taste, 121
  equal, 122
Tathāgata, 144
Tathāgatagarbha (Buddha-nature), 65, 81, 131, 132
Teacher, 76
  pray to, 77
Teachings
  integrating them into one's being, 168
Ten
  directions, 222
  levels, 84
  negative actions, 23
    definition, 218
  positive actions, 23, 218
  powers, 93
    definition, 223
Thirty-five Buddhas of Confession, 69
Thought of enlightenment. *See* Bodhichitta
Thoughts, 114
  absence of tangible existence, 142
  analysis of, 108
  how they arise, 107
  chain of, 108
  constant awareness of, 160
  how to deal with, 145
  as Dharmakaya, 94
  as display of awareness, 81

Index

Index